Natural Law Jurisprudence in U.S. Supreme Court Cases since *Roe v. Wade*

Natural Law Jurisprudence in U.S. Supreme Court Cases since *Roe v. Wade*

Charles P. Nemeth

ANTHEM PRESS

Anthem Press
An imprint of Wimbledon Publishing Company
www.anthempress.com

This edition first published in UK and USA 2025
by ANTHEM PRESS
75–76 Blackfriars Road, London SE1 8HA, UK
or PO Box 9779, London SW19 7ZG, UK
and
244 Madison Ave #116, New York, NY 10016, USA

First published in the UK and USA by Anthem Press in 2020

Copyright © Charles P. Nemeth 2025

The author asserts the moral right to be identified as the author of this work.

All rights reserved. Without limiting the rights under copyright reserved above,
no part of this publication may be reproduced, stored or introduced into
a retrieval system, or transmitted, in any form or by any means
(electronic, mechanical, photocopying, recording or otherwise),
without the prior written permission of both the copyright
owner and the above publisher of this book.

British Library Cataloguing-in-Publication Data
A catalogue record for this book is available from the British Library.

Library of Congress Control Number: 2024945221

ISBN-13: 978-1-83999-380-0 (Pbk)
ISBN-10: 1-83999-380-4 (Pbk)

This title is also available as an e-book.

To my son Joseph Aloysius who is blessed with a bright intellect and wonderful future in the law. And he is sure to carry on the natural law tradition.
To St. Thomas Aquinas who remarked,

Now laws are written for the purpose of manifesting both these rights, but in different ways. For the written law does indeed contain natural right, but it does not establish it, for the latter derives its force, not from the law but from nature: whereas the written law both contains positive right, and establishes it by giving it force of authority.

Hence it is necessary to judge according to the written law, else judgment would fall short either of the natural or of the positive right. (St. Thomas Aquinas, *Summa Theologica*, II-II, Art. 5, sed. Contra.)

CONTENTS

Preface	xi
Acknowledgments	xvii

1	A Short Summary of the Natural Law Tradition	1
	Natural Law Predecessors: A Short History	3
	Ancient and classical vision	3
	Early medieval legal thought on the natural law	6
	Medieval conceptions of the natural law	8
	St. Thomas Aquinas on the natural law	13
	Law as the rule and measure of reason	14
	Law as an instrument of the common good	15
	Law as good and end	15
	Law: The supremacy of reason over will	16
	Law and its correlation to virtue	17
	Law is hierarchical	18
	Conclusion	21
2	The Content and Substance of the Natural Law	29
	Natural Law Jurisprudence and Its Principles	31
	The various kinds of law	31
	The eternal law	32
	The natural law	34
	The content of the natural law	36
	Secondary precepts of the natural law	37
	Self-preservation	39
	Procreation and sexual attraction	41
	Family and care of offspring	42
	A social, communal life	44
	Belief in a deity	45
	The divine law	46
	The human law	47
	The necessity of human law	48
	Human law is derivative	49
	Conclusion	50

3	**Natural Law and Abortion: A Post-Roe Evaluation**	57
	Background and History	57
	Roe v. Wade, 410 U.S. 113 (1973)	62
	History and tradition in Roe v. Wade: *A natural law inclination without natural law application*	65
	Roe v. Wade *and the natural law: Potentiality, actuality, personhood and self-preservation*	69
	Doe v. Bolton, 410 U.S. 179 (1973)	74
	Thornburgh v. American College of Obstetricians and Gynecologists, 476 U.S. 747 (1986)	79
	Viability and self-preservation	80
	Care of offspring	83
	Webster v. Reproductive Health Systems, 492 U.S. 490 (1989)	85
	Viability, personhood and self-preservation	86
	Planned Parenthood of Southeastern Pennsylvania v. Casey, 505 U.S. 833 (1992)	89
	Viability, personhood and self-preservation	92
	Informed consent, self-preservation and viability	93
	Family and care of offspring	94
	Minor's consent	95
	Spousal consent	97
	Stenberg v. Carhart, 530 U.S. 914 (2000)	100
	Self-preservation, viability and personhood	102
	Gonzales v. Carhart 550 U.S. 124 (2007)	109
	Family and care of offspring	112
	Summary and Conclusion	115
4	**Natural Law and the Supreme Court: Sexuality, Sexual Attraction and Procreation**	125
	Bowers v. Hardwick, 478 U.S. 186 (1986)	127
	Bowers: *The law of nature and the natural law*	128
	Bowers: *Family, procreation and the natural law*	132
	Romer v. Evans, 517 U.S. 620 (1996)	135
	Romer: *Moral tradition, family and the natural law*	136
	Boy Scouts of America v. Dale, 530 U.S. 640 (2000)	141
	Boy Scouts v. Dale: *Tradition, natural order and the natural law*	143
	Lawrence v. Texas, 539 U.S. 558 (2003)	146
	Lawrence v. Texas: *Nature, moral tradition, procreation and the natural law*	148
	Obergefell v. Hodges, 135 S.Ct. 2071 (2015)	151
	Obergefell: *Nature, procreation, family and care of offspring and the natural law*	154
	Conclusion	158

5	Natural Law and the Supreme Court: Suicide, Euthanasia and Mercy Killing	165
	Vacco v. Quill, 521 U.S. 793 (1997)	167
	Nature, self-preservation and respect for life	168
	Washington v. Glucksberg, 521 U.S. 702 (1997)	169
	Natural law, legal tradition and history	170
	Natural law, self-preservation, family life and the value of every human being	172
	Conclusion	176
6	Natural Law, Religious Expression and the Freedom to Believe	181
	Marsh v. Chambers, 463 U.S. 783 (1983)	183
	Natural law, legal tradition and religious belief	184
	Employment Division v. Smith, 494 U.S. 872 (1990)	187
	Natural law, religious freedom and belief in a deity	188
	Locke v. Davey, 540 U.S. 712 (2003)	191
	Natural law, free exercise and belief	192
	Christian Legal Society of the University of California v. Leo P. Martinez, 561 U.S. 661 (2010)	195
	The natural law, religious expression and belief	198
	Burwell v. Hobby Lobby Stores, 134 S.Ct. 2751 (2014)	200
	Natural law, religious expression and belief	202
	Masterpiece Cakeshop v. Colorado Civil Rights Commission, 138 S.Ct. 1719 (2018)	206
	Natural Law, belief in a Deity, sexual attraction and procreation	207
	Conclusion	210
Postscript to *Roe v. Wade*: The *Dobbs* Decision		217
Index		221

PREFACE

Natural law, as a school of jurisprudence or a means to decide or consider legal cases, is considered by some as nothing more than an emotive reminiscence and by others as a foundational system upon which legal reasoning must depend. To be sure, the once mighty method of natural law scrutiny has seen better and more prolific days. Critics often allege that natural law thinking borders on religious dogmatism or some sort of strange superstition. Those who still see its relevance are caricatured as sentimentalists wishing and hoping for a previous time and an earlier reverence for traditional moral principles. Of course, neither conclusion is correct, even though often argued.

The jurisprudence of natural law, the school and its advocacy, is something far more complicated than the caricature. For most of our legal history and legal tradition, the idea of a "law of nature" or a "natural law" was not so foreign. Indeed, the founders and framers of this extraordinary nation were comfortable with arguing on its behalf—and the Founding documents clearly manifest this hierarchical mindset with a higher more transcendent power reigning above the promulgations of man.[1] Edward S. Corwin's masterpiece, *The "Higher Law" Background of American Constitutional Law*, ties these jurisprudential and historical threads together neatly when he claims,

> The men we meet in the pages of this essay—Demosthenes, Sophocles, Aristotle, Cicero, Seneca, Ulpian, Gaius, John of Salisbury, Isidore of Seville, St. Thomas Aquinas, Bracton, Fortescue, Coke, Grotius, Newton, Hooker, Pufendorf, Locke, Blackstone—all insisted that the laws by which men live can and should be the "embodiment of essential and unchanging justice," and we may salute them respectfully as founding fathers of our experiment in ordered liberty.[2]

In short, nothing happened by chance in this magnificent republic but instead is the product of a long-standing tradition of human dignity and human liberty, which meant something to the citizenry. Princeton's esteemed Robert George cogently ties the natural law connection to our nation's founding documents and its founding fathers—a conclusion that should never be minimized or forgotten. He remarks,

> Most modern commentators agree that the American founders were firm believers in natural law and sought to craft a constitution that would conform to its requirements, as they understood them, and embody its basic principles for the design of a just political order. The framers of the Constitution sought to create institutions and procedures that would afford respect and protection to those basic rights ("natural rights") that people possess, not as privileges or opportunities granted by the state, but as principles of natural law.[3]

It would be a tragedy to forget the power and persuasion of the natural law in this nation's birth and in whatever form the natural law might be construed. For example, the founding fathers display some undeniable affection for Ciceronian naturalism and natural law reasoning quite evident at the time of the American Revolution. In addition, the framers hardly were melded together by a strong, common theology, although most adhered to some sort of higher authority in affairs—both human and divine. In other words, the foundational documents and rationales for America were not strictly based on a theological justification alone but at times were driven toward a natural philosophy that sought to determine what was natural and good for every human person and citizen. English common law never abrogated the idea or concept known as natural law and, in some sense, enshrined and assigned it a permanent place in Western jurisprudence. The links between Coke, Bracton, and other English legal commentators never sever the integration of natural law reasoning from a secular legal system. And as the new colonies and states unfolded, a bevy of earlier judicial decisions, at the nation's highest court, were unapologetic about using natural law reasoning in its published decisions, many of which shall be covered and analyzed throughout the pages of this text. That sort of reasoning was part of the jurisprudential nomenclature or toolbox for up to and including most of the twentieth century.[4] In fact, many of the more controversial legal decisions dwelling upon moral issues or the complex ethical thickets often relied upon the natural law for resolution.

That dependency or reliance appears to have broken down at the time of *Roe v. Wade*—a case that still stirs up both sides of the abortion spectrum. If laws, especially case decisions, are to settle a legal question and deliver a resolution that assures domestic tranquility and favorable public acceptance, the Roe decision has failed miserably. On both sides of the ideological fence, for both advocates and jurists, the matter is a ghastly failure. The rancor and division caused by its announcement, implementation, and recurring challenges is an unrivaled example of how legal reasoning can fail to solve or resolve any specific legal case. Why this occurred is a question with many answers. One of those answers might be that our system, our way of legally reasoning through cumbersome topics in the ethical domain, forgot about the natural law. If there is anything to properly ascribe to the natural law, it is that when applying its principles, solutions are possible. These solutions are unlikely to garner universal support, but unlike the relativistic irrationality so common in today's legal reasoning, the natural law guidepost delivers a more predictable conclusion—a judgment of legal cause and effect.

Part of this text's purpose is to demonstrate that the natural law has never been completely eradicated for this theory of law operates like a sleeping giant—still discernible in the words and language of legal opinions issued by the nation's highest court. On top of this, there have been, in recent years, a few justices of the Supreme Court who display an affinity for traditional natural law reasoning. Some justices, like Clarence Thomas, have candidly and forthrightly admitted that they see merit in natural law jurisprudence. And while Thomas' decisions never state, "I reach this conclusion because of the natural law," a quick reading of his powerful body of work manifests this natural law understanding. In fact, Justice Thomas has been known to comment on how the institution of slavery would not have been possible if natural law principles had been front and center in slave cases. The same could be said, as Heinrich Rommen, the great legal German philosopher during the time of Nazi Germany, has pointed out, that Auschwitz and the Final Solution could never have occurred if Germany had not abandoned the natural law.[5]

Aside from Justice Thomas, there are some who make a similar claim about the late Justice Antonin Scalia—whose opinions are often brilliant reflections that could only emerge from a jurisprudence like the natural law. Over the course of my professional lifetime, I had some written and personal communications with him about being a natural law thinker on the bench—but he politely and respectfully never concurred with my observation. Let us just say that Justice Scalia was utterly bound up in natural law jurisprudence—a condition he thought not possible for a judge, although his reasoning proving quite the opposite. In Justice Scalia's case, his entire jurisprudential approach reflected some of the chief aims and underpinnings of the natural law. With the nomination and confirmation of Justice Neil Gorsuch in 2017—another "sympathizer" at least—found a place on this nation's highest court. It is difficult to envision Justice Gorsuch not having some affection for natural law reasoning given his studies at Oxford University, under the directorship of Dr. John Finnis, for a doctoral dissertation in legal philosophy on a matter directly correlated to natural law reasoning. While this reality does not prove that Justice Gorsuch will ever rely on natural law reasoning in judicial decision making, it is a safe bet that he at least thinks about it. These three do not act alone over the last 50 years since Roe—for reading the judicial opinions of Justice Burger, Rehnquist, Roberts, Alito, and others illuminates that natural law jurisprudence is not comatose or dead in the workings of the US Supreme Court.[6]

Each of these justices argues the natural law from various slants and angles, although never explicitly. For example, Justice Alito holds tight to tradition as a barometer for determining whether a right is either naturally presumptive or essentially suspect. Tradition, what has been, likely will continue as a reasoning bulwark in deciding cases. In other words, if a right or legal claim has been around a long, long time, and has been uniformly applied, one should be more than cautious about its overthrow. In this sense, tradition is much like the natural law.[7]

For Antonin Scalia, the thrust has similarities, yet the emphasis could be said to be more historical and in this way, one looks to how cultures, societies, and communities have resolved particular moral and legal dilemmas since the earliest times of the Western civilization. Even Justice Anthony Kennedy, a less than always popular jurist in natural law circles, can edify some aspects of natural law jurisprudence. His critique of partial birth abortion is quite critical of his colleagues and other courts seemingly denying the existence of fetal human life. While he displays some affinity for natural law reasoning in late-term abortion cases, that sympathy is lacking at the early stages. His opinions on matters of religious belief and expression also display this quality, though his musings on cases involving homosexuality appear completely devoid of natural law reasoning.

What is clear is that the court's docket, whether it intends it or not, is often filled with cases that border and touch natural law principles. No term of the court ever fully evades the concepts and principles of the natural law. Given this state of affairs, it might make sense to examine how the tenets and conceptual threads of the natural law have played out in court decisions since Roe v. Wade. Might the natural law be discoverable in Washington v. Glucksberg—a rare 9–0 decision striking down the constitutional right to self-inflicted or assisted suicide? Or, in a series of cases dealing with same-sex marriage, polygamy, religious expression, sterilization, or infanticide, are there still natural law nuances, glimmers of natural law reasoning, or, as Aquinas would call it, "phantasms" of a once-vaunted reality where natural law played without much limitation. That is what this project yearns to accomplish—to lay out a status report on the condition of natural law jurisprudence in US Supreme Court decisions since Roe. v. Wade. In the final analysis, the conclusion may be that this school of jurisprudence is in critical stage or on its deathbed, or better described as a minor intellectual influence in judicial reasoning, or possibly a jurisprudential school on the road to greater influence. Hence, the text shall examine case decisions since Roe that involve abortion, infanticide, partial birth abortion, homosexuality and same-sex marriage, the conflict of religious belief with governmental policy on birth control, religious belief and its free exercise, and end with a close look at suicide, both self-inflicted and physician-assisted.

One final note, all this analysis is offered for a variety of reasons. First, the intellectual interest and challenge that this form of jurisprudence delivers is not to be discounted, for natural law analysis has been part of the legal landscape since the age of Rome and Greece. Second, the analysis will be honest yet always charitable and never condemnatory. Because the natural law is tough on modern liberal social and sexual mores, one should never impute a lack of charity on the part of natural law advocates. Holding fast to natural law principles does not impute or signify any sort of animus or insult. Readers who do not agree with the conclusions of the natural law should not reject either its proponent or the sincerity of the concepts. Disagreements over whether specific conduct or actions rest in or out of the natural law should never be personalized nor taken as a personal attack. Simply put, the text has no animosity toward anyone but attempts to analyze the application of natural law principles in particular cases and calls for resolutions that are at odds with a world witnessing far too much intolerance under regimes of political correctness. Charity and justice, virtues that are part and parcel of the natural law, demand that even those we disagree with are entitled to respect and personal deference. In a sense, this debate may be a good starting point for an agreement to agree to disagree, yet still manifest honor and respect for all points of view.

Finally, imagine a world dependent on natural law jurisprudence—be open to it and not instinctively retaliatory. Natural law jurisprudence admirably served Martin Luther King, Jr., when he mounted and moved forward the most effective civil disobedience program since Gandhi. Natural law would have, as Justice Thomas indicates, been a bulwark against slavery and similarly, as Heinrich Rommen observes, the Holocaust would have faltered if Germany would have adhered to a natural law philosophy of life and governance. To fear natural law jurisprudence is to avoid its magnificence of purpose and its exceptional capacity to elevate the value of life, the flourishing of the human person, and, just as critically, a constant reminder that some judgments are perennial, immutable, and universal.

It shall be an interesting journey.

Charles P. Nemeth, JD, PhD, LLM
Chair and Professor
City University of New York—John Jay College of Criminal Justice

Notes

1. Edward S. Corwin, *The "Higher Law" Background of American Constitutional Law* (Ithaca, NY: Cornell University Press, 1955).
2. Ibid., vii.
3. Robert P. George, "Natural Law, the Constitution, and the Theory and Practice of Judicial Review," *Fordham Law Review* 69, no. 6 (2001): 2269, 2269–70, http://ir.lawnet.fordham.edu/flr/vol69/iss6/1. Accessed October 1, 2018.
4. See Corwin, "Higher Law"; Gary L. McDowell, "Coke, Corwin and the Constitution: The 'Higher Law Background' Reconsidered," *Review of Politics*, 55, no. 3 (993): 393–420; William Blackstone, *Blackstone's Commentaries on the Laws of England*, 3rd revised ed. (Clark, NJ: The Lawbook Exchange, 2003).
5. See Heinrich A. Rommen, *The Natural Law*, trans. T. Hanley (St. Louis, MO: B. Herder, 1948).
6. The Tradition Project, Law and Religion Forum, https://lawandreligionforum.org/tradition-project/. Accessed October 1, 2019; Neil S. Siegel, "The Distinctive Role of Justice Samuel Alito: From a Politics of Restoration to a Politics of Dissent," *Yale Law Journal* 126 (2016): 164–77.
7. Todd W. Shaw and Steven G. Calabresi, "The Jurisprudence of Justice Samuel Alito," *George Washington Law Review*, 87 (2018): 507–78; See also Justice Alito's recent speech in Italy on the "Value of Tradition in the Global Context" at https://www.lumsa.it/en/value-tradition-global-context. Accessed October 1, 2018.

ACKNOWLEDGMENTS

This endeavor was made possible by the generous sabbatical policy of the City University of New York and John Jay College. Few institutions are as generous in allowing senior faculty, especially chairs, the opportunity to engage in research on such a grand level. I am fully aware of the system's gracious accommodation and, more particularly, express personal gratitude to President Karol Mason and Provost Yi Li for allowing this leave.

My host institution, Franciscan University of Steubenville, Ohio, has been welcoming and supportive since the day of my arrival. My heartfelt appreciation is extended to Dr. Stephen Krason, Chair of Political Science, who made the invitation to spend a year at Franciscan. It has been not only an exhilarating experience but also a transformational one. After 35 years as a chair, I had almost forgotten what it was like to simply teach and write, and it is a state of being I have always cherished. Franciscan has been supportive at every level, at the office of the provost, Dr. Daniel Kempton, to the warm and helpful Franciscan library staff and facility where I spent hours writing this and other texts. To say I am rejuvenated is an understatement.

To Anthem Press, I am most thankful, especially Megan Grieving, who can only be described as encouraging and most innovative. I look forward to a long association with this press.

To my longtime editorial colleague, Hope Haywood, I reiterate my constant awareness of her unrivaled talent to keep my work intact, to assure its quality and integrity, and to pull together all that is needed to make any text a reality. Hope has been overseeing my projects for nearly thirty years and with each work, her skill increases.

At John Jay College, a great deal of advance research was conducted and exceptionally so by a graduate student, Chris Singh, whose work made this project possible. Chris is presently the assistant director of security at New York's Metropolitan Museum of Art. Additional funding for this work was provided by a grant from the Office for the Advancement of Research at John Jay College.

Two faculty colleagues who provided greatly appreciated insights and a critique that surely made this a better work than first authored, were:

Dr. Dan Feldman of the City University of New York and John Jay College, a distinguished author-gorunded in a long history of political life in New York State, and Dr. Kevin Govern, an exceptional scholar and retired military officer who teaches at Ave Maria Law School. Both colleagues could not have been more generous on this project and even if in disagreement with the conclusions, saw the project as worthwhile in our quest for a meaningful jurisprudence.

Finally, my impetus to write largely arises from my unceasing intellectual interest in the subject matter but also because I am blessed with an amazing family—Jean Marie, for 47 years my closet friend and partner for life, and my seven children, Eleanor, Stephen, Anne Marie, John, Joe, Mary Claire, and Michael Augustine.

Chapter 1

A SHORT SUMMARY OF THE NATURAL LAW TRADITION

Natural law has long been a part and piece of Western jurisprudence—around 4,000 years or so. Its longevity alone made its contemporary demise even more remarkable. Either its adherents are utterly stubborn or its principles attractive enough to capture the legal imagination for millennia. Most other schools of jurisprudence are almost infantile in length and duration, for example, the utilitarianism of the eighteenth century, the critical legal theory of the twentieth or Hobbsian moral determinations based on power alone in the recent centuries. By contrast, natural law's lineage can be traced to early Greek and Roman thinkers and in fact is discoverable, in whole or in part, in ancient religious texts like the Bible, the Torah and the Koran. It is no secret that the idea of a law of nature or a natural law has long been on the minds of the world's greatest thinkers. So, when Plato spoke of gardening as a form of law, or Augustine looked to music as evidence of a natural principle, or Cicero espoused nature as the rule and arbiter of things lawful or not, the jurisprudential club has exceptional company. The line of thought reached its apex in Isidore, Albert the Great, Gratian, Peter of Abelard and, of course, Thomas Aquinas, up to the thirteenth century and extended its influence on our Founding Fathers and its notion of natural rights and their bestowal by a transcendent power.[1]

As a result, the natural law's demise in legal reasoning in continental philosophy and the late nineteenth until the mid-twentieth century in America is all the more puzzling. How could something of this legal and jurisprudential substantiality lose its punch and power so quickly? Since its general fall from grace, what has happened to our culture, our legal system and our notions of justice? In fact, some have argued that any saving of the currently beleaguered legal system must recognize that the abandonment of the natural law has had grave consequences for our society. John Lawrence Hall makes this argument with clarity.[2]

That debate is for another day. In the interim, the question is whether jurisprudence is necessary in the broadest sense and whether the natural law should be revisited. More particularly, whether the tenets, the principles of the natural law, might have meaning and relevance in legal decisions since *Roe v. Wade*. Side by side, with this argument, is whether the natural law has really been abandoned in full. While the school has fallen out of favor with the legal intelligentsia and law school academics, it is a safe bet that there are still judges and legal arguments that find their foundation in natural law principles.

Considering these foundational questions, the thesis posed here depends upon a natural law content that reached its pinnacle in the thought and analysis posed by St. Thomas Aquinas. Clearly, even his detractors realize that his treatment of the natural law was the most comprehensive and systematic then and now. Writers like Alisdair McIntyre, Robert George and John Finnis would all attest to this primacy of coverage.[3] As such, that is how natural law will be assessed in light of specific cases since the abortion decision. In a nutshell, natural law can be discovered in those reasoned opinions, especially as to its tenets and precepts, namely:

- doing good and avoiding evil,
- self-preservation,
- procreation and sexual attraction,
- care of offspring,
- communal and social living, and
- belief in a deity.

Those entrusted with the enactment, enforcement, decision making and advocacy of law in contemporary settings must possess a conception, an idea, a meaning of what law is. Each judge and jurist, each scholar of jurisprudence, each lawyer must yearn to discover the essence of what the law means. Every judge and lawyer, by nature, must ask hard questions about law, many of which extend far beyond the language of law or its precedent and principle. Where is the law rooted? From whence does the law derive its legitimacy and authority? What is the basis for the justness of any law? How can the law guarantee consistency, universality or the capacity to apply to individual circumstances? In what way are laws properly interpreted? On what theory or legal principle can the notion of right, goodness and justice be discoverable? Over history, while natural law has never been declared "extinct," other schools of jurisprudence come and go while others hang on despite a failure to prove effectiveness. Whatever school of jurisprudence is adopted, from the secular positivist, the utilitarian or the relativist, each camp seeks a suitable rational for any law. Each jurisprudential school desires formal approval and legitimacy among legal colleagues and peers. The aim and ambition of natural law finds it fundamental home in teleology—of the human person's relationship with his or her Creator. Natural law is primarily cosmological and ontological, driven deep and unreservedly into the nature of man, his constitution, reason, intellect and rationality. By contrast, the positivist, those who solely ground jurisprudence in a philosophy of enactment, constructs his legal edifice on the indemonstrable, sociological foundation that issues no definite philosophy of man.[4] Utilitarians in the tradition of Jeremy Bentham,[5] manufacture a law's legitimacy from its inherent usefulness, a utility for the most part and for the most moments. To the Hegelian,[6] law is an expression, an unfolding of man as some historical form; to the Marxian,[7] law reflects the power base that wrenches both its authority and its corresponding materialism from the powerless and less influential. In any backdrop of jurisprudence, from the extremely rational to the reactionary, legal philosophy yearns for a foundation. Natural law articulates a legal ideology that is grounded in a teleological approach, where law is a far more esoteric principle than simple enactment, where law draws in the comprehensive whole, the perfection of God and his creation, the natural, rational orders of the human species and the ends and purposes of human existence.[8] Natural law discovers law in the pure reality of human operations—what is normative, predictable, inclined or disposed toward.

The natural law is incapable of bifurcating law from the operation of the human species since law is the rule and measure of reason itself.[9] The essence of law resides in human intellectual operations. Law is a rational plan and rule of operation, proper only to the rational being.[10] Promulgation, however, never fully embraces the context and essence of law but is but "a necessary condition that law be observed."[11] Western thought, since the time of the Hellenic world, takes for granted that law is a grander enterprise than only its making. For most of legal history, law had both transcendent and earthly qualities. The idea of law in a tiered sense, the higher over the lower, the superior over the inferior, the supernatural over the natural, is a long-standing theme in historical, natural law jurisprudence.

Natural Law Predecessors: A Short History

Ancient and classical vision

In the ancient world, the idea of nature as law or a natural law somehow being part of the cosmos, the universe itself, was not foreign or alien to the Hellenic and Roman world. Plato writes with regularity about law, the gods, divine and human justice and a hierarchical perspective on morality, truth and perfection. Plato accepts, without much argument, the existence of divine forces in human reality.[12] The "orderliness" of the universe recognizes that life, and by association, the law, depends upon or is subject to beings beyond the finite dimension. Heaven before earth so to speak.

Early on, Plato portrays a reality twofold in design: one human, where the vagaries of day-to-day existence are grounded; another divine, where the divine god or gods (as the case may be) set the example and provide or detract from human experience. In this sense, man makes or breaks his world by his adherence to law but, as is typical in Greek theology, may be an unwitting recipient of a divinely generated justice or injustice. In "Book I," in the *Laws* this position is urged from the outset. "They are correct laws, laws that make those who use them happy. For they provide all the good things. Now the good things are two-fold, some human, some divine. The former depends on the divine goods, and if a city receives the greater it will also acquire the lesser. If not, it will lack both."[13]

In Plato's world, human agents depend upon and pray to the gods for justice. Man alone is inadequate to assure a just society for "if the gods are willing, the laws will succeed in making our city blessed and happy."[14] At the level of the divine, there is perfection, beauty and justice—traits difficult to achieve in a changeable and terminal world. In the divine, all things reach perfection, whether art, music or a craft. The divine provides the blueprint for what law is and should be, since the divine is encased without error, capable of self-movement and generation and the cause of all else.

Nature too plays a pivotal role in Plato's perspective on law. That Plato has long been associated with some type of natural law reasoning has been the subject of scholarly debate. This connection to nature further buttresses Plato's resistance to positivism and supports this loftier jurisprudence discussed thus far. To latch onto nature signifies Plato's comprehensive legal formula, a formula that readily accepts enactments and promulgations, though not in a metaphysical vacuum. Plato perceives nature as a grounding station, a panoply of norms and universal expectations. Nature is not exclusively a hodgepodge of occurrences without rhyme or design but, more appropriately, is a rule and measure, an operation with not only means but also proper ends and an added entanglement with the divine. Nature is not mere chance but a divinely executed action. In *Timaeus*, Plato asserts that "all souls are said to have been made according to one formula, and the myth of the *Politicus* speaks of the whole human flock and of one divine shepherd."[15] In *The Phaedo*, Plato dwells intently upon how man's soul is guided by nature's prescription. "The subject of the Phaedo is not the soul of Greeks or Persians but the soul of man."[16]

Whether horses, eyes, organic or inorganic matter, Plato discerns a law of nature or natural law in every facet of existence. The order of things, in general, according to Leo Strauss, "is established by nature."[17] In all facets of

Plato's jurisprudence, nature stands neither alone nor in domination over man or the gods. Platonic conceptions of divine law and nature's order will be central and undeniable tenets in his legal philosophy.

Aristotle's major contribution to the formulation of a natural law theory is less extensive than his counterparts, yet still powerfully relevant. It is Aristotle's view that every law should direct the citizen to virtue—and since virtue conforms with human reason best, he sets out the compelling view that law is not about will or whim, emotion or choices but rather rooted in reason and rationality. This finding delivers extraordinary implications for the natural law school—that law, reason and virtue are blended and amalgamated. Reason is consistent with a good and virtuous existence and, therefore, a lawful life, while its contrary, vice, aligns itself with irrationality and illegality. Aristotelian thinking[18] adopts an alternative to the *Forms*, replacing this dualistic reality with a philosophy of being, *actuality* and *potentiality*, an ordering of life, means, ends and goods, which the natural law urges. Aristotle's ideas of justice, reason and law in a human and transcendent sense are now central to natural law reasoning.[19] Just as compellingly, Aristotle discerns the habituating tendencies in law since law and legislation are the means by which "all men become virtuous."[20] Aristotle poses the law's training propensity, as a form of shaping civic-minded inhabitants, especially for the young who "must be regulated by laws."[21] Aristotle exhorts the human agent "to become immortal as far as that is possible and do our utmost to live in accordance with what is highest in us"[22] to live life "guided by reason,"[23] for such an existence "is the best and most pleasant for man."[24] To be a lawful person, the actor must carry out existence in accordance with the "nature proper to each thing."[25] For Aristotle, the state, the law, exists for happiness and the advancement of virtue and wisdom.[26] Individual virtue leads a collective of virtuous agents comprising the community and the communal good, Aristotle claims. Aristotle is incapable of differentiating individual conduct from its effect on the collective whole, for "it is evident that the same life is best for each individual, and for states and for mankind collectively."[27] That virtue is synonymous with law will be Aristotle's legacy. Both Plato and Aristotle fix their eyes toward the heavens, knowing that any chance for temporary happiness in a mutable environment will depend on the celestial heights.

Roman jurists, in the mold of Cicero, affirmed the connection between a higher and lower form of law. Cicero's masterpiece, *De Legibus*,[28] expends considerable time laying out multiple levels in law, allowing for the necessity of positive human laws, then passionately reminding his readers not to forget the law's ultimate source that is beyond the temporal. Cicero poetically argues that the human person, due to his or her reason and rationality, lives in communion—a state connecting God and the human person. "Inasmuch as there is no attribute superior to reason, and it is present in both God and man, it must be the essential basis for communion between man and God."[29] When Cicero declares that God is the "supreme"[30] law, by implication and explicit meaning, he admits a continuum of laws, a series of law forms that stand atop one another, integrated, yet simultaneously existing in separate or diverse domains.

Cicero's legal dialogue anticipates the role of reason in jurisprudence. Cicero recognized that human beings are capable of reason and, as a result, are qualified to create laws. Reason, especially *recta ratio* (right reason), presumes a legal product in tune with the drafter's essential nature. Cicero describes how reason is the glue for both person and culture.

> The essential justice that binds human society together and is maintained by one law is right reason, expressed in commands and prohibitions. Whoever disregards this law, whether written or unwritten, is unjust.[31]

Nature, Cicero declares, is our other dependable guide, and, in fact, justice itself is derived from or discoverable in nature. Cicero foretells of the natural law model proffered by Aquinas, particularly the natural law's instructive powers that are permanent fixtures and guideposts in moral activity.[32]

"Goodness is not just a matter of opinion—what idea is more absurd than that? Since then we distinguish good from evil by its nature, and since these qualities are fundamental in nature, surely by a similar logic we may discriminate and judge between what is honorable and what is base according to nature."[33]

Early medieval legal thought on the natural law

By the time of St. Augustine, the rudimentary, pagan conceptions of law donned a Stoic, yet religious, Christianized attitude, a sort of supreme cosmic rationality, although that sort of pantheism seems fully rejected by Cicero. In Cicero, God creates and oversees, not just participates, in the workings of the universe. Augustine picks up by fully rejecting God as being nature or one in the same and his laws a part of how the universe works. The law's supremacy was not simply a perfection, a form without force, but the active deliberation of a creating, perfect and all-loving God. Augustine, throughout his brilliant inquiries, erects a multilevel edifice where law resides. According to St. Augustine, the eternal law of God, the *lex aeterna*, served as the starting point for human operations since God is the author of the universe. Augustine declares God the primordial truth where "truth is one and common to all, just as much as it is true."[34] Creation itself manifests this eternal perfection, the eternal law of the Supreme God who is its author. "And this physical and moral order, which in its sublime rationality and perfection is eternal and immutable, possesses all the characteristics of a law or norm which is also declaratory of an absolute and perfect universality, necessity, and rationality."[35]

In his *Confessions*, Augustine determines the futility of existence without reference to the perfection of God. "Wheresoever I found truth, there I found my God, truth itself, and since I first learned the truth I have not forgotten it. Therefore, ever since I learned about you, you abide in my memory, and I find you there when I recall you to mind and take delight in you."[36] Augustine's *lex aeterna* is not a pantheistic ideal, where God is the universe itself. Instead, it is "the ineradicable and sublime administration of all things with proceeds from the Divine Providence.[37]

The *lex aeterna* is a "divinely ordained orderliness"[38] covering every aspect of human existence. St. Augustine states, "To put in a few words, as best I can, the notion of eternal law that has been impressed upon our minds: it is that law by which it is just that everything be ordered in the highest degree."[39] Hovering over all levels of human existence, Augustine's *lex aeterna* perfectly represents law as the act of legislator, lawyer and the judge interpreting its content, in submission to a divine plan and a divine will.[40]

For Augustine, happiness and orderliness is a function of the self-will and of self-control, in tune with God's rational legal plan. Augustine portrays the happy life as choosing in sync with God's reason.

> Or how does a man gain a happy life through his will, when although all want to be happy, there are so many unhappy men [...] The eternal law, to which it is time now to turn our attention, established with immutable firmness the point that merit lies in the will, while happiness and unhappiness are a matter of reward and punishment.[41]

Besides this, Augustine's contribution to the hierarchical ideal in law is quite evident in his discussion of the *lex naturalis*, the law of nature. Descending from the apex of the eternal law is the imprint of the Creator on beings created. This imprint, this inherency, Augustine terms the *lex naturalis*, is participatory in the *lex aeterna*. Transcribed, implanted in the soul of man, the *lex naturalis* is man's imperfect participation in the perfection of the eternal law. The *natural law* opens a door to the eternal perfection of our Creator and "is written in the hearts of men, which iniquity itself effects not."[42]

Augustinian legal thought is essentially derivative in design. Natural law "is to be discovered in the divinely ordained ontological order. It is the observance of this infinite natural and moral order which forms the true substance of the Augustinian concept of law and right, justice and morality."[43] Human laws are not independent of this order and are, in fact, partners to the natural and eternal laws. Human laws are crucial to individual and social operations and are, according to St. Augustine, "helpful to men living in this life."[44] Nations and states cannot exist without temporal laws.

When a human law is inconsistent with and contrary to the tenets of the eternal and natural law, it loses its force and identity as law. Augustine's maxim, "an unjust law is not a law at all,"[45] imparts the derivative quality of his jurisprudence. He issues this provocative argument in *De Libero Arbitrio*. "We shall not, shall we, dare say that these laws are unjust—or rather, are not laws at all, for I think that a law that is not just is not a law."[46]

During the centuries following Augustine's contribution, various insights were added to this metaphysical conception of the natural law. For example, the writings of Isidore of Seville[47] whose seventh-century analysis of the natural law struck a chord in Aquinas relative to human law and its relationship to the natural law.[48] In St. Thomas's *Treatise on Law*, two questions are posed that expressly mention Isidore:

> Whether Isidore appropriately described the quality of positive law?[49]
>
> Whether Isidore's division of human laws is appropriate?[50]

Isidore surely firmed up the natural law as being a hierarchical construct for human laws are not severable from the higher laws that justify their enactment. Isidore's "natural law is a law common to all peoples (nations), and is held to be not something established by man himself, but rather a common natural instinct."[51] Isidore's willingness to author a series of particular determinations that represent the content of the natural law, most of which is instinctual, including marriage,[52] procreation and education of offspring,[53] and other prescriptions will further shape natural law content in the centuries to follow.

Finally, quite evident in Isidore's work is the recognition of how authority, legal or otherwise, descends from God. Government and individuals both function because of it. Kings as well as subjects were bound by the law identically. These same characters compel king and citizen to obey the law so that justice might be nurtured. Truth is the ruler's guide.[54] Isidore's prevailing imperative was to demand and search for certitude because each thing tends "one end of truth."[55]

Medieval conceptions of the natural law

Between the time of Isidore and the eleventh century, there were scant contributions to a natural legal theory, with most authors remaining true to the Augustinian model. In time, St. Anselm of Canterbury affirmed the hierarchical structure inherent in the natural law theory. Anselm's *Cur Deus Homo* declared that God is "the supreme good, is justice himself and is the perfection all beings seek."[56] Law can only be law when compatible with justice, God being its highest and greatest good. Anselm's *De Conceptu Virginalia et de Originali Peccato* also affords insight into how God is enthroned above any theory of law and justice. Nothing in God is injustice or unjust.[57] At the pinnacle of justice is truth itself, and justice instructs the human person on how to live with self and others.[58] In this truth, God subsists and nothing else can corrupt.[59] Anselm advances a theory of justice based on the rectitude of will, in contrast to those espousing the centrality of reason in natural law reasoning. Rectitude seeks the mean between extremes; rectitude is only possible when a man orders and directs "his life according to the rules of divine or eternal law."[60]

In the later medieval period, philosopher-ethicist Peter Abelard's philosophic approach further solidified natural law jurisprudence. Abelard made notable contributions to a theory of jurisprudence by his threefold category of law: God-given law, natural law and the law of the Old and New Testaments.[61] Mixing the transient reality of man with divine revelation bespeaks a commitment to teleology. Replaying St. Paul's message that there is a law inscribed or written in the hearts of men, "which enables them naturally to do the things which the written law commands,"[62] attests to Abelard's multidimensional perspective. Abelard's conceptual approach accepts the dominant position divine law assumes. Not only is man, by committing crimes, displeasing his nature, he is displeasing his Creator. Abelard summarizes in his *Ethics*:

> If perhaps someone asks whence we can infer that the transgression of adultery displeases God more than overeating, I think divine law can teach us, which has not instituted any satisfaction of punishment to penalize the latter, but it has decreed that the former be damned not with any penalty but with the supreme affliction of death. For where the love of our neighbour, which the Apostle says is "the fulfilling of the Law," is more fully damaged, more is done against it and sin is greater.[63]

The significance of Abelard's thought rests in his emphasis on particular legal and moral situations. Abelard builds a more complex series of rules that were derived from not only the Testaments but also the natural law impressed in the psyche of the human species. Abelard's ethical theory stresses the universality and immutability of our natural law imprint. The natural law, impressed on Christian, Jew and Pagan, is simultaneously revealed in Scripture and encapsulates "the basic moral prohibitions of murder, stealing and so on."[64] Abelard also comments on the relationship of justice, the ethical life of the individual and the common good. Justice is not exclusively what is due another since any theory of reciprocity and equality is impossible without reference to the collective whole. Abelard clearly delivers this principle:

> For it often happens that, when we give someone what is his due on account of his merits, what we do for one individual brings common harm. Therefore, in order to prevent the part being put before the whole, the individual before the community, to the definition [of justice] there is added "provided that the common utility is preserved." We should do all things so that we each seek not our own, but the common good, and provide for the public welfare rather than that of our families and live not for ourselves but our fatherland.[65]

By the twelfth century, it would be difficult to find a legal thinker who did not share the basic sentiments outlined to this point. The law, structured in tiers and escalating dimensions, anchored its legitimacy in a higher–lower continuum. The legal thought of Gratian, particularly his *Decretals*, and more specifically his *Treatise on Laws* at DD 1–20, provides a confirmation of a developed and well-defined natural law jurisprudence. In Gratian, virtue is presented as essential to any definition of law, and the overall purpose of the law is to lead men to virtue so that "human temerity can be controlled, innocence can be protected in the midst of wicked people, and the capacity of the wicked to harm others can be restrained by fear of punishment."[66] These same human laws, prodding man to virtue, are legitimate only to the extent compatible with a natural law, infused by the Creator. Gratian further comments, "Now natural law similarly prevails by dignity over custom and enactments. So, whatever has been either received in usages or set down in writing is to be held null and void if it is contrary to natural law."[67] Further, Gratian's natural law, just as Abelard attempts, delivers a series of general precepts, "common to all nations"[68] and to all peoples. These primary tenets of the natural law are, by way of example,

> the union of men and women, the succession and rearing of children, the common possession of all things, the identical liberty of all, or the acquisition of things that are taken from the heavens, earth, or sea, as well as the return of a thing deposited or of money entrusted to one, and the repelling of violence by force. This, and anything similar, is never regarded as unjust but is held to be natural and equitable.[69]

At this stage, definite signs of the natural law's participatory qualities, its binding and obligatory power and its resistance and condemnation of human laws enacted contrarily to its content are evident. As a rule, Gratian argues, "dispensation"[70] from its content is not permitted.

Alexander of Hales dwelled upon similar subject matter in his *Summa Universae Theologiae*. A hierarchy of laws underscores Alexander's legal formula, for every law, even the positive variety, is bound to the eternal law of God.[71] This eternal law is impressed and imprinted in the souls of rational creatures.[72] Alexander's legal thinking is undeniably derivative, maintaining that every law, human or divine, derives its force from the *lege aeterna*[73] assuming that the law is just and good. The *legis aeternae* is immutable[74] and absolute.[75] An unjust law is not derived from the eternal law and properly described as maliciously evil and defectively ordered.[76] Both human law and the natural law are derived from the eternal law as well. At the lower part of the legal continuum, human laws are integrated into his hierarchical plan,[77] just as the natural law, since every good is undeniably and universally from the eternal good, just as the natural law is derived from the eternal law.[78]

Alexander is reverential about the natural law, its immutability,[79] its rationality,[80] its mandatory connection to the positive law.[81] Finally, the tenets of the natural law help the human agent to do what is right and to forever journey toward the God who implants its directives. Alexander's natural reasoning is an intensely intimate participation with the eternal law of God. Its precepts ordinate us toward God[82] and assure that we love God over all things.[83] Alexander's law concerns itself with justice,[84] the blessed, the beautiful and the sacred.[85]

Natural law tradition and jurisprudence finds a vigorous advocate in Johannes Fidenza, more commonly known as St. Bonaventure. Bonaventure's natural law is a blend of imprints, scriptural instruction and universal truths. He sums up the idea as the natural law impressed on the human mind and soul by the eternal law.[86] The dictates of the natural law reflect "the eternal law, which is the ultimate rule of all human action and the principal source of the order of human life."[87] The dictates include, but are not limited to, a natural knowledge of God, an instant realization of His perfection and that *good is to be done and evil to be avoided*. Bonaventure poses positions that will be adopted in the centuries ahead such as the role of practical reason in decision making, habits and virtues; the idea of *synderesis*, where the human person chooses the good, not by compulsion but from desire; and how the intellect is subject to habituation, in the form of right reason, a *recta ratio*, where it deliberates and counsels rightly without coercion or enticement. Bonaventure's portrayal of the human player concludes that will moves the intellect, while most natural law thinkers prioritize reason and the intellect as the driver of natural law content and reasoning. Certainly, Bonaventure fails to fit the Thomistic ideal as to reason's supremacy since the natural law binds the will.[88]

Taken as a whole, Bonaventure's thought posits practical reason as "infallibly connected with volition,"[89] but this interaction never detracts from the primacy and celebration of will.[90] Similar to Augustine, Bonaventure's man needs some form of illumination, a divine gravitational pull so to speak. The Aquinian man, whose will chooses, can only do so because it is "impregnated by reason."[91] For Bonaventure, the imprint is in the human constitution, starting with Adam and Eve.[92] The intellect "exercises final causality in moving the will, i.e., the intellect's judgment presents some good which as a goal moves the will to act."[93] The arguments made, though contrary to one another, still assume a teleological vision of law. In either case, whether intellectualized or willed, the content of the natural law trumps the moral legitimacy of positive law alone.

The shift toward a natural law jurisprudence grounded in the primacy of reason becomes quite evident in the work of St. Albert the Great. Albert devised a philosophical approach that merges the temporality of the human agent, his or her astounding freedom of intellect, and a theory of law that encompasses the supremacy of reason as the knowledge doorway for natural law principles.[94] The influence of Albert is felt most keenly by the greatest natural law thinker, St. Thomas, whose relationship with Albert was one of student-professor with St. Thomas studying "under Albert for four full years at Cologne."[95] By most accounts, their mutual experiences were characterized by respect and admiration,[96] and throughout both their respective lives their intellectual interests largely were in concurrence. Albert perceives law in both a personal and political sense: to control the masses, to maintain order and to compel nations and states to unite. Law is a sanction, an authoritative reminder as well as a tool for human advancement and virtue, making both individual citizen and the nation good.[97]

Albert's definition of the natural law includes universality in design and principle, a content instinctually and inherently known and understood and written and inscribed in reason.[98] While positive human law differs across the world's stage, the natural law is the same for all[99] since it is innately and inherently possessed and discoverable as dictates and commands in human reason.[100] Such a law cannot be banished from memory, but its extent and quality may diminish or differ in the consideration of particular dilemmas. No dispensation from its content is possible, nor can it be altered or eliminated, Albert holds, for the natural law is part of our fundamental makeup, in the same way reason is a component of the human agent.[101]

Albert confirmed that the intellect is the central basis for law, both in deliberative and command capacity, that law is an obligatory act, not because a law is willed but because reason and the intellect have ends and goods that are nonnegotiable. Only intellect can discern truth, objective reality—the essence of obligation. Only reason binds the human action and, as a result, nothing but reason can provide the underpinning for law. Albert connects reason to the obligatoriness of the natural law;[102] only intellect is capable of discerning reality and Albert recognized that reason was the link, the conduit between the will and objective reality. Obligation emerges not from choice but from truth itself. The intellect alone discovers prima facie truth. The will must choose among many options in objective and subjective reality. It is in the contemplative life, not the active life, where man reaches the fullness of his being. Contemplation is the province of reason, not will. Reason is what makes the man and the law. Albert characterizes the essence of man as reason, not will. Reason is therefore nobler than the will and serves as the legitimate anchor for law and legal thinking. Reason is the *mensura*[103] that insures a lawful person and community. In this way, reason is law.[104,105]

Albert is equally dedicated to a perpetual dialogue on justice and injustice, a tendency comparable to his student, Thomas. Justice as well as other virtues are intimately part of Albert's jurisprudence. Justice, in its most general sense is giving one another that *debitum*[106]—what is due. Justice is rectitude, ordination of people and things; legal justice is communal relationships in balance; and, justice is always toward another. Justice is concerned with every act of virtue.[107]

St. Thomas Aquinas on the natural law

From Albert forward, the apex of natural law jurisprudence resides in the great systematic philosopher—theologian, St. Thomas Aquinas. Building on the depth and breadth of those preceding him, St. Thomas would author a natural law jurisprudence that has no rivals even to the present. St. Thomas's insight into the nature of law is erudite and profound. As comprehended by St. Thomas, law is juridical[108] but only partially. St. Thomas paints the broadest picture of law possible. First, law is synonymous with God, rationality and a rational plan of creation and operations. Even the irrational creature, as directed by God through natural inclination, has a legalistic quality. Law pertains to the species. Modern-day legal thinkers would be confused by the comprehensiveness of his definition:

> Just as the acts of irrational creatures are directed by God through a rational plan which pertains to their species, so are the acts of men directed by God inasmuch as they pertain to the individual, as we have shown. But the acts of irrational creatures, as pertaining to the species,

are directed by God through natural inclination, which goes along with the nature of the species. Therefore, over and above this, something must be given to men whereby they may be directed in their own personal acts. And this we call law.[109]

Therefore, Thomistic law defines itself in a more profound sense beyond promulgation, for the law's essence mirrors the fullness of God's creation, the nature of his creatures and the unfolding of species and their corresponding operations. Law is supreme, divine legislation in addition to its positive codification or ordinance; it is the plan for a life consistent with this divine rationality—a life of virtue, and it is the order "whereby man clings to God."[110] St. Thomas lays out other attributes and characteristics regarding the concept of law, a summary of the more poignant features, in the sections ahead.

Law as the rule and measure of reason

As his predecessors, particularly Cicero and Albert the Great, St. Thomas firmly and unequivocally ties reason to his definition of law. In St. Thomas's view, law is a "certain rational plan and rule of operation"[111] and especially proper "to rational creatures only."[112] St. Thomas confidently asserts that "law is something pertaining to reason"[113] and a measure of human activity. If it is a measure of human action, one must presuppose there is a connection to human reason, since only the human species analyzes, deliberates and counsels about activity and movement. Law is entwined with being itself and is the handmaiden of reason itself. When dealing with the law's essence, St. Thomas imparts primary stature to reason:

> Law is a rule and measure of acts, whereby man is induced to act or is restrained from acting; for *lex* [*law*] is derived from *ligare* [*to bind*], because it binds one to act. Now the rule and measure of human acts is the reason, which is the first principle of human acts, as is evident from what has been stated above. For it belongs to the reason to direct to the end, which is the first principle in all matters of action, according to the Philosopher.[114]

By contrast, human activities and movements contrary to reason's operations will lack the stature of law and legality. The model St. Thomas provides is not one of will but of intellect, of reason in the human person.[115] St. Thomas indicates that law is a dictate, an ordination of reason, standing in a superior position to human will. Reason mirrors the law of our being, our consistent and compatible dispositions toward particular goods and ends.[116] Reason tells the human actor not simply what law is in form but what should be done to be consistent with the laws of our nature. Reason instructs and guides us.

Law as an instrument of the common good

Since man is a social animal, any legitimate theory of law extends to a culture, a community and a civilization. St. Thomas understands that the ordinating influence of law does not terminate with individual activity, because it just as pertinently applies to the common good of a nation as it applies to the common good of its individual citizenry. In response to whether a law should be crafted for the individual or common case, St. Thomas indicates that every human law derives legitimacy from its relationship to the common interest. Laws consist of far more than individual applications but are germane to the life of a nation. "Hence human laws should be proportioned to the common good. Now the common good comprises many things. Therefore, law should take account of many things, as to persons, as to matters, and as to times."[117]

With keen insight, St. Thomas discerns the futility of a law that applies in the individual scenario alone. Laws are implemented not for the single person or the one-time circumstance, but instead law is a common precept applicable to a community of men.[118] It is for the multitude that laws exist, because laws for the community are nothing more than the social sum of its members. Law, particularly the human variety, "is framed for the multitude of beings."[119] Law is equated with the happiness in both individual and culture. If lacking a communal component, the enactment would be "devoid of the nature of law."[120]

Law as good and end

Any Thomistic understanding of law considers the concept of the good, whether temporal, temporary ones or the ultimate good, the penultimate end of man—God. Holistic in style, universal in approach, Thomistic law pulls in all that is good, beautiful and perfect and finds final solace only in the beatific vision. Thomistic jurisprudence embraces more than the functionality of utilitarianism, the artificiality of Marxism[121] or any relative, transformative humanism. A theory of law, so says St. Thomas, is loftier, rising above "prejudice and passion"[122] and fixing "upon eternal reasons to reaffirm a forgotten truth, formulate a new principle, or overturn an established error."[123]

To be consistent with reason, man seeks perfection in every category of life. He or she can will otherwise, but in the intricate and incomprehensible act of creation itself, God could not fashion a being who would command his or her own destruction. Since the Creator is all-good, so too the creatures molded in his image. These ideas will be more easily understood in the context of Aquinas's various kinds of law, specifically the eternal, natural, divine and human. Man's reason, the artifice of law itself, can readily discover these ends. Perfect, unreserved happiness resides only in the splendor of divine perfection. "Perfect orderliness,"[124] as Chroust terms it, is "declaratory of the *summum bonum*, that is, of God."[125]

At every level of Thomistic thinking, legal or otherwise, God is the ultimate end of the reasoning, intellectual creature. St. Thomas urges us,

> Now, from what has been seen earlier, it is established that God is the ultimate end of the whole of things; that an intellectual nature alone attains to Him in Himself, that is by knowing and loving Him, as is evident from what has been said.[126]

Law: The supremacy of reason over will

At its foundation, law is an ordinance of reason since every human agent is endowed with rational faculties. In a similar way, God's eternal law is His own intellect, the divine exemplar, the blueprint for existence. Incredibly, God and man share rationality, although man's version is imperfect. St. Thomas indicates that this rational force in the human person is his or her chance to participate in the Eternal Law of the Divine intellect, in Divine Reason. God's reason embraces, by its perfect nature, incalculable goodness, purity and perfection. Man's nature, which is identified by its rationality, will essentially apprehend these same ends. It will have no other choice. It is will that corrodes this settled order. It is intellect that knows worthy goods.[127]

The will of man, contrasted with reason, can and does what it wills. The will's willing can be about bad, evil ends, while reason is powerless to identify destructive purposes. Early on, Aquinas poses this inevitable and unstoppable path reason takes. Reason does not elect as will does—will can only command; reason moves the will but cannot force the will. In will, the beauty and tragedy of human freedom unfolds. The complete human act has both qualities, that of intellect and will, with intellect reigning supreme.[128] In choosing intellect and rationality as his foundation, St. Thomas speaks loudly of his preference for the permanent, the dependable and the certain. St. Thomas's law is not subject to the whims of individual will but is planted in the firm earth of reason.

From the earliest pages of the *Treatise on Law*, St. Thomas places reason in its primary place and context when judgments are rendered about acceptable human behavior. Laws, if effective and meaningful, must be the product of a rational being, using and employing reason to adhere to what nature demands of us. To live in accordance with nature is to live a fully reasoned and virtuous existence for only "reason issues its commands as regards things ordained" to our proper end.[129] Aquinas never ceases to blend reason and virtue with his jurisprudence for he sees law as a "dictate of reason,"[130] its primary effect being to "lead its subjects to their proper virtue."[131] When St. Thomas delineates his theory of natural law, he commences that discussion by referencing how the human agent can naturally know its content and how by "the light of natural reason [...] we discern what is good and what is evil."[132] When connecting human law, primarily the promulgation of the legislator, St. Thomas characterizes these practical applications, these "particular determinations, devised by human reason,"[133] as dependent upon the identical theory of reason as does the natural law. Human law is still a "dictate of the practical reason," which depends on "human reason to proceed."[134] At the same time that reason is trumpeted as the rule and measure of law, its effects and impacts are directed to the good, to the virtuous and ultimately our natural and final end—God.

Suffice it to say, Thomistic jurisprudence, and especially the natural law, is one planted in the mind of man, forged and burned into the intellect, delivering predictable and reliable messages about what our ends are. The messages are unambiguous and universal. Whether their content is understood is not in dispute; whether the instructions are adopted and adhered to is a matter of will. Reason is law for it ordains the actor toward those ends the intellect unequivocally prescribes.

What is so reassuring about Thomistic jurisprudence is its teleological permanence. Anton-Herman Chroust describes St. Thomas's enterprise, where the intellect of God is the *lex aeterna*, as the "measure of every corner of being."[135] St. Thomas's picture of human operations is psychologically complicated, yet beautifully accurate. Man engages the universe in greater ways than the appetitive, the sensual or the pleasurable. Man, like the laws enacted, mirrors the wholeness of human life. In *Love and Friendship*, St. Thomas uses a broad brush to describe man.

> The good man wishes and performs good because of himself, i.e., because of his intellectual nature, which is principal in man. (That seems most important which is principal in a being.) Thus, the virtuous man always strives to act according to reason. Therefore, it is plain that in so doing he also always wishes that which is good for himself.[136]

Law and its correlation to virtue

St. Thomas's jurisprudence never defines law as the sole act of the legislator but a product intended toward a specific end, of happiness and the virtuous life. It is within the "social, moral and intellectual context"[137] that the human species moves "towards the end of a perfected science, in which a finally adequate comprehension of first principles has been achieved, that the Aristotelean and Thomistic conceptions of truth and rational justification find their place."[138] Law unsupportive of these goals will not train or educate the young or old. Good laws, by friendly coercion, make the actor "accustomed to good things which will not be distasteful but pleasant after the habit has been formed."[139] The objective of human law is to look to the heavens and to prod man toward a life of virtue. A Thomist discovers early on that law has a formidable relationship with virtue, and that every human law should contribute to the advancement of individual and collective virtue. Law should foster not inhibit self-perfection.[140] Human law transforms the citizenry "who live under common legal institutions into perfect citizens."[141] The law, as an instrument of the state, wishes perfection and happiness for its community. The positive or human law cannot possibly extinguish human imperfection in every case, but it can gradually lead men to a life of virtue.[142]

Throughout his natural law analysis, St. Thomas discerns the interplay and the compatibility of law and virtue. Virtue is the ordered disposition of the soul, the proper habituation and inclination to acceptable goods and, thus, a suitable exercise of reason. As such, virtue experiences the effect of law and by implication is within its general definition. St. Thomas repeatedly refers to virtue in the *Treatise on Law*, for to be a law it must make the subject good.[143]

Law is hierarchical

As in many of his predecessors, the law will be interdependently weaved into the other forms of law. Human law will need higher forms for any real legitimacy—whether it be the eternal, natural or divine. Aquinas offers up types of law that cannot be severed from one another and, in fact, are thoroughly dependent on each classification. So human laws need the natural law for determinations of propriety, and the natural law is tethered to the eternal law of God as his creative imprint. The divine law shall provide revelatory instruction on how to live one's life in conformity with the natural and the eternal. All of this will become more obvious and apparent when covering the content of the natural law and its applications to particular legal dilemmas.

In sum, the contributions of Aquinas in natural law jurisprudence serve as the benchmark for this school—the Thomistic system achieving a fullness and richness unparalleled in our intellectual history. Little has really been added to the debate and content since the thirteenth century, and while there are some variations in more contemporary thinkers, such as John Finnis, Jacques

Maritain and Germain Grisez, to name just a few examples, there is a tendency to be strikingly less doctrinaire and less confident in the discernment of the natural law content.[144] Finnis, in particular, has tended to question the "innateness" of the natural law content and is more apt to conclude that each human being learns from the experiences derived from particular inclinations.[145] He also displays a tendency to diminish the idea that "goods" are mandatorily part of the eternal law and more to living reasonably and consistently with a series of designated goods: Life, health, knowledge, play, friendship, religion, and aesthetic experience have an intrinsic value because of our human nature and are readily discoverable in every culture.[146] But, despite his extraordinary brilliance, Professor Finnis affirms most of what Aquinas has offered for seven centuries. The same is also true of Jacques Maritain, whose classic work, *Man and the State*, affirms the need for and necessity of a natural law philosophy but uses differing terminology than posed by Aquinas.[147]

In particular, Maritain, like Finnis, is less likely to concur in the view that every human being can discover, self-evidently, principles of the natural law beyond to seek the good and avoid evil. It is through experience and human life that we tend to fathom our natural inclinations and then reach other conclusions about the natural law. For Aquinas, the basic content of the natural law is already innate and within the confines of reasons, but for Maritain, the only innate principle is the first one. Maritain argues that the intellect does not discover these moral principles by the speculative intellect alone and, as does Finnis, argues that further knowledge about our natural law tendencies is learned through our inclinations. Instead of being self-evident, those precepts or tenets are not clearly discernible but rather "obscure, unsystematic, vital knowledge by connaturality or congeniality, in which the intellect, in order to bear judgment, consults and listens to the inner melody that the vibrating strings of abiding tendencies make present in the subject."[148]

In contrast to Aquinas, Maritain displays a poetic although highly imprecise method for this discovery—for the "inner melody that the vibrating strings of abiding tendencies" will be hard to pin down. In any event, the distinction and differentiation do little to change the fundamental understanding of what the natural law means and is.[149]

The writings of Germain Grisez, often referred to as the founder of the "New Natural Law Movement," manifest a break—seemingly needless and hyper technical distinction with the old natural law. Grisez, like Finnis and Maritain, suspects that speculative intellect cannot know automatically all the precepts of the natural but must depend upon practical application and practical reasoning as the human agent lives out their lives on a day-to-day basis. In addition, the work of Grisez places less emphasis on the metaphysical dimensions of the natural law and more on the human inclination version.[150]

Most of the natural law precepts are discoverable after practical reason encounters its content and our dispositions or inclinations must contend with that content. Then and only then will the principles of the natural law become evident. Grisez remarks,

> Practical reason, equipped with the primary principle it has formed, does not spin the whole of natural law out of itself. It is true that if "natural law" refers to all the general practical judgments reason can form, much of natural law can be derived by reasoning. But reason needs starting points. And it is with these starting points that Aquinas is concerned at the end of the fifth paragraph. The primary precepts of practical reason, he says, concern the things-to-be-done that practical reason naturally grasps as human goods, and the things-to-be-avoided that are opposed to those goods.[151]

As in Finnis and Maritain, the arguments posed change the path to knowledge but not the knowledge itself. In the former natural law, the precepts are embedded, imprinted and discoverable. In the latter instance, only the primordial principle of the natural law is utterly impressed, while the remainder is findable after experience with the content. The subtleties do not change the fundamental notion of what natural law jurisprudence has been and is to this day.

A host of other characters have tinkered with the Thomist conception of the natural law or fully affirmed it. Bernard Lonergan's examination of the natural law and Aquinas elevates the role desire plays when choosing courses of conduct, of value judgments in the decision making and feelings as being part of the overall mix when discerning what should be done in accordance with the natural law. It is a very different bent to be sure.[152]

Lonergan's method, before full deliberation, asks questions regarding conduct and its alternatives and then weighs and evaluates the chosen conduct. This is achieved "affective insights attained by feelings as intentional responses to value."[153]

As a group, the view that natural law rules, moral norms and specific content are readily accessible seems too idealistic for the bulk of the citizenry. Only through experience will a human agent discover the "good" needed for compliance with the natural law—and while we may understand the primary tenet of the natural law on seeking the good and avoiding evil, the remaining content has a harder and more imprecise road to discovery.[154]

This is but a mere fraction of more contemporary natural law thinkers—all of whom could never be covered in a work of this scope and magnitude. And while some modern thinkers tinker with the method of the natural law, and even its substance as to precepts, many others resolutely affirm the genius and brilliance of the Thomistic version. Jean Porter's *Nature's Reason: A Thomistic Theory of the Natural Law* (2005) is a magnificent compendium of natural law reasoning that finds Aquinas and his natural law are to be seen in the fullness and comprehensiveness of both his substance and his method. She remarks,

> On the Thomistic account of the natural law, [...] there is nothing particularly mysterious about the phenomenon of human morality itself. On the contrary, morality on this account is an expression of the natural life of the human creature. As such, it is an expression of the creative wisdom of God, a reflection of the Divine Image borne by each human being, and an expression of the distinctively human mode of God's eternal providence; for all these reasons, it deserves our respect, even our reverence.[155]

Just as compellingly supportive has been the masterful work of Alisdair MacIntrye, whose two texts, *Whose Justice? Which Rationality?* and *After Virtue*, unequivocally endorse Aquinas and his Aristotelian heritage as a crucial philosophical system for the West's survival.[156]

When evaluating Aquinas and his overall penchant for rules and guideposts for human operations, gleaned from the natural law, MacIntyre observes,

> The moral life begins with rules designed to direct the will and desires to its and their good by providing a standard of right direction (rectitudo). This rectitude is valued, not for its own sake, but as leading to that perfected will and those perfected desires which happiness requires. Consequently the rules are to be valued as constituting the life which leads to perfect happiness, and they can only be understood insofar as their point and purpose is understood.[157]

Conclusion

Just completed was a short course in the history and meaning of the natural law and how that legal philosophy has conceptual depth and breadth for an eventual jurisprudence. The natural law can be typed as more than a singular idea and is properly designated a complete philosophical system covering everything from being and essence, God and the human person, both theological and philosophical principles, nature and natural science, heaven and its counterpart and, of course, the nature of law, legislation and the occupations related to it. Simply put, it is an immense field of ideas, not only in its range of coverage but also its long-standing influence. If the natural law lacked substantiality, it would have disappeared long ago. However, for nearly 4,500 years, the world has dabbled and debated in the notion of a natural law or a law of nature—probably because its participants live in the natural world and have already observed the many manifestations of law in the natural realm.

From the early Greeks to the Romans, from the diverse periods of the Middle Ages to the crowning glory of thirteenth-century Thomism, the path of the natural law has been persistent. Natural law jurisprudence is a mirror reflection of Thomistic thought, not because our intellectual history has become stunted or halted but because Aquinas offered up the most comprehensive and systematic examination imaginable. Even to the present, so many challenges to its legitimacy, especially the elites of academic environments and higher courts, have not succeeded in its full banishment. This persistence in natural law thinking is most likely because there is not only an appeal but also a perennial tug at truth in this jurisprudential school. For ethical dilemmas, moral and legal challenges and complicated human operations, few legal schools offer the type of reasoning that natural law does. This attractiveness might be related to the transcendent nature of the natural law, its fundamental passion about finding justice and truth and its optimistic and vivifying look at how the human actor connects and intersects with his or her neighbors and, more importantly, the Creator who fashions all human persons.

While critics may discount the natural law and call for its banishment into the dust pile of bad ideas, and others challenge the entire theory empirically and scientifically as a fantasy or theological wizardry, or others literally dance on the head of conceptual pin as to what this term means or what does one really know, the natural law remains as fixed and permanent as a lighthouse. In the end, it cannot be banished; it cannot be blotted out; it cannot be eradicated from the human person's intellect because the essence of the natural law directly mirrors our very being.

Notes

1 Vernon Bourke, "The Ethical Justification of Legal Punishment," *American Journal of Jurisprudence*, 22, no. 1 (1977): 1–18; Roberti Bellarmini, *Opera Omnia, Del Summo Pontefice, Tomus Primus* (Naples: Neapoli, 1872); Albert the Great, *Opera omnia*, ed., P. Jammy (Lyons, 1651); Albert the Great, *Opera omnia*, ed., A. Borgnet (Paris: Vives, 1890–99); Cajetan (Thomas de Vio), *Commentaria in Summam Theologicam S. Thomae*, ed. Leonine (Antwerp, 1568; Rome, 1888–1906); Dominic Soto, *De ustitia et jure* (Venice, 1602); Jacques Maritain, *The Rights of Man and Natural Law*, trans., Doris C. Anson (New York: Charles Scribner's, 1943).

2 John Lawrence Hill, *After the Natural Law: How the Classical Worldview Supports Our Modern Moral and Political Views* (San Francisco, CA: Ignatius Press, 2016). See also Charles

P. Nemeth, *Aquinas in the Courtroom: Lawyers, Judges, and Judicial Conduct* (Santa Barbara, CA: Praeger Press, 2001).

3   Alasdair MacIntyre, *After Virtue: A Study in Moral Theory*, 2nd ed. (Notre Dame: University of Notre Dame Press, 1984); Alasdair MacIntyre, *Whose Justice? Which Rationality?* (Notre Dame: University of Notre Dame Press, 1988); Alasdair MacIntyre, *First Principles, Final Ends, and Contemporary Philosophical Issues. The Aquinas Lecture* (Milwaukee, WI: Marquette University Press, 1990); Robert P. George, *Natural Law Theory: Contemporary Essays* (Oxford: Clarendon Press, 1992); Robert P. George, *In Defense of Natural Law* (Oxford: Oxford University Press, 1999); Robert P. George, *Natural Law, Liberalism, and Morality* (Oxford: Oxford University Press, 2001), Robert P. George, *Embryo: A Defense of Human Life* (New York: Doubleday, 2008); John Finnis, *Natural Law and Natural Rights*, 2nd ed. (Oxford: Oxford University Press, 1980); John Finnis, "Aquinas' Moral, Political, and Legal Philosophy," in *The Stanford Encyclopedia of Philosophy*, ed. Edward N. Zalta (Stanford, CA: Stanford University, Summer 2018 Edition); John Finnis, *Aquinas: Moral, Political and Legal Theory* (Oxford: Oxford University Press, 1998).

4   The classic treatise *The Nature of Law*, by Thomas E. Davitt, assesses the comparative foundations of positivism and Thomism (St. Louis, MO: B. Herder, 1951).

5   See Gerald J. Postema, *Bentham and the Common Law Tradition* (Oxford: Clarendon Press, 1986).

6   See Georg Hegel, *Science of Logic*, trans. A.V. Miller (London: George Allen & Unwin, 1969).

7   See Heinrich A. Rommen, *The Natural Law* (St. Louis, MO: B. Herder, 1948) 91, 125.

8   Vernon Bourke characterizes St. Thomas's legal school as a "workable philosophy of law" that "requires acceptance of the view that the human mind knows universal meanings." Bourke, "Ethical Justification," 14.

9   St. Thomas Aquinas, *Summa Theologica*, trans. English Dominican Friars, vol. I (New York: Benziger, 1947), Book I, Part II, Q. 90, a. 1.

10 St. Thomas Aquinas, *Summa Contra Gentiles*, 2nd ed., trans. Vernon Bourke, vol. 4 (Garden City, NY: Hanover House, 1956; Notre Dame: University of Notre Dame Press, 1975), Book III, Part II, Ch. 114, 3.

11 George Quentin Friel, *Punishment in Philosophy of Saint Thomas Aquinas and among Some Primitive Peoples*, diss., Catholic University of America (Washington, DC: Catholic University of America Press, 1939), 121.

12 An example being: "First, there's the earth, the sun, the stars, and all things, and this beautiful orderliness of the seasons, divided into years and months. Then there's the fact that all Greeks and barbarians believe the gods exist." Plato, *The Laws of Plato*, ed. Thomas L. Pangle (New York: Basic Books, 1980), b X 886a.

13 Pangle, b I 631b–c.

14 Pangle, b IV 718b.

15 John Wild portrays nature's underpinnings in Platonic thought. "The unwritten laws of nature hold universally and underlie the written positive laws of every genuinely human community." *Plato's Modern Enemies and the Theory of Natural Law* (Chicago, IL: University Of Chicago Press, 1953), 153.

16 Ibid.

17 Leo Strauss, *The Argument and the Action of Plato's Laws* (Chicago, IL: University of Chicago Press, 1975). See also Jerome Hall, "Plato's Legal Philosophy," *Indiana Law Journal*, 31, no. 2 (1955–1956): 204.

18 Aristotle's rejection of *Forms* is at "Metaphysics," in *The Basic Works of Aristotle*, ed. Richard McKeon (New York: Random House, 1941), 1040 b-27–30.

19 Aquinas, *Theologica*, I, Benziger I-II, Q. 90, a. 1, ad 2, referring to Aristotle's *Ethics*.
20 Aristotle, *Nicomachean Ethics*, trans. Martin Ostwald (New York: Bobbs-Merrill, 1962), X, 9, 1180a.
21 Ibid..
22 Ibid., X, 8, 1178a.
23 Ibid.
24 Ibid.
25 Ibid.
26 Aristotle, "Politics," *The Basic Works of Aristotle*, ed. Richard McKeon (New York: Random House, 1941), VII, 3, 11325b.
27 Ibid.
28 Cicero, "On the Laws," in *Selected Works of Cicero* (New York: Walter J. Black, 1948).
29 Ibid., Book One at 228.
30 Ibid., Book One at 228–29.
31 Ibid., Book One at 237.
32 Charles P. Nemeth, *A Comparative Analysis of Cicero and Aquinas: Nature and the Natural Law* (New York: Bloomsbury Academic, 2018).
33 Cicero, "Laws," Book I at 239. See also Cicero's *De Republica*, ed. Clinton Walker Keys (London: William Heinemann, 1927).
34 St. Augustine, *On Free Choice of the Will*, trans. Anna S. Benjamin and L. H. Hackstaff (New York: Macmillan, 1964), Book 2, 10, 115.
35 Anton-Hermann Chroust, "The Philosophy of Law of St. Thomas Aquinas: His Fundamental Ideas and Some of His Historical Precursors," *American Journal of Jurisprudence*, 19, no. 1 (1975), 3.
36 St. Augustine, *Confessions*, trans. John K. Ryan (New York: Doubleday, 1960), Book 10, Ch. 24 (35).
37 Augustine, *Free Choice*, Book I, 6.
38 Chroust, at 2, n. 6.
39 Augustine, *Free Choice*, Book I, 6, 51.
40 Anton-Herman Chroust's precise inquiry into legal thought preceding St. Thomas captures the Augustinian way. "The *lex aeterna*, according to St. Augustine, defines and determines man's relations to God, to the universe, and to his fellow men. In brief, it constitutes the surest road to God. At the same time the *lex aeterna* is the most concise as well as the most sublime manifestation of God's infinite wisdom, perfect intellect, and boundless love. In this it is a deliberate act of God and as such, the ultimate and absolute justification and, at the same time, encompasses everything created." Chroust, at 3.
41 Augustine, *Free Choice*, Book I, 14, 100–1.
42 Aquinas, *Theologica*, I, Benziger I-II Q. 94, a. 6, sed contra.
43 Anton-Hermann Chroust, "The Philosophy of Law from St. Augustine to St. Thomas Aquinas," *New Scholasticism*, 20, no. 1 (1946): 27.
44 Augustine, *Free Choice*, Book I, 6.
45 Ibid., Book I, 5, 33.
46 Ibid., Book I, 5, 33.
47 St. Thomas references Isidore 25 times in I-II, Q 90–97 and 7 times in I-II, Q 98–108. See Jean Tonneau, "The Teaching of the Thomist Tract on Law," *Thomist*, 34, no. 1 (1970): 31.
48 Aquinas, *Theologica*, I, Benziger I-II Q. 95, a. 3. See also Aquinas, *Theologica*, III, Benziger 386 & 387

49 Ibid., I-II Q 95, a. 3. See also Aquinas, *Theologica*, III, Benziger 386.
50 Ibid., I-II Q 95, a. 4. See also Aquinas, *Theologica*, III, Benziger 387.
51 St. Isidore, *Isidori Hispalensis Episcopi Etymologiarum sive Originum Libri XXX*, ed. W. Lindsay (London: Oxford Press, 1962), Bk V, 4–6.
52 Ibid., V, iv, at 2.
53 Ibid., V, iv, at 2.
54 Marie R. Madden, *Political Theory and Law in Medieval Spain* (New York: Fordham University Press, 1930), 26.
55 Isidore of Seville, *The Letters of St. Isidore of Seville*, 2nd ed., trans. Gordon B. Ford, Jr. (Amsterdam: Adolf M. Hakkert, 1970), Letter VI, 32,33.
56 St. Anselm, *Cur Deus Homo*, vol. II, Capit I, p. 98, 3–5.
57 Anselm, *De Conceptu Virginali et de Originali Peccato*, Capit. IV, p. 145, 30–31.
58 Anselm, *De Veritate*, Capit. XII, p. 191, 27–29.
59 Ibid., Capit. XIII, p. 199, 27–28.
60 John F. Quinn, C.S.B., "The Moral Philosophy of St. Bonaventure," in *Bonaventure & Aquinas: Enduring Philosophers*, eds. Robert W. Shahan and Francis J. Kovach (Norman: University Of Oklahoma Press, 1976), 28.
61 See Prof. E. M. Buytaert, ed., *Peter Abelard: Proceedings of the International Conference, Louvain, May 10–12, 1971* (Louvain: Leuven University Press, 1974).
62 John Marenbon, *The Philosophy of Peter Abelard* (Cambridge: Cambridge University Press), 267.
63 Peter Abelard, *Ethics*, trans. D. E. Luscombe (Oxford: Clarendon Press, 1971), 75.
64 Marenbon, *Philosophy of Peter Abelard*, 270.
65 Peter Abelard, *Collationes* (Oxford: Oxford University Press), 118: 2068–119: 2075.
66 Gratian, *The Treatise on Laws* (Washington, DC: Catholic University of America Press, 1993), D. 4, C. 1.
67 Ibid., D. 8, Part 2.
68 Ibid., D. 1, C. 6 § 2.
69 Ibid., D. 1, C.7 § 3.
70 Ibid., D. 13, Part 1.
71 Alexander of Hales, *Summa Universae Theologica* (Florence: Ex Typographia Collegii S. Bonaventurae, 1948), IV, pars II, Inq 1, Q Unica, Caput VII, Article IV, olution.
72 Ibid., Q I, Caput I, ad obiecta 3.
73 Ibid., Caput VII.
74 Ibid., Caput V, Ad oppositum, a.
75 Ibid., Caput VI.
76 Ibid., Caput VII, articulus I.
77 Ibid., Caput VII, Art. III, Solutio.
78 Ibid., Caput VII, Art. IV, Ad oppositum.
79 Ibid., Inq. II, Q III, Caput II.
80 Ibid., Q I, Caput I.
81 Ibid., Q IV, Membrum II, Caput II.
82 Ibid., Q IV, Membrum II, Caput I.
83 Ibid., Q IV, Membrum II, Caput III.
84 Ibid., Inq. I, Q I, Caput VIII, Art 5.
85 Ibid., Inq. I, Q I, Caput VIII, Art 5–6.
86 St. Bonaventure, *Quaestio disputata, De perfectione evangelica*, V, 117–98. See also Bonaventure's intricate discussion of God, grace and nature as imprint in: S.

Bonaventure, "Sentiarum," in *Opera Omnia*, ed. Ludovicus Vivies (Paris: 1865), Book II, dist. XXXIX at Art. i.

87 Quinn, "Moral Philosophy of St. Bonaventure," 33. See also Matthew M. Dr. Benedictis, *The Social Thought of St. Bonaventure* (Connecticut: Greenwood Press, 1972); Etienne Gilson, *The Philosophy of St. Bonaventure* (New York: Sheed & Ward, 1938).

88 John Quinn summarizes the debate. "Reason and will have free choice rather than free judgment, Bonaventure maintains, for choice regulates reason by a command of the will, but judgment regulates it by the rule of truth, or the eternal law. A judge is one who decides a case according to law, but an arbiter is one who decides it by his own will. The faculty of freedom, therefore, is named properly from choice, because the decisions of free choice, properly considered, are made more according to will than according to precept of law." Quinn, "Moral Philosophy of St. Bonaventure," 39.

89 Lawrence David Roberts, "John Duns Scotus and the Concept of Human Freedom," (PhD diss., Indiana University, 1969), 23.

90 Ibid., 23.

91 Ibid.

92 St. Bonaventure, *Breviloquim* (Venetiis, 1894), V. I, part III at 6.

93 Roberts, "John Duns Scotus and the Concept of Human Freedom," 27.

94 George Reilly deems Albert a remarkable pathfinder. "Now there is nothing remarkable about this nor is it difficult to explain. St. Albert the Great was a pioneer in the use of the entire Aristotelian philosophy for the service of Christian truth; this he was by his own efforts." George C. Reilly, *The Psychology of St. Albert the Great Compared with that of Saint Thomas* (Washington, DC: Catholic University of America Press, 1934), 75.

95 James A. Weisheipl, *Thomas d'Aquino and Albert His Teacher* (Toronto: Pontifical Institute of Mediaeval Studies, 1980), 7.

96 Albert the Great and Thomas Aquinas, *Albert & Thomas: Selected Writings*, ed. and trans. Simon Tugwell (New York: Paulist Press, 1988), 11.

97 Alberti Magni, *De Bono* (Monasterii Westfalorum in Aedibus Aschendorff, 1951), t 5, Q. II, Art. 1, Solutio.

98 Ibid., Q. I, Art. I, Solutio.

99 Ibid., (23).

100 Ibid., Solutio (16).

101 Ibid., Art. 4, (3).

102 Ibid., Art. I, Solutio (2).

103 Alberti Magni, *Opera Omnia, Super Ethica* (Monasterii Westfalorum in Aedibus Aschendorff, 1968), XIV, pars I, Liber V, Lectio XI.

104 Alberti, *Super Ethica*, XIV, Pars I, Liber V, Lectio XI, Octavo videtur, Solutio (1).

105 Stanley Cunningham describes the views advanced by Albert as trail-breaking yet evolutionary. Albert, says Cunningham, does "validate and emphasize, to a greater extent than any of his predecessors, the purely rational and natural factors in the morality of acts. Every *naturally* virtuous act is a morally good act. Every *rational* act is a moral act (with the added stipulation that futile or idle acts are evil). In relation to his predecessors and contemporaries, Albert's position represents an advance." Stanley B. Cunningham, "Albertus Magnus and the Problem of Moral Virtue," *Vivarium*, 7, no. 2 (1969): 102.

106 Alberti, *De Bono*, t 5, Q. III, Art. I.

107 Ibid., Q. IV, Art. 2, Respondeo.

108 Daniel Nelson, *The Priority of Prudence* (University Park: Pennsylvania State University Press, 1992), 107. See also Daniel J. Sullivan, *An Introduction to Philosophy: The Perennial Principles of Classical Realist Tradition* (Rockford, IL: Jan Books, 1992); Bernard Beodder, *Natural Theology* (New York: Longmans, Green, 1927); Etienne Gilson, *The Christian Philosophy of St. Thomas Aquinas*, trans. L. K. Shook (New York: Random House, 1956), 266; Thomas E. Davitt, *The Nature of Law* (St. Louis, MO: Herder, 1951), 39–54.
109 Thomas Aquinas, *Summa Contra Gentiles*, trans. Vernon J. Bourke, vol. 4 (Notre Dame: University of Notre Dame Press, 1975), Book III, part II, Chapter 114, 1.
110 Ibid., 115.
111 Ibid., 114.
112 Ibid., 114.
113 Thomas Aquinas, "Summa Theologica," *Basic Writings of Saint Thomas Aquinas*, ed. Anton C. Pegis, vol. 2 (New York: Random House, 1945), I-II, Q. 90, a. 1, sed contra.
114 Aristotle, *Phys.*, II, 9 (200a 22); Aquinas, *Theologica*, Pegis I-II, Q. 90, a. 1, c.
115 Walter Farrell, *The Natural Moral Law According to St. Thomas and Suarez* (Ditchling: St. Dominic's Press, 1930), 10. See also Davitt, 39–54; Robert J. Henle, "St. Thomas Aquinas and American Law," in *Thomistic Papers II*, eds. Leonard A. Kennedy, C. S. B. and Jack C. Marler (Houston, TX: Center for Thomistic Studies, 1986), 67.
116 Aquinas, *Gentiles*, III-I, Chapter 2.
117 Aquinas, *Theologica*, Pegis I-II, Q. 96, a. 2, c.
118 Ibid., a. 1, ad 2.
119 Ibid., a. 2.
120 Ibid., Q. 90, Art. 2, c.
121 Jeremy Bentham, *The Principles of Morals and Legislation* (New York: Hafner, 1948).
122 J. V. Dolan, "Natural Law & Modern Jurisprudence," *Laval Theologique et Philosophique*, 16 (1990): 40.
123 Ibid.
124 Anton-Hermann Chroust, "The Fundamental Ideas in St. Augustine's Philosophy of Law," *American Journal of Jurisprudence*, 18 (1973): 67.
125 Daniel Nelson appreciates this comprehensive view of *law* when he states, "Law in all of its manifestations derives from God's reason." Nelson, *Priority of Prudence*, 107. See also Chroust, "Fundamental Ideas," 67.
126 Aquinas, *Gentiles*, III-II, Ch. 112, 3.
127 Thomas Aquinas, *Summa Contra Gentiles*, trans. Vernon J. Bourke, vol. 3 (Notre Dame: University of Notre Dame Press: 1975), Book Three, Chapter 3, 8.
128 Aquinas, *Theologica*, I, Benziger I-II Q. 90, a. 1. See Charles D. Skok, *Prudent Civil Legislation According to St. Thomas and Some Controversial American Law* (Rome: Catholic Book Agency, 1967), 31.
129 Aquinas, *Theologica*, I, Benziger, 994.
130 Ibid., 1001, Bk. I-II, Q. 92, art. 1.
131 Ibid.
132 Ibid., 997, Bk. I-II, Q. 91, art. 2.
133 Ibid., art. 3.
134 Ibid., 997–98.
135 Chroust, *Philosophy of Aquinas*, 25.
136 Thomas Aquinas, *On Aristotle's Love and Friendship*, trans. Pierre Conway (Providence: Providence College Press, 1951), Book IX, chapter 4.

137 MacIntyre, *First Principles*, 43.
138 Ibid..
139 Thomas Aquinas, *Commentary on the Nicomachean Ethics*, trans. C. I. Litzinger (Chicago, IL: Henry Regnery, 1964), X. L.XIV:C 2149.
140 Raymond Dennehy addresses the law's ultimate aim in "The Ontological Basis of Human Rights": "For, as a rational being, man attains his self-perfection by transcending the limitations of his finite, temporal self. Through the immanence of knowing, he achieves ever higher levels of reality as he identifies himself ontologically with Being and its facets. Truth, Goodness, Beauty, and ultimately with the fullness of Being, God; and all the while he retains his own unique selfhood." *Thomist* 42, no. 2 (1978): 455.
141 Heinrich A. Rommen, *The Natural Law*, trans. T. Hanley (St. Louis, MO: B. Herder, 1948), 54–55.
142 Aquinas, *Theologica*, I, Benziger, 1018, Bk. I-II, Q. 96, art. 2.
143 Aquinas, *Theologica*, Pegis I-II, Q. 92, a. 1, c.
144 Jean Porter, *Nature as Reason: A Thomistic Theory of the Natural Law* (Grand Rapids, MI: Eerdmans, 2004), 38–39
145 John Finnis, *Aquinas: Moral, Political and Legal Theory* (Oxford: Oxford University Press, 1998), 90–91.
146 Ibid.
147 Jacques Maritain, *Natural Law: Reflections on Theory & Practice*, ed. William Sweet (South Bend: St. Augustine's Press, 2001).
148 Jacques Maritain, *Man and the State* (Washington, DC: Catholic University of America Press, 1998), 91–92.
149 Gregory Doolan, "Maritain, St. Thomas Aquinas, and the First Principles of the Natural Law," in *Reassessing the Liberal State: Reading Maritain's Man and the State*, eds. Timothy Fuller and John P. Hittinger (Washington, DC: Catholic University of America Press, 2001), 127–39.
150 Germain G. Grisez, "The First Principle of Practical Reason," in *Aquinas: A Collection of Critical Essays*, ed. Anthony Kenny (London: Palgrave Macmillan, 1970), 340–382. See also Craig Paterson, "Aquinas, Finnis and Non-Naturalism," in *Analytical Thomism: Traditions in Dialogue*, eds. Craig Paterson and Matthew S. Pugh (Aldershot: Ashgate, 2006), 171–93.
151 Grisez, "First Principle," 168–201 (176).
152 Lonergan, 395.
153 Frederick G. Lawrence, "Finnis on Lonergan: A Reflection," *Villanova Law Review*, 57, no. 5 (2012): 849, 865.
154 See also: Robert George's *In Defense of the Natural Law* (Oxford: Oxford University Press, 2001) for some unique interpretations of classical natural theory.
155 Porter, *Nature as Reason*, 398.
156 MacIntyre, After Virtue; MacIntyre, *Whose Justice? Which Rationality?*
157 MacIntyre, *Whose Justice?*, 194.

Chapter 2

THE CONTENT AND SUBSTANCE OF THE NATURAL LAW

Any reasoned view of how the natural law plays out in US Supreme Court decisions since the period of Roe must depend on the natural law's composition, its content, principles and precepts. As most natural law thinkers have done, they begin at the beginning but see promulgation as inherently insufficient by and through itself. Whatever version of natural law jurisprudence relied upon, natural law thinkers, as we have noted many times, think and reason hierarchically—viewing every law in light of a higher order—a transcendency that guides the decision making. However, there are degrees of thinking at a higher level. For the medievalist, in the mold of Aquinas, the natural law schema commences at the heights—at the eternal law of God—and descends downward to the precepts of the natural law, the human law promulgations enacted with consistency and in conformity with revelation. Others tend to rely more heavily on how the natural order unfolds—how each being and creature acts in conformity with its essence and nature. Cicero could readily be described as this sort of character.[1]

And there is even a "secular" portion in the natural law ideology—those that hold that natural rights exist due to our nature as human persons. In this way, our nature alone suffices to assure rights. Thinkers like Lon Fuller and Lloyd Weinreib tend toward this limited view of the natural law. Weinreib argues,

> It is a theory that locates the normative aspect of our existence within the natural order, in the irrefutable designation of human beings as persons. [...] The theory does not itself provide us with a moral calculus, nor even a moral compass. It requires us to look toward and beyond the actual conditions of the community in which we live. But it is not without significance. Its largest significance is that it rejects a utilitarian calculation of the good as sufficient in itself. It insists that the recognition of persons as persons, honoring their rights, is the only path to the good, not the highest good perhaps, but the humanly good. And it tells

us, without providing a certain guide to success, the manner and means for achieving it.[2]

Whichever version of the natural law is adhered to, its proponent, whether judge, lawyer, legislator or citizen, rejects exclusive reliance on promulgation as the barometer of right and at the same time will not rely on text as the sole basis for legal conclusions. Natural law advocates, while giving extraordinary deference to the language of the law, will or should disregard that text if the law does not comport with a higher, transcendent order. In the real world of law practice, judicial decision making and appellate analysis, natural law adherence is easy to propose but difficult to implement. The esteemed Honorable Robert Bork wrote extensively on the natural law and its place in law and legal reasoning and displayed some reticence—not about the principles of the natural law but how judges can employ it in decision making—something also concerning to Antonin Scalia. Bork notes in 1992,

> "Natural law." The words have an attractive, even a seductive, resonance. They refer to principles about ultimate right and wrong that transcend particular nations and cultures and are true for all people at all times. Most of us feel intuitively that natural law exists, though we differ, both as to its source and its content. For some, it is ordained by God; for others, it arises from the nature of human beings, even if we are evolutionary accidents; or it may simply express the requirements for anything recognizable as a society. Whatever its source, natural law's content is discovered by reason.[3]

Precisely how a case should be judged affirmatively using natural law is a much more difficult endeavor. Even horrid legal decisions in the Supreme Court's past have errantly used natural order arguments to justify slavery and other dubious legal conclusions. The genetics movement, eugenics—a law of the jungle mentality—has also relied on naturalistic arguments to justify the worst sort of injustices. Terms like "inferior race" or "sub-species" or "defective persons" all harken to a survivalist mentality under the measure of the stronger winning out. All of these conclusions distort the essence of the natural law as traditionally defined.

In the end, the natural law advocate considers both the procedural elements of a law, such as notice and pronouncement, clarity and equal application, as well as the legitimacy of the subject matter. Once the procedural elements are considered, the law needs to be evaluated in light of its consistency with reason and the content of the natural law that is discoverable and fully discernable in reason and the fullness of human operations. Other natural law proponents will head to a higher level—to the creator—to God who makes all being possible. In God, the eternal law exists in the eternal being. Descending downward on the creatures fashioned by God will be the natural law that is burned, impressed into our very essence. The natural law will consist of various precepts including its primary precept—*doing good and avoiding evil*. With a little more reflection, the human agent easily discovers the secondary precepts of the natural law—self-preservation, procreation and sexual attraction, care of offspring, social and communal living and belief in a Deity.

How that natural law content resides in legal decisions that deal with moral and ethical problems is this text's chief aim—how in suicide, birth control, abortion, same-sex marriage and consensual homosexual activity, to illustrate the applications, the jurisprudence of the natural law may or may not work.

Finally, the legitimacy of any law, in light of natural law jurisprudence, may also be measured by a divine law—that revelatory guidance outlined in the Old and New Testaments. While not all natural law thinkers refer to this source, most traditional natural law thinkers rely upon divine revelation to evaluate legal dilemmas.

Natural Law Jurisprudence and Its Principles

To understand the natural law requires that it be viewed in terms of its hierarchy, not as a jurisprudence in isolation from other laws or legal traditions. What follows is a short examination of what the content of the natural law consists of as well as its dependency on other forms of law; its primary content principle being "seek the good and avoid evil" and the many secondary precepts that are most pertinent in this examination, namely self-preservation, procreation, sexual attraction of the opposite sexes, marriage and family, care of offspring and living in community.

The various kinds of law

To fathom natural law jurisprudence, one must always look beyond the promulgation or a mechanistic view of law. Positivism, the present penchant of jurisprudence, the idea that laws are laws because they are promulgated, sits in contrast to a natural law thinker. While the natural law thinker will be impressed with the power of human law, and simultaneously aware of its limitations, a grander system, a hierarchical architectonic of four types of law will be crucial to the natural law, those four being the eternal, the natural, the divine and the human. None of these types exists without the other, for each

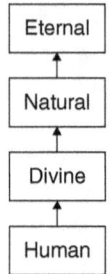

Figure 1 St. Thomas' Hierarchy of Laws.

is dependent, yet distinct; each is unified and integrated with one another. Succinctly put, the hierarchy implies unity but is dedicated to a priority of one type of law over the others. An elementary depiction would be as shown in Figure 1.

At the apex, in the plan of God, the higher, eternal law descends to the lower forms of law. This "derivative"[4] quality commences with the eternal law, the Divine exemplar that is the blueprint for the universe and its law. Divine revelation, centrally exposed in biblical instruction, gives clarification to the people of God. Creation, especially the rational variety, participates in the eternal law by and through the natural law. Positive laws, the promulgations of man, are a necessary component for a civil society, which are evaluated in light of the eternal, divine and natural laws. God's eternal law watches over the other categories being the "exemplar of divine Wisdom."[5] In this sense, as Aquinas relates, "all laws proceed from the eternal law."[6]

At the human level, each derives its legitimacy from its superior counterpart. A judge, jurist, lawmaker and lawyer cannot differentiate or chop up their legal inquiry, for example, forgetting man's natural inclination in a case of sodomy; proclaiming a humanistic notion of individual rights at the expense of common welfare; and enacting a statute, interpreting a case, applying a principle, without regard for spiritual, moral or revelatory considerations. Pure functionalism, legal emotivism or subjectivism, lacks the larger framework advanced by a natural law jurisprudence.

A more thorough examination of these four types of law follows, with special reliance on the pinnacle of natural law reasoning, Thomas Aquinas.

The eternal law

God, as rational architect of the universe and its creatures, and as an omniscient and omnipotent Being, by and through his eternal law, fashions an exemplar for man and his universe. The eternal law, as Gilson urges, is that which "makes us what we are."[7] The lex aeterna is the blueprint for an ordered existence, the benchmark for perfection in every facet of existence. It is "the objective and absolute a priori of everything that may properly be called a rule and a measure."[8]

In calling God's law the "supreme exemplar,"[9] the natural law school of jurisprudence foundationally sets the basis for all legal practice and theory in this perennial, permanent and immutable dimension. God, the artist and the craftsman, makes only good things and, as a result, molds creatures with lawful inclinations and components. Every object or being created by God is an "emanation"[10] from God's being, containing or being the law itself and the "extensiveness" of God's influence on reality itself.

Despite this perfection, our access to God is not an unbridgeable valley due to God's creative relationship with his authorship of the world. Creation possesses an artistic or demonstrative quality that inevitably and intimately bonds Creator with the created. The Divine God moves "all things to their due end"[11] and "bears the character of law."[12]

The perfect God naturally has a perfect legal constitution, though His complete content and subject matter are unknowable to temporal species like man. The eternal law is incapable of promulgation since such promulgation is meaningless.[13] In this sense, all temporal beings are incapable of grasping and fully understanding the eternal law, since this law is God Himself and only God knows his own eternal law in its fullness. As imperfect beings, we can struggle only to know the effects of the eternal law and "cannot know the things that are of God as they are in themselves; but they are made known to us in their effects."[14] All that is created by God, "whether contingent or necessary, is subject to the eternal law."[15] God's law is the supreme norm for all living beings and creation. Governance of the universe by God imputes a law of operations, a sort of "government" when God is described as "the ruler of the universe."[16] This rule and ruler has the quality of and the "nature of a law."[17] All human affairs are subject to the eternal law while even the wicked and the perverse are subject to the eternal law. Even the "blessed and the damned are under the eternal law."[18] Even the ignorant cannot disavow some knowledge of the eternal law since their being still reflects the Creator by its effects. Even the lustful and the slaves of flesh cannot "dominate"[19] and destroy the good of one's nature, for "there remains in man the inclination to do the things which belong to the eternal law."[20] Nothing and no one can evade the eternal law. The eternal law, residing within, or more accurately inherently within, the God of Creation is the measure of all activity.

But God does not leave his creatures stranded without the necessary knowledge to know what we need and must do to live in accordance with His creation for in this sense, man and woman participate with God by and through the natural law that is impressed and imprinted on all rational creatures.

The natural law

The natural law has both eternal and scientific qualities, the latter designation tightly bound to the order of nature and how beings operate. In this manner, human beings discover what is right when something is consistent with or beneficial to our natural operations. This includes what is in reason the imprinted principles of the natural law. Since the human species is powerless to fully learn the mind of God and His eternal law, natural law jurisprudence looks to the natural order. Nature, in a scientific, physical sense has an order, a series of operational rules. Nature "in its purity [...] is rather like the word life."[21] Man is a creature of nature and thereby subsists of rules and operational qualities. C. S. Lewis's critical mind poses the foundational meaning of nature. "By far the commonest native meaning of *natura* is something like sort, kind, quality, or character. When you ask, in our modern idiom, what something 'is like', you are asking for its *natura*. When you want to tell a man the *natura* of anything you describe the thing."[22] Aquinas gets to the core of nature in his work, *On Kingship*, for "whatever is in accord with nature is best, for in all things nature does what is best."[23]

As author of nature, God could not and would not forge a creation of disorder and anarchy but, more predictably, infuses and imprints an orderly, lawful, natural sequence in each of his creatures. "The manifold and beautiful order of nature is the work of a designing mind of vast intelligence; and must be ultimately explained by the existence of a personal God."[24] Undoubtedly, human beings, like other beings, display natural inclinations, preferences, propensities and dispositions that mirror the wisdom of the author. Gilson artfully offers this analysis:

> Granted this, it is clear that the precepts of natural law correspond exactly with our natural inclinations and that their order is the same. Man is, to begin with, a being like all others. More particularly, he is a living being, like all other animals. Finally, by the privilege of this nature, he is a rational being. Thus it is that three great natural laws bind him, each in its own way.[25]

The term, natural law, references two critical ideas: (1) the nature of a being itself and (2) law as an operation of that nature. To say someone or something has a nature is to typify its very existence. Then, apply law to that nature and that nature unfolds before us—doing what it must and should do to preserve its existence signifies nature as well.[26] Nor is the natural law some changeable phenomena deposited in the creature for the moment, nor a transitory habituation in the form of virtue or vice.[27] Instead, the natural law is a fixed, perpetual state in human operations, a reflection of the eternal law is God Himself, a mirror of really what we are as beings and an imprint of the Creator.[28]

More than strict biological design, the natural law is the human person's participatory opportunity with the Creator, by and through our rational natures where the content of the natural law is fully discernable, not as a series of legal annotations, codifications and enactments but more like dispositions and inclinations that are conducive to a productive and flourishing life. Ignatius Eschmann cogently defines the natural law as "not a statute enacted by the divine Legislator, but is the self-same act by which the Creator brought into being our rational nature."[29] Inclinations, tendencies and propensities are not blank, intellectual exercises, especially since the natural law theory centrally depends upon reason for its discernment. Only rational creatures possess the natural law. Natural law is about inclinations and imprints—how the human creature lives in accordance with their overall constitution. The human player living compatibly with these natural impressions lives as the Creator intended. Natural law cannot be removed, "blotted out";[30] moreover, neither can it be forgotten nor can its content be denied on the basis of ignorance. Natural law is the human person's participation in the eternal law of God. "Thus man has a natural inclination to know the truth about God, and to live in society; and in this respect, whatever pertains to this inclination belongs to the natural law: e.g., to shun ignorance, to avoid offending those among whom one has to live, and other such things regarding the above inclination."[31]

The human person is forged so tightly with the natural law that he or she cannot extricate him or herself from its influence. We can't even intend contrary to what we are, though we can will the difference—choosing evil—which "is a result apart from intention."[32] Wickedness, unlawfulness, does not reside in reason or our constitution, for "such a thing is not the necessary result of what is intended; rather, it is repugnant to what is intended."[33] Every inclination in the human actor, particularly those touched or controlled by reason, deals with our natural law imprint.[34] Those who argue its relativity, inapplicability and selectivity as to person or precept would be at odds with the natural law doctrine. Therefore, in human conduct, reason rules and commands the other powers, and this universal condition labels permanently the natural law.[35] This unchangeable, immutable reflection of the eternal law, this participation, albeit imperfect, by man in the eternal law, this imprint, messaging inclinations and ends for the human person, is the essence of the natural law. Quoting Gratian's *Decretals*, Aquinas summarizes the permanency of the natural law as follows: "It is said in the *Decretals:* The natural law dates from the creation of the rational creature. It does not vary according to time, but remains unchangeable."[36]

The content of the natural law Thus far, descriptive terms, like inclinations and imprints, have been employed to describe the natural law, but this is inadequate. What is it that we are inclined about? Since law is reason's rule and measure, and since all human beings seek the good, the natural law must be rooted in one, basic tenet or the first principle of the natural law that "good is to be done and promoted, and evil is to be avoided."[37] This primary and common precept is part of our very fabric of being, Gilson argues: "To say that we must do good and avoid evil is not arbitrarily to decree a moral law; it is merely to read a natural law which is written in the very substance of beings and to bring to light the hidden spring of all their operations. We have to do it, because it is our nature to do it. Such a precept is but a verification of fact."[38] This doing good and avoiding evil provides, at best, a generalized prescription for life and, at worst, gives fodder to those who challenge or debate the content or ingredients of its recipe. In the first instance, this primary precept is only a call that the human actor "act in accordance with reason [...] with the created pattern of our nature and species."[39] While only rational creatures intellectualize natural law precepts, every being moves toward its proper end or goal.[40]

This fundamental precept, doing good and avoiding evil, is known equally by all, although determinations of practical rectitude are "not equally known to all."[41] This "golden rule of the natural law"[42] is effortlessly understood "without investigation [...] known and approved by all humans."[43] The matter of the natural law's instruction does not end with this common precept. For in each human actor there are basic inclinations, predispositions and predilections that reflect our fundamental makeup as a being and these inclinations are what are best for the human person and hence part of the natural law. Natural law thinkers sometimes refer to these propositions as "self-evident principles" of operation, deduced from the primary precept of the natural law.

In this way, one determines the lawfulness or the unlawfulness of conduct by its compatibility with these inclinations—all of which are essentially self-evident and discoverable by all who engage in "slight reflection."[44] Aquinas lays out an excellent catalog of precepts that make up the content of the natural law at Question 94, Article 2:

> For there is in man, first of all, an inclination to good in accordance with the nature which he has in common with all substances, inasmuch,

namely, as every substance seeks the preservation of its own being, according to its nature; and by reason of this inclination, whatever is a means of preserving human life, and of warding off its obstacles, belongs to the natural law. Secondly, there is in man an inclination to things that pertain to him more specially, according to that nature which he has in common with other animals; and in virtue of this inclination, those things are said to belong to the natural law which nature has taught to all animals, such as sexual intercourse, the education of offspring and so forth.[45]

These inclinations of social existence, propagation of the species, self-preservation and the inherent desire to know truth and God are universally true in all rational beings.[46] They are unavoidably consistent with human experience and are naturally discernable.[47] Being self-evident propositions, the actors have no choice but to make decisions compatible with their subject matter. This is why a natural law theorist has little or no quandary reconciling the current debates over abortion, homosexuality or assisted suicide. These first principles of the natural law set out a formula, a series of criteria that forbid each of these activities.

Secondary precepts of the natural law While no person "can have an erroneous judgment about"[48] the first principles of the natural law, those emanating further down the continuum are not as readily discoverable. These other principles are labeled secondary, or by some tertiary,[49] derivations of fundamental natural law principles. The clear-cut, undeniable tenets of first principles can be discerned easily but as one moves to more particular cases, a growing and natural remoteness regarding the applicability of the natural law happens. Put another way, it is easier to resolve physician-assisted suicide under natural law reasoning than a case involving divorce. Even Aquinas remarks that our legal reasoning "will be found to fail the more, according as we descend further towards the particular."[50] Surely one may properly conclude that there is a natural law resolution for other problems such as adultery, masturbation, artificial birth control and the like, but the correct application will require a bit more deductive reasoning than a question like self-preservation and suicide.

So the trick for the natural law thinker is to find a relationship between the first principles and those secondary questions that are "proximate"[51] to the first principles and properly derivable therefrom. There may even be times when following the natural law would create an ironic injustice, for example, the maintenance of life of a fetus over the life of the mother or the condemnation of a soldier who, by giving up his life for comrade, fails to preserve himself[52]—all of these cases dispel any notion that the natural law is absolute in each and every case.

Secondary precepts are so designated because of their intimate relationship to the ends and goods suitable for man. Conduct, in the most particularized categories, can be evaluated for moral legitimacy and legality by the ends promoted. If the ends are contrary to human perfection, the conduct or law would be contrary to the natural law. Aquinas writes splendidly about this interplay between lawfulness, natural law and ends in the *Summa Contra Gentiles*.

> Now, it is good for each person to attain his end, whereas it is bad for him to swerve away from his proper end. Now, this should be considered applicable to the parts, just as it is to the whole being; for instance, each and every part of man, and every one of his acts, should attain the proper end.[53]

Furthermore, a series of predictable ethical dilemmas can be speedily reconciled by adhering to these basic propositions. Polygamy is contrary to the natural law because "one female is for one male is a consequence of natural instinct."[54] Incestuous marriage is inconsistent with natural law precepts since "it is unfitting for one to be conjugally united with persons to whom one should naturally be subject."[55] Promiscuity, inordinate affections and gluttony are distortions of the ends man normally seeks and to engage in such vice is a departure from "the order of reason."[56]

Behavior can also have licit and illicit qualities. For example, sexual desire drives propagation and procreation, yet that inclination has parameters, guiderails so to speak, so what is natural does not evolve into the unnatural. Hence, the natural law insists that sexual intercourse remain within the confines of a loving marriage and at the same time be open to the procreative possibility; otherwise, the act may metamorphosize into other goals and ends, compulsions, addictions or promiscuity, to name a few. As always, Aquinas delivers the highest level of insight in matters involving the nature law. In his *Summa Contra Gentiles*, he comments,

> Now, since the use of food and sexual capacities is not illicit in itself, but can only be illicit when it departs from the order of reason, and since external possessions are necessary for the taking of food, for the upbringing of offspring and the support of a family, and for other needs of the body, it follows also that the possession of wealth is not in itself illicit, provided the order of reason be respected. That is to say, a man must justly possess what he has; he must not set the end of his will in

these things, and he must use them in a fitting way for his own and others' benefit.[57]

While the list of natural law principles is surprisingly short, their impact extends to nearly every aspect of human operations. The natural law closely assesses life's most cumbersome difficulties—abortion, suicide and euthanasia, same-sex marriage and homosexuality, marriage and parental obligations— the stuff our US Supreme Court encounters with regularity.

Self-preservation When weighed as a group, there is no precept of the natural law as instructive as the self-preservation principle. To live and preserve is an inherent tendency in every living being, from mammal to man. It is not that we merely desire to live on but that we preserve the quality of our natures and our existence, for self-preservation assumes a rational being's hope for continued life and a productive and rewarding day-to-day existence. To wish for the contrary is to act and live unnaturally, for it is absolutely "natural to everything to keep itself in being, as far as possible."[58] Criminal and civil laws fully recognize the idea of self-preservation for killing another in proportionate self-defense because it is "lawful to defend one's life" and to "kill another in defense of his own life."[59] In self-defense, the moral agent confronts a precept of the natural law so powerful that the legitimate defense may include, depending upon circumstances, the destruction of another's life. Self-preservation, when justifiable and proportionate, signifies complete adherence to natural law principles since the human agent is "bound to take more care of one's own life than of another's."[60]

Suicide provides another telling illustration of natural law application. At no place will suicide be accepted or tolerated under natural law reasoning, for to advance or aid or abet its commission is to act in contravention with self-preservation principles. Current advocates for physician-assisted suicide cannot find any support in natural law jurisprudence because the act brazenly and unequivocally undermines the essence of self-preservation. Calling it mercy, care for the dying, dying with dignity or other benign descriptor does not change the fundamental reality that suicide antagonizes and confronts natural law reasoning. Aquinas lays out three rationales for why suicide, which would also include euthanasia and versions of mercy killing, would be contrary to the natural law.

> It is all together unlawful to kill oneself, for three reasons. First, because everything naturally loves itself, the result being that everything naturally keeps itself in being, and resists corruptions so far as it can. Wherefore suicide is contrary to the inclination of nature, and to charity whereby

everyman should love himself. Hence suicide is always a mortal sin, as being contrary to the natural law and to charity.

Secondly, [...] he belongs to the community. Hence by killing himself he injures the community. [...] Thirdly, because life is God's gift to man, and is subject to His power, Who kills and makes to live.[61]

Suicide causes injustice to self and others, and its complete lack of charity as to self and others edifies how far the act "departs from the order of reason."[62]

Abortion and infanticide are equally instructive regarding the self-preservation precept of the natural law. Since the chief aim of the procreative act, the conjugal joining of the married couple, is the propagation of the species, any interference with that furtherance works at odds with this principle. While there has been recent debate on the early period of conception as not having met the necessary stage of human development for the claim of murder to be alleged, there is little tolerance for abortion at any stage of development.[63] While it is true that both Aristotle and Aquinas declared that an animated fetus be essential to the charge of murder, a judgment made in the criminal justice system and a matter of prosecutorial discretion, the earlier natural law rejection of murder does not imply approval or consent. As most medievalists would hold, until quickening, the fetus lacks "ensoulment," although this developmental question never justifies abortion. For abortion is an attack on the natural order, always in opposition to the natural law's self-preservation principle and a sin against nature. The issue of ensoulment was a trickier question for the medievalist than the contemporary neo-natal scientist. Hence, the earliest stages of human development, while more tolerantly construed by Aquinas, cannot be read as a permissive stance on abortion. Aquinas lays out the contrast:

> In the first case, the necessity of the action itself results from the form by which the agent is made actual, because in order for this kind of action to exist, nothing extrinsic, as a terminus for it, is required. Thus, when the sense power is actualized by the sensible species, it necessarily acts; and so, too, does the intellect when it is actualized by the intelligible species.[64]

If the soul provides the form for the human person, Aquinas states that semen, as a physical composition, cannot transmit the qualities of a noncorporeal soul—that it cannot "extend its action to the production of an immaterial effect."[65] St. Thomas states that the soul "comes from without"[66] and arrives at some undetermined time.[67] Admittedly, according to John Finnis, the crude biology of the time and the infancy of the science led Aquinas to findings that are in opposition to the current understanding of human formation. On top of this, the natural law reasoning in the most traditional sense gives little deference to the competing interests of reproductive choice, life plans, family size and planning and other forces. And this resistance to other variables in the abortion debate often causes natural law proponents in the abortion question the greatest criticism. Joshua Greene's "moral tribes" call upon those wishing to deny the right to abortion to be a bit more utilitarian—a condition not to be naturally abhorred as it is so often in natural law circles.[68] However, utilitarianism operates under conditions that are properly described as fully relative—something deeply in contrast with the absolute tenets of natural law reasoning.

Procreation and sexual attraction Sexuality undeniably is a necessary component of the maintenance and advancement of the human species, but to be in line with the natural law theory, sexuality must take place in the marital state with a procreative mindset "for the welfare of the whole human race."[69] The sexual act has a specific purpose in the natural world and should be undertaken in "due manner and order, in keeping with the end of human procreation"[70] and "the preservation of the whole human race."[71] Sexual activity in the proper context is good while illicit purposes and motives are rooted in "lust"—a condition that cannot serve as a rational basis for sexual activity for lust creates a feverish frenzy where the actor loses all rational moorings and sows pleasure for its own sake, obsesses with carnal desire and seeks the wanton and the debaucherous. Lust wreaks the "greatest havoc in a man's mind, yet secondarily applies to any matters pertaining to excess,"[72] and promotes a warped and distorted view of the procreative act. This wantonness seeks only the sensory and cares not for the objects or the means of its pursuit, gravitating toward the lower rather than higher ends. Many sexual acts run counter to the end of human procreation. Acts of sodomy have no other end except pleasure, which crosses the end and aim of all sexuality. In this way, sodomy between same-sex persons has been adjudged under natural law reasoning as an unnatural vice, a "special kind of deformity whereby a venereal act is rendered unbecoming."[73] In light of this, any activity between two men, two women or between man and animal resides outside of the true meaning of human sexuality. These unnatural acts are deemed unnatural not because the bulk of humankind does not engage in these sexual practices, but because the sexual agency in question acts in contravention to the biology of sexuality and sexual function, but more importantly because by engaging in unnatural acts "man transgresses which has been determined by nature with regard to the use of venereal actions, it follows that in this matter the sin is gravest of all."[74]

Incest, sexual intercourse between those related by blood, affinity or proximity, additionally illustrates the natural law principle of sexual attraction and procreative purpose and suffers from "unbecomingness."[75] Aquinas denounced incestuous acts by portraying the natural aversion humans possess to such activities.

> There is something essentially unbecoming and contrary to natural reason in sexual intercourse between person related by blood, for instance between parents and children who are directly and immediately related to one another, since children naturally owe their parents honor.[76]

Although lower in severity when compared to relationships built on consanguinity, this unbecomingness extends to relationships with an adoptive parent, stepfather, stepmother or guardian. Sexual activity with a blood relative can only be described as "unseemly" and "most prejudicial to charity."[77]

Family and care of offspring In the natural world, most creatures instinctively care for their offspring, as birds and mammals can readily be observed caring for their offspring. In natural law thinking, that same conclusion is reached that every human being has an instinctual desire to protect and nurture children born into the family setting. Even strangers to children and infants in need pressingly feel a desire to protect the innocent child from every sort of harm. And while human beings may instinctively and rationally know the nature of this obligation, they are quite capable of neglecting the responsibility. With 61 percent divorce rates and illegitimacy rates as high as 80 percent in selected communities, the human agent can be just as malfeasant in this case as he or she can be loving and nurturing. Because of this freedom—to care dutifully or with neglect—the natural law combines offspring with the marital state, the institution of marriage as a formal setting that lays out fundamental responsibilities of parents to their children. In short, it is much more likely that two parent families, in a blessed state of matrimony, will care responsibly for their offspring than a plague of illegitimate births with abandoning fathers or even mothers who are not quite sure who the father might be. In a world of promiscuity, it is difficult if not impossible to raise any offspring with the same order and structure natural to the nuclear family. For natural law thinkers, the institution of marriage acts as the stabilizing force in sexual relations and the fortifier assuring healthy communities. Marriage provides a structured environment, more dependable relationships and protection for the family members. In contrast, the instability of one-night stands and cavalier sexual behavior cannot deliver positive settings for the proper care and feeding of children. Hence, a promiscuous lifestyle, driven by fornication and lust, is "an indeterminate union of the sexes, as something incompatible with matrimony, it is opposed to the good of the child's upbringing."[78]

In marriage, the husband and wife commit and promise to one another, not as mere whim or for the temporary moment but a lifetime. Those engaged in fornication, bigamy, adultery and polygamy have far more challenges in the care and provision for offspring. In the marital state, one knows more naturally the essential obligations. In the state of promiscuity and unchastity, the child matters far less if at all to the participants. And the "mistakes" that arise in pregnancy from nonmarital relationships are beings far more disposable than those born of wedlock. It is this cruel detachment from offspring—erecting barriers from essentially no more than a male figure depositing sperm and semen into a female figure uncommitted to a lifetime partnership—that fosters this indifference in children. Dare one also say that this state of emotional alienation makes abortion all the more tolerated and even demanded in order that mistakes might be corrected. This is a calculating and heartless view of children and how parents are to be naturally responsible. As a result, sexual intercourse must remain in the context of a loving marriage. Pursuing sexual activity outside of marriage leads only to sin and emptiness.[79]

Most natural law thinkers staunchly defend the sanctity of marriage and reject disrespect for the sacrament of matrimony. Marriage is a bond of unity, and any action that undermines that relationship is judged contrary to the natural law.[80] The bond of matrimony instills the social and spiritual structure for a "common life in family matters."[81] For these reasons, under natural law reasoning, bigamy cannot be defended or tolerated. Bigamy destroys the unity between the marital partners and undermines the very definition of marriage. The multiple marital relationships inherent in bigamy eliminate the bond and contractual promise that any marriage entails—to love and cherish one another till death. Bigamy creates coexistent relationships that operate in secrecy and fraud. The bigamist lives in the underworld of multiple relationships, instead of a world of "fidelity," boldly breaking the promise of charity in the marital state. Bigamy leads to the ruination of marital integrity and "causes irregularity, because it destroys the perfect signification of the sacrament: which is seated both in the union of the minds, as expressed by the consent, and in the union of the bodies."[82] Bigamy runs contrary to the marital ideal because marriage "requires the husband to have only one wife, and the wife to have only one husband."[83] Bigamy is "incompatible with spirituality, inasmuch as it makes a man to be wholly carnal,"[84] and causes the spouse to be "unwilling to be content with one wife"[85] and more inclined to promiscuity and lust.

In addition, the natural law cannot brook or accept polygamy since these multiple husbands or wives cause injustice among the members and the disproportionate relationship dooms the subservient parties. A multitude of wives is antagonistic to "nature's dictate to every animal according to the mode befitting its nature."[86] This also applies to the children born from these unions "since the rearing of whose offspring demands the care of both, namely the male and female, by natural instinct clings to the union of one with one, for instance the turtle-dove, the dove and so forth."[87] Polygamy leads to a state of confusion for the offspring who experience the uncertainty of multiple mothers.

In sum, the natural law rightfully holds that sexual intercourse between opposite sex parties, within the confines of the matrimonial state, being part of a nuclear family, best represents the natural order. Nothing in nature displays the chaos of the bigamist or polygamist or the fornicator or lust-driven offender. Of course, begetting children is merely the first step in the procreative process, for parents have a life-long obligation to not only beget but also rear.[88]

A social, communal life Since man is a social animal, any legitimate theory of law extends to a culture, a community and a civilization. Promoters of the natural law are well aware that the ordinating influence of law does not terminate with individual activity, because it just as pertinently applies to the common good of a nation as it applies to the common good of its individual citizenry. In response to whether a law should be crafted for the individual or common case, Aquinas indicates that every human law derives legitimacy from its relationship to the common interest.

> Hence human laws should be proportionate to the common good. Now the common good comprises many things. Wherefore law should take account of many things, as to persons, as to matters, and as to times.[89]

With keen insight, Aquinas discerns the futility of a law that applies in the individual scenario alone. Laws are implemented not for the single person or the one-time circumstance, but instead law is a common precept applicable to a community of men.[90] It is for the multitude that laws exist, because laws for the community are nothing more than the social sum of its members. Law, particularly the human variety, "is framed for a number of beings."[91] Law is equated with the happiness in both individual and culture. If lacking a communal component, the enactment would be "devoid of the nature of a law."[92]

Since the human person is a social and political being, he or she cannot live in isolation according the natural law. By our very nature, we tend to gravitate to others, to live in groups, to erect familial structures for a lifetime and to be part of a larger whole. History makes plain that no man is an "island" but is part of a larger collective of beings living in harmony with one another. All observable reality makes this condition inherent in the human agent. Finally, to live a virtuous life fundamentally depends on relations, an associative quality with others since it is impossible to be just with a lone self without other beings. Charity has little meaning if not relational nor courage or temperance. Every human action need be measured in light of others as one carries out a virtuous life. In this sense, the natural law school displays no tendency to idyllic isolationism of complete separation from the world but a full integration into it.

Belief in a Deity Another self-evident principle of the natural law involves the spiritual side of the human person, that tendency, that inclination and disposition to believe in God, in a Deity, a higher and more transcendent power. For natural law adherents, this belief serves as the bedrock for everything else that matters for natural law jurisprudence. And while some parts of the school of the natural law may be a bit more biological or cosmological, or even naturalistic, it is difficult to fully apply and extend natural law reasoning without resorting to higher, more hierarchical levels that manifest ultimate truths. Since the human person is so transitory, nothing much permanent, in matters or ethics or anything else, could ever be captured. In natural law reasoning, God serves as bedrock and foundation for its pronouncements and conclusions. In this fashion, natural law displays no penchant for relativity or individualized or situation ethics. This observation is what makes modernism so wary of it for that school concludes a trap without exception or any form of tolerance. That viewpoint is more a stereotype than reality. History shows that it better to live under the alleged tyranny of metaphysics than the whims and musings of exclusive human operations. In natural law reasoning, the eternal exemplar, the divine intellect, gives rationality and sense to the universe. God's very being is the eternal law itself. Everything in the universe depends upon the eternal law, literally every being and every form of matter. Nothing escapes the watchful oversight of the eternal law. Yet, as noted previously, no human person can fully fathom the eternal law, although we are most capable of deriving knowledge about from its effects, nature and creation being the most poignant examples. To be educated about the eternal Godhead and the plan for the universe, the human agent will have to master what the Creator imprinted in our very essence, our reason—the content of the natural law. God has equipped the human actor with this fundamental understanding, although the degrees to which we shall encounter and understand it may vary depending on our fortitude to discover its proper applications and our capacity to discern its principles. All of these factors lead to the power of our belief in God, a natural law understanding of the Creator and the creative process of which we are part. Human beings are God's most ambitious project and the only other being operating with reason.

The divine law

In natural law circles there are other proofs of God's tutelage and guidance, namely the role and function of the divine law. Divine law, while having the qualities of God's rationality and plan, is not the same as the eternal law. Divine law consists of the Old and New Testaments of the Bible and documents of revelation, of God giving instructions on how to live in accordance with his commandments and plan for human life. The divine law is scriptural authority for how to live in accordance with God's overall plan for human fulfillment. Scripture explains the mind and particular commands of a transcendent, perfect God. Scripture directs the human person to happiness.[93] Man and man alone is simply incapable of operating without divine instruction for "human reason is not infallible and with the best will in the world people fall into subjective error in working out the details of right and wrong."[94]

It is just this quality of the "directing of human conduct"[95] that makes divine law central to many natural law thinkers. Accepting the condition of human frailty and imperfection, realizing the historical evidence for both success and failure on the part of God's people, the natural law advocate looks to scriptural instruction as a guide in a world of competing moral claims. When in doubt, God's word can and does resolve dilemmas, legal or otherwise. To assure salvation, God's divine instruction helps man "know without any doubt what he ought to do and what he ought to avoid."[96] Man's inability to do what is right and God's unbridled generosity in His revealing through Scripture the plan for human operations, the divine law anchors humankind in God's great scheme.[97]

In short, the divine law directly enunciates the faith since human reason alone cannot fully discern the things of God.[98] In both the Old and New Testaments, many natural law thinkers see the divine law as proof of our natural belief in God and the necessity of having God lay out a plan of salvation. Whether by the Old Testament's stern deterrent mentality or the New Testament's all-encompassing charity, both scriptural domains lay out a map for salvation. The Decalogue, as an illustration, represents the divine law's capacity to guide, instruct and lead man to proper ends, on the way giving one another their due.[99] Divine law continually serves as a reminder to the citizen and moral agent, transmitting its luminous beacon of moral truth to those "habituated to sin"[100] and "obscured in the point of things to be done in detail."[101] Eternal happiness is an end that "exceeds man's natural ability"[102] and the divine law fills the void.[103] St. Thomas agrees with this relational quality of the divine law since its prime aim is leading man to God, "either in this life or in the life to come,"[104] for the foremost purpose of the law "is for man to cling to God."[105] Much more could be said about this component of natural law philosophy, but suffice it to say, the divine law is yet another reflection of God's love for His creation.

The human law

In the natural law construct, the higher forms of law, namely the eternal, natural and divine, descend downward to human promulgations, enactments and law. Human law is not to be devalued in the natural law theory but prized for its application; it is where the rubber meets the road. Assessing human law gives us the opportunity to see the natural law in action for speculative theory alone is but one piece of the natural law puzzle, because human law is prompted by the practical side of our intellect. Human laws will fundamentally comply with these higher forms of law or act in contravention or opposition thereto. In this way, while there is no such thing as a bad natural or eternal law, human laws can be both good and bad. In the latter case, in natural law analysis, the human law directly attacks the principles of the natural law. Thus, abortion laws that permit the destruction of the fetus, especially in later developmental stages, would be bad laws, while a law that protects the fetus, good. From another perspective, one can conclude the human law making and promulgating is an imperfect and often incorrect process. Despite the imperfection, human laws are essential to the natural law theory since their content aims "at the ordering of human life [...] under the precepts of a life we have to lead."[106] Moreover, human law maintains its integrative place in natural law jurisprudence because of its relation to reality, to social and political living and governance and to the advancement of temporal happiness. Undeniably, the human or positive law can never be as comprehensive or as perfect as its relational superiors—the eternal, natural and divine laws—and if its terminus and enforceability depend solely on its human, secular object, then such a law, if not today, will tomorrow exact an injustice. This inevitable tragedy that results when human law is the centerpiece of a legal system is easy enough to predict. Since human law is promulgated by human beings, it will always be subject to error and mistake. Nevertheless, human law is driving toward and is concerned with the same goods as its counterparts. Law, as previously defined, is an exercise of reason, a rule and measure of it. Human laws directly reflect the exercise of practical reason—assessing individual facts and circumstances and then deliberating, enacting and infusing authority by actual laws. Human laws are not the exclusive province of the positivist. Not because man is the author of the human law but more persuasively because man, in exercising practical reason, entwines himself with the God who fashioned him.[107]

As in all other forms of laws posed here, each depend upon one another for natural law jurisprudence, the lower form of law; for example, human depends on the natural and eternal for its legitimacy. And human law plays a central role in the development of both the citizenry and the community, for each enactment has the power to mold and shape both forces and to do so virtuously. Human law cannot, if true to justice, stand isolated or independent of its legal counterparts but holds firmly to the truths fully discoverable in the natural law. Human law habituates the populace, sets parameters for behavior and gives notice on the acceptability or unacceptability of conduct.[108] Human law is not only language but a mechanism to habituate, a force to reign in the unreasonable and the untrue and a prescription for the virtues. Indeed, for the natural law theorist, "it is difficult to see how man could suffice"[109] without it.

The necessity of human law Natural law thinkers correctly conclude that human law is absolutely necessary for a civil and moral society—a belief that human existence would fail without legal promulgations. Human beings need commands, proscriptions and prohibitions to carry out their individual and collective obligations. Human laws serve as a series of parameters and controls for human conduct. Although human beings are fundamentally geared to the good, and by their rational nature can identify proper ends, experience delineates the value of control. Wills, passions and appetites tug and, at times, overwhelm the rational creatures who choose conduct that is contrary to their nature. While some persons are naturally in need of less control than others, most individuals need the guidance and corresponding control of human laws. In this manner, human law is necessitous for the bulk of humanity.[110] Those already disposed to virtue have less need for legal regulation while those whose "disposition is evil are not led to virtue unless they are compelled."[111]

The world's own imperfections necessitate the role of human law in human affairs, for human law has the capacity to remove evil from the world.[112] Human law can purify and defend the onslaught of moral barbarism and deliver tranquility and peace to communal settings. Neither in anarchy nor in isolation does the human person carry out a social and political existence reliant upon law. Henle argues that human law is necessary not because of its own necessity but because of the "state of fallen man."[113] The law is not inherently coercive, but it is consistent with all its other purposes, "directive" of what ought to be done. To be sure, human law has the power to coerce and mold, but since law is a pure exercise of reason, the human actor should be comfortable with its content. Those exercising behavior in accordance with reason are willing properly and thus not in need of coercive power of the law. In this sense, "the good are not subject to law, but only the wicked."[114] Hence, human law is necessitous for both reasons of utility and man's current lack of perfection. It is, for lack of better description, a libation that the virtuous can avoid and the wicked must drink.

Human law is derivative Any legal professional such as a judge or lawyer soon discovers that most law has a precedential legacy. Cases of first instance are rare events, since legal pronouncements eventually attract a following. When enough people praise the decision and enough support is generated among the legal community, a legal maxim and principle is borne. To have any credibility, a human law withstands the test of time and the clamor of the crowd. Good laws are not drafted in isolation but rooted in tradition. For those following natural law tradition, human law is derived from other sources including the theological and philosophical underpinnings, none more compelling or relevant than natural law jurisprudence. In the end, every human law needs to be measured by the principles and tenets of the natural law. Even speeding, jaywalking, taxes, and so on, have a derivative quality, especially in the justness behind their enactment. Kings, too, derive their authority from a higher power, although history is replete with examples of those who turn the crown into an anointing, who would "usurp that right, by framing unjust laws, and by degenerating into tyrants who preyed on their subjects."[115]

Human law, to assure its legitimacy, must look to the eternal, natural and divine laws. By measuring law integratively and hierarchically, the lawmaker or legislator is confident that the law posed or sponsored passes natural law muster. So too, the judge on the bench, the policy maker pushing an agenda or the cop on the street carrying out a particular tactic, all evaluates a law by referencing the law's other forms, namely natural, divine and eternal. Since law is an exercise of human reason, and reason is the rule and measure of law, a natural law advocate reminds us that reason contains the precepts of the natural law, it already understands and has mastered them. "Human law is derived from the natural and eternal law and, consequently, every human law has just so much of the nature of law as it is derived from the law of nature."[116] Since positivism zealously excludes any rootedness beyond its promulgation, it has stripped away, gutted moral inquiry in human law analysis. Rights are based on codifications, the mutterings of "some tiny little minority of an elite,"[117] rather than inherencies or perennial truths.

The derivative relationship between the positive law and "higher" law is not one based on confrontation but one of unity and integration. Human laws that are contrary to the tenets of the natural law are, by implication, an affront to the eternal law and not really laws in the truest sense. Some natural law thinkers cannot even allow the label of bad law to exist, for a bad law is not a law at all and because it deviates from reason and the content of the natural law "has not the nature of law in any sense."[118] A human law, inconsistent with the natural, does violence to the very notion of what law is and ergo cannot bind in conscience.[119] Neither, therefore, is it nor can it be law as popularly understood. Human laws inconsistent with the higher forms of law are, in some natural law circles, simply not recognized since the enactment "has not the nature of law."[120] An unjust human promulgation antagonistic to the eternal, divine and natural laws "has the nature, not of law but of violence."[121]

Conclusion

Natural law jurisprudence encompasses far more than codification or enactment but instead a full, esoteric integration of God's plan, the supreme exemplar for all being. The natural law not only reflects the eternal law, whereby the human person "participates" in the God who authors all life, but also provides a cohesive and unified plan for social, governmental and personal living; it lays out a schema of moral and human rights; it insists upon an unbridled attentiveness to nature and endorses conduct consistent with our nature. More particularly, there is recognition that the law of God is neither severable nor any different from any other legal approach. Despite efforts to shape or craft a "secular vision" of the natural law, the bulk of natural law thinkers remain interested in a higher order. The natural law without the eternal law is only partially justifiable. The stamp of its ancestry causes the natural law adherent to think teleologically, always searching for the ultimate end of man, that supernatural dimension in the human agent's existence, while simultaneously living in the trenches and realities of legal practice and theory. From the foxholes will arise laws consistent with unity and derived from the natural and eternal law or promulgations that trigger violence to the nature and essence of law.[122]

Natural law encourages the human player to imperfectly interact with the eternal law of God by following the blueprint implanted by God in his rational creatures and always driven by a fundamental theorem—doing good and avoiding evil. Other first principles and even secondary principles are deduced therefrom, namely self-preservation, sexual attraction based on the opposite sex, procreation, belief in a Deity, family and care of offspring and living in community rather than isolation. Natural law jurisprudence posits "that there are right answers to moral questions and those lawmakers can and should be guided by such moral truths."[123] That this form of jurisprudence is allegedly out of the mainstream, supplanted by the trendy variations of positivism, makes it no less persuasive.

Attacked by a host of critics for pontificating a rigid formula of ethical choice, the natural law theory is assuredly at odds with those espousing any theory of relativity. The relativists, after angrily reviewing the natural law's dictates and conclusions, can't accept restrictions in human activity. These restrictions are invariably labeled the enemies of freedom. Freedom, for a natural law thinker, is more than the will to act, to do what one chooses, since activity, like law, must be measured and evaluated in light of reason's instruction. All the natural law does is guarantee the freedom of the human person to be exactly who they are.

Finally, natural law jurisprudence affords the legal practitioner, whether a police officer, judge or lawyer, or any involved citizen or legislator, a reliable indicator of justice. Instead of power groups forcing the law, or screaming crowds demanding a particular law, or relative whims or fads for the moment insisting on legal rights or protections, the natural law weighs the propriety of any law based on a higher power, a transcendent God coupled with his only rational creature in the human person—who has the capability of discerning the content of the natural law and applying it to particular case and circumstance. No other school of jurisprudence offers this level of dependability and universality.

Notes

1 Charles P. Nemeth, *A Comparative Analysis of Cicero and Aquinas: Nature and the Natural Law* (London: Bloomsbury Academic, 2017).
2 Lloyd L. Weinreb, "A Secular Theory of Natural Law," *Fordham Law Review*, 72, no. 6 (2004): 2299–2300.
3 Robert H. Bork, "Natural Law and the Constitution," *First Things* (March 1992), https://www.firstthings.com/article/1992/03/natural-law-and-the-constitution.
4 St. Thomas Aquinas, *The Treatise on Law*, ed. R. J. Henle (Notre Dame: University of Notre Dame Press, 1993), 149.
5 St. Thomas Aquinas, "Summa Theologica," in *Basic Writings of Saint Thomas Aquinas*, ed. Anton C. Pegis, vol. 2 (New York: Random House, 1945), I-II, Q. 93, a. 3, sed contra.
6 Ibid.
7 Etienne Gilson, *The Christian Philosophy of St. Thomas Aquinas*, trans. L. K. Shook (New York: Random House, 1956), 266.
8 Anton-Hermann Chroust, "The Philosophy of Law of St. Thomas Aquinas: His Fundamental Ideas and Some of His Historical Precursors," *American Journal of Jurisprudence*, 19, no. 1 (1974): 25.
9 Aquinas, *Pegis* I-II, Q. 93, a. 1.
10 Ibid., I, Q. 45, a. 3.
11 Ibid., I-II Q. 93, a. 1, c.
12 Ibid.
13 Ibid., I-II, Q. 91, a. 1.
14 Ibid., Q. 93, a. 2, ad 1.
15 Ibid., a. 4, c.
16 Ibid., Q. 91, a. 1, c.
17 Ibid.
18 Ibid., Q. 93, a. 6, ad. 3.
19 Ibid., ad. 2.
20 Ibid., Q. 93, a. 6, ad. 2.
21 C. S. Lewis, *Studies in Words* (Cambridge: Cambridge University Press, 1960), 37.

22 Ibid., 24.
23 St. Thomas Aquinas, *On Kingship*, trans. Gerald B. Phelan (Toronto: Pontifical Institute of Mediaeval Studies, 1982), ch. 2, 19.
24 Bernard Boedder, *Natural Theology* (New York: Longmans, Green, 1927), 46.
25 Gilson, *Christian Philosophy of St. Thomas Aquinas*, 266.
26 Alasdair MacIntyre's often-cited work, *Whose Justice? Which Rationality?*, warns the critic and ally alike that the natural law is not merely a registry of pre- and proscriptions. "Obeying the precepts of the natural law is more than simply refraining from doing what those precepts prohibit and doing what they enjoin. The precepts become effectively operative only as and when we find ourselves with motivating reasons for performing actions inconsistent with those precepts; what the precepts can then provide us with is a reason which can outweigh the motivating reasons for disobeying them, that is, they point us to a more perfect good than do the latter." (Notre Dame: University of Notre Dame Press, 1988), 194.
27 Aquinas, *Theologica, Pegis*, I-II, Q. 94, a. 1.
28 Ibid., Q. 91, a. 2, c.
29 Ignatius T. Eschmann, *The Ethics of St. Thomas Aquinas* (Toronto: Pontifical Institute of Mediaeval Studies, 1997), 187.
30 Aquinas, *Theologica, Pegis*, I-II, Q. 94, a. 6.
31 Ibid., a. 2, c.
32 Aquinas, *Gentiles*, III-I, ch. 4, 2.
33 Ibid., ch. 6, 5.
34 Aquinas, *Theologica, Pegis*, I-II, Q. 94, a. 2, ad. 2.
35 Ibid., a. 4, ad. 3.
36 Gratian, *Decretum*, I, v, prol. (I,7); Aquinas, *Theologica, Pegis* I-II, Q. 94, a. 5, sed contra.
37 Aquinas, *Theologica, Pegis*, I-II, Q. 94, a. 2, c.
38 Gilson, *Christian Philosophy of St. Thomas Aquinas*, 266.
39 Nelson, 107.
40 Even the appetitive process exhibits a certain inclination. "This certitude is based on the nature of the being. Things are constituted in a determined way, and their inclination follows and is one with their determination, so that, even without knowledge of what is and what is not appetible, a natural inclination will seek the appetible." Gustaf J. Gustafson, *The Theory of Natural Appetency in the Philosophy of St. Thomas* (Washington, DC: Catholic University of America Press, 1944), 71.
41 Aquinas, *Theologica, Pegis*, I-II, Q. 94, a. 4, c.
42 Eschmann, *Ethics of St. Thomas Aquinas*, 188.
43 Ibid.
44 Aquinas, *Theologica, Pegis*, I-II, Q. 100, a. 3.
45 Ibid., Q. 94, a. 2, c.
46 Ralph McInerny cautions interpreters not to confuse natural law reasoning with the physical laws or imperatives. "Natural law is not simply the rational recognition of physical imperatives, nor is it a judgment of how we should act which ignores the given teleology of the physical. Natural law relates to inclinations other than reason, which have their own ends, by prescribing how we should humanly pursue them. For St. Thomas, natural law is a dictate of reason, not a physical law." *Ethica Thomistica: The Moral Philosophy of Thomas Aquinas* (Washington, DC: Catholic University of American Press, 1982), 46.

47 Aquinas, *Theologica*, I-II, Q. 94, a. 2 and a. 4, quoted in R. A. Armstrong, *Primary and Secondary Precepts in Thomistic Natural Law Teaching* (The Hague: Martinus Nijhoff, 1966), 125.
48 Aquinas, *Theologica, Pegis*, I-II, Q. 100, a. 11.
49 See Henle, *Treatise on Law*.
50 Aquinas, *Theologica, Pegis*, I-II, Q. 94, a. 4, c.
51 Ibid., a. 5.
52 Ibid, c.
53 Aquinas, *Gentiles*, III-II, ch. 122, 4.
54 Ibid., ch. 124, 1.
55 Ibid., ch. 125, 7.
56 Ibid., ch. 127.
57 Ibid., ch. 127, 7.
58 St. Thomas Aquinas, *Summa Theologica*, trans. Fathers of the English Dominican Province, vol. 2 (New York: Benzinger Brothers, 1947), 1471, Bk. II-II, Q. 64, art. 7, corpus.
59 Ibid., sed contra.
60 St. Thomas, *Summa*, Benzinger, 1471, Bk. II-II, Q. 64, art. 7, corpus; see Joseph Rickaby, *Aquinas Ethicus: Or, the Moral Teaching of St. Thomas*, vol. 1 (London: Burns & Oates, 1892), 47–48.
61 St. Thomas, *Summa*, Benzinger, 1469, art. 5, corpus.
62 Ibid., 1467, art. 2, r. obj. 3.
63 Charles P. Nemeth, *Aquinas on Crime* (South Bend: St. Augustine's Press, 2009), 58–59.
64 St. Thomas, *Gentiles*, 88–89.
65 St. Thomas Aquinas, *Summa Theologica*, trans. Fathers of the English Dominican Province, vol. 1 (New York: Benzinger Brothers, 1947), 574, Bk. I, Q. 118, art. 2.
66 Ibid.
67 See Daniel A. Dambrowski, "Rachels, Abortion and the Seventeenth Century," *International Journal of Applied Philosophy*, 9, no. 2 (1998): 38.
68 Joshua Greene, *Moral Tribes: Emotion, Reason, and the Gap between Us and Them* (New York: Penguin, 2014).
69 St. Thomas, *Summa*, Benzinger 2, 1811, Bk. II-II, Q. 153, art. 2.
70 Ibid.
71 Ibid.
72 Ibid., 1810.
73 Ibid., 1825, art. 11.
74 Ibid.
75 Ibid., 1824, art. 10.
76 Ibid.
77 Ibid.
78 Ibid., 1816, Bk. II-II, Q. 154, art. 2.
79 Ibid.
80 Ibid., 2722–23, Bk. III, Q. 44, art. 1.
81 Ibid., 2724, art. 3.
82 Ibid., 2814, Q. 66, art. 1.
83 Ibid.
84 Ibid.
85 Ibid.

86 Ibid., 2808, Q. 65, art. 1.
87 Ibid.
88 Ibid., 2809.
89 St. Thomas, *Summa*, Benzinger 1, 1017, Bk. I-II, Q. 96, art. 1, corpus.
90 Ibid., 1018, r. obj. 2.
91 Ibid., art. 2, corpus.
92 Ibid., 994, Q. 90, art. 2, corpus.
93 Ibid., 1026, Q. 98, art. 1, corpus.
94 Noel Dermot O'Donoghue, "The Law beyond the Law," *American Journal of Jurisprudence*, 18, no. 1 (1973): 158.
95 St. Thomas, *Summa*, Benzinger 1, 998, Bk. I-II, Q. 91, art. 4, corpus.
96 Ibid.
97 Patrick M. J. Clancy, "St. Thomas on Law," in St. Thomas Aquinas, *The Summa Theologica*, vol. 3, trans. Fathers of the English Dominican Province (New York: Benziger Brothers, 1947), 3275.
98 St. Thomas, *Summa*, Benzinger 1, 1037, Bk. I-II, Q. 100, art. 1.
99 Ibid., 1045, art. 8, corpus.
100 Ibid., 1032, Q. 99, art. 2, r. obj. 2.
101 Ibid.
102 Aquinas, *Theologica*, Pegis, I-II, Q. 91, a. 4.
103 Gilson artistically blends this divine law and human agent into a *union*, a *unity*, a bridge spanning the chasm of the temporal and the eternal, attaching him to God by means of His love. Gilson, *Christian Philosophy of St. Thomas Aquinas*, 333.
104 Aquinas, *Theologica*, Pegis, I-II, Q. 100, a. 2, c.
105 Aquinas, *Gentiles*, III-II, ch. 128, 2.
106 Aquinas, *Theologica*, Pegis, I-II, Q. 99, a. 4, ad. 1.
107 For some well-grounded discussion of positive law in Thomistic jurisprudence, see Vincent McNabb, *St. Thomas Aquinas and Law* (Blackfriars: Aquin Press, 1955); and Barry F. Smith, "Of Truth and Certainty in the Law: Reflections on the Legal Method," *American Journal of Jurisprudence*, 30, no. 1 (1985): 119.
108 Aquinas, *Theologica*, Pegis, I-II, Q. 63, a. 1; Q. 94, a.3; Q. 95, a. 1, c.
109 Ibid., Q., 95, a. 1.
110 Charles Skok portrays St. Thomas's vision as realistic rather than pessimistic. "St. Thomas often made reference to men in their present condition. Not many men are truly virtuous or highly virtuous. Laws have to be made for the general run of the people in the state in which they are found. This is not pessimism but realism." Charles D. Skok, *Prudent Civil Legislation According to St. Thomas and Some Controversial American Law* (Rome: Catholic Book Agency, 1967), 119.
111 Aquinas, *Theologica*, Pegis, I-II, Q. 95, a. 1, ad. 1.
112 Ibid., a. 3.
113 Henle, *Treatise on Law*, 335.
114 Aquinas, *Theologica*, Pegis, I-II, Q. 96, a. 5, c.
115 Ibid., Q. 105, a. 1, ad 5.
116 Ibid, Q. 95, a. 2, c.
117 M. Gilson, *Law on the Human Level: Moral Values and Moral life the System of St. Thomas*, trans. L. Ward (St. Louis, MO: B. Herder, 1931), 204.
118 Aquinas, *Theologica*, Pegis, I-II, Q. 93, a. 3, ad. 2.
119 Ibid., a. 3.

120 Ibid., Q. 93, a. 3, ad. 1.
121 Ibid., Q. 93, a. 3, ad. 2.
122 Ibid., Q. 96, a. 2; Q. 69, a. 1; Q. 77, a. 1; Q. 78, a. 1, ad. 3.
123 Henry Mather, "Natural Law and Right Answers," *American Journal of Jurisprudence*, 38, no. 1 (1993): 334; See also Skok, *Prudent Civil Legislation*, 22.

Chapter 3

NATURAL LAW AND ABORTION: A POST-ROE EVALUATION

Background and History

That *Roe v. Wade*[1] has caused extraordinary consternation, dispute and an unsettled state of legal affairs has not been a contention from either the right or the left. There are many reasons for this. First, the decision exhibits all the draconian traits of an unrestrained and unchecked federalism—manifesting little, if any, regard for our 50 states that in the majority had favored some type of oversight and prohibition of abortion at the time of Roe. Coupled with this state's rights disregard—which dominated the legal landscape over many decades in the American experience—was a general federal arrogance that states seem incapable of resolving this question. Such arrogance is bound to generate a backlash against the scope of the decision and its general disregard for a huge segment of the population.[2] Others have argued that Roe stifled any attempt to a compromise or alternative due to its sweeping and very noninclusive ruling.

However, criticisms of Roe go beyond the conventional backlash narrative.[3] Scholars, Supreme Court Justices, and grassroots activists argue that the 1973 decision did broader political damage.[4] Richard Posner suggests that Roe cut off a promising, state-by-state negotiation about the scope and rationale of abortion rights.[5] If the Court had not imposed a single, national result on a divided polity, Posner reasons, lawmakers might have arrived at an approach that commended itself to those on both sides of the issue.[6,7]

Even Justice Ginsburg, an avid supporter of reproductive rights, has frequently expressed reservations about the sweep of Roe. She commented in a 1985 law review article,

"Roe v. Wade sparked public opposition and academic criticism, in part, I believe, because the Court ventured too far in the change it ordered and presented an incomplete justification for its action."[8] The Court's subliminal tendencies in Roe are many and varied, one being a thirst or lust for universality in abortion application. This state of affairs, gazed at in hindsight, that is an inordinate desire to make abortion some sort of universal right, seems almost immature when compared to the previous legal structure. Antonin Scalia often urged his colleagues to return to these "good old days" when states were the arbiters of this complex system, not the federal leviathan.[9]

In short, let Texas or Mississippi and New York or California decide on its own moral, cultural, spiritual and religious terms. In either case, the people of those jurisdictions speak for what their citizenry find compatible. In Roe, any dissenting voice is squashed without hesitation or reservation and, as a result, a chasm between the decision and those that disagree now appears unbridgeable. To those who might claim that the identical argument would have justified and maintained a "slavery" exception, the conclusion seems an apple over an orange. In slavery, a universal deduction about human equality, the essentiality of the human person and natural freedom to live and prosper are the stuff of consensus and in a very universal sense. When applied to abortion, the dynamics generate competing conclusions, especially in light of competing lives: the mother and the potential or actual life of the fetus. Even neonatal science cannot deny the existence and operation of a human life at earlier stages than ever dreamt of or anticipated at the time of Roe.[10] The science of Roe is properly termed "incredibly weak."[11] Add to this an admission by the court that the decision as to when life begins cannot be decided today, and yet, "the Court did decide that question" with its trimester invention.[12]

To be sure, the foundational science of Roe, when compared to the current state of fetal development, appears quite elementary.[13]

Aristotle's conception of "quickening," when life could be measured forward, was strangely more scientifically accurate than the Roe science. For in Roe, the ends are what matter; how one gets to abortion's legalization drives the legal enterprise and secures the abortion becomes the undergirding for the legal conclusion. The fetus lacks personhood in Roe and eventually becomes marginalized. Roe's conclusion suffers from its novelty too since a demand for a right was posed on conduct never previously agreed to or even enumerated in the Constitution.

Third, the decision's legal inventiveness and almost illusory quality has long been an impediment to Roe acceptance. For those who operate as textualists, it will never be satisfactory because this "right" is never referenced or enumerated, nor is it part of our common law or our legal tradition, nor for that matter has it ever been a staple of Western jurisprudence. Indeed, if one had to compare, for most of Western jurisprudence, the practice has been prohibited or severely restricted. The decision, as enunciated, "for a nearly unlimited right to abortion was deeply flawed from the outset."[14]

For those who believe in a "living and breathing" Constitution, it is a decision that keeps up with the times, just as the court has recently done in the same-sex marriage cases and others. While this sort of legal reasoning may give the advocates what it wants and hopes for, on what foundation does the decision rest? Even Justice Ginsburg has critiqued Roe for its specious legal rationale—calling on the court to root its reasoning in a more legitimate legal basis.[15]

In other words, one can exhort the right to privacy, with both passion and good intentions, but where in our express constitutional authority does that right exist? Even more squarely, did the framers ever envision privacy being applicable to the practice of abortion? Roe's conceptual foundation has always been suspect, whether one agrees with abortion or not. This sort of shaky, intellectual grounding further causes dissent, dissension and an inability for the reasoning to ever really take hold in American law. Bad law rots the communal good a day at a time and one need only witness the ferocity of disagreement between pro-life and pro-choice to see the unsettled and unstable landscape of Roe.

Fourth, not only are the diverse arguments posed for the legalization of abortion at the federal and constitutional level overly creative, the decision has been hijacked by those who want to advance abortion at any cost. By hijacked I mean that if the reader looks closely at Roe, there are truly critiques and admonitions to those who indicate that Roe is "abortion on demand," or that it is always an "undue burden" to place any restriction, of any sort, on the practice, or that call into question any relevance or competing interest of the fetus or as it indicates "potential human life." So intense are the arguments for access and unbridled, unrestricted and literally unchecked levels of oversight that some abortion advocates are urging that doctors be eliminated from the equation of reproductive rights when the woman chooses "medication-induced" abortions, performed at home. Doctors should not be required in these settings—an extreme extension of Roe if there ever was one.[16]

Oddly and curiously, any inspection of Roe, textually, finds a court repeatedly arguing against abortion on demand and how states rightfully can impose reasonable restrictions on the practice.

Most tellingly, the court sets up a trimester system where rights aligned with abortion practice slowly but surely dissipate the more the fetus develops. The third trimester is particularly troubling, even under the historic Roe legacy, the case reasoning does not appear comfortable with either partial birth abortion or infanticide. Roe's majority opinion, despite its outcome, displays an excellent philosophical understanding of abortion from a Western perspective and, to be sure, does not demonize those that disagree, an unfortunate by-product that the Roe authors never intended. On top of this, the Roe majority never laid waste to the idea of restriction, notions of viability or the proper role of the state in protecting the fetus and all potential life. Almost surreally the court reiterates, over and over, that the right of any abortion need to be properly evaluated in light of a competing life. The court remarks,

> The third reason is the State's interest—some phrase it in terms of duty—in protecting prenatal life. Some of the argument for this justification rests on the theory that a new human life is present from the moment of conception. The State's interest and general obligation to protect life then extends, it is argued, to prenatal life. Only when the life of the pregnant mother herself is at stake, balanced against the life she carries within her, should the interest of the embryo or fetus not prevail.[17]

In a way, Roe has become a caricature of its own reasoning for it is not an impulsive conclusion nor some unbridled diatribe against those who wish fetal life to be part of the mix. Justice Blackmun uses the West's greatest thinkers, Hellenic and Roman philosophers like Aristotle and Seneca, and expends equal amounts of time on great theological thinkers like Gratian and Aquinas—both crucial players in the natural law tradition. The use of Aquinas at least indicates an awareness of the natural law tradition in matters of moral and ethical import. As Aristotle had done, Aquinas gives credence to the human person being a human person when "ensouled," that vivification of human person which occurs 40–80 days after conception. Both thinkers thought a charge of murder at this stage unwarranted due to the developmental questions. The court, however, leaves out that while murder may not be a proper charge in this first period of the trimester, abortion is never an act consistent with natural law. In this early stage, the party procuring the abortion would be committing a mortal sin, punishable by perpetual damnation.[18]

Finally, there is the matter of a factual foundation for Roe that has been in severe dispute. To arouse the highest level of sympathy, the advocates for Roe—namely Norma McCorvey—concocted a legal claim that she subsequently was not fully informed about and felt she had been duped by her counsel and outside advocacy groups.[19] Ironically, Norma McCorvey never procured the abortion and had that child placing it up for adoption.[20] In repeated interviews and memoirs, Norma makes plain that her own sense of events and conditions was based on being kept ignorant and essentially an outlier in a case that caused so much social and ethical turmoil.

All of these currents and cross-currents cause *Roe v. Wade* to be a legal decision that cannot garner the necessary respect since the issuance of the decision. The decision's inherent complexity, in a moral, ethical and legal sense, makes its language and implementation as precedent in subsequent cases, a tool that confuses and befuddles. In other words, the problem is not going away anytime soon. Yet, this is precisely why the natural law may be the proper arbiter, conciliator and mediator in this troublesome question. Roe hardly accomplishes any sort of moral framing or helpful debate on the question either but tends to foster polarization and entrenched positions, something completely at odds with the purpose of law in a natural law framework. In the natural law domain, law habituates citizens to the good, assures domestic tranquility and peace among competing members, enabling "fruitful relationships between individual freedom and communal values."[21] Roe does nothing of the kind. For in the natural law, there are certain guideposts that are neither relative nor changeable and, because of this fixed state, are dependable measures in select, although not all, ethical dilemmas. It is not enough to bandy about slogans about "coat hangers" or "my body– my right" or keep your "rosaries out of my ovaries." This is polemical and utterly devoid advocacy in a legal sense. Roe conveniently and very comfortably just dispenses with any woman not favorable to abortion when reality dictates at least a split in women's views and among younger women, the trend has moving in the pro-life direction, a movement often labeled "pro-life feminism."[22] Castigating those who disagree with Roe will never generate a consensus.[23]

Roe is just the case to foster and fester this type of emotional maelstrom since its reasoning was too political rather than legal and since the end sought gave rise to an any means mentality. In addition, Roe's often seen contradiction between the viability and compelling state interest to protect that viability appears almost incomprehensible upon a third and fourth reading. By contrast, the natural law measure might deliver some dependable certitude in this ethical thicket, for in the natural law various precepts are undeniable for every event and every situation. Hence, the natural law seeks and craves self-preservation of all beings, and at the same time, the natural law, as posed by Cicero, has a penchant for living naturally and not interfering with the natural processes evident in human operations. Finally, the natural law advances a "care of offspring" and family preference throughout its content. Abortion was once justified as an assurance that its implementation would guarantee that care of children would be greatly advanced. The current state of child neglect, abuse, broken families and human destruction from crumbling familial structures has long shattered that promise. Because of all this, readers should make a new attempt to see how, even in this abortion on demand world, there are increasing calls for a return to natural law principles. That journey is far from over but commences with an examination of *Roe v. Wade*.

Roe v. Wade, 410 U.S. 113 (1973)

During the bulk of the last 200 years of the Republic, Texas, like the majority of American States, had a prohibition on the practice of abortion. During the late 1960s and into the early dawn of the 1970s, Texas residents could not readily gain access to any abortion services, and the procedure was rare to be sure and usually involved exceptional circumstances such as saving the life of the mother. The statute, the Texas Penal Code, read in part:

> [2] Article 1191 Abortion
>
> If any person shall designedly administer to a pregnant woman or knowingly procure to be administered with her consent any drug or medicine, or shall use towards her any violence or means whatever externally or internally applied, and thereby procure an abortion, he shall be confined in the penitentiary not less than two nor more than five years; if it be done without her consent, the punishment shall be doubled. By "abortion" is meant that the life of the fetus or embryo shall be destroyed in the woman's womb or that a premature birth thereof be caused.
>
> Article 1192 Furnishing the Means
>
> Whoever furnishes the means for procuring an abortion knowing the purpose intended is guilty as an accomplice.
>
> Article 1193 Attempt at Abortion
>
> If the means used shall fail to produce an abortion, the offender is nevertheless guilty of an attempt to produce abortion, provided it be shown that such means were calculated to produce that result, and shall be fined not less than one hundred nor more than one thousand dollars.
>
> Article 1194 Murder in Producing Abortion
>
> If the death of the mother is occasioned by an abortion so produced or by an attempt to effect the same it is murder.
>
> Article 1196 By Medical Advice
>
> Nothing in this chapter applies to an abortion procured or attempted by medical advice for the purpose of saving the life of the mother.[24]

The court concluded, without any explicit or express authority to constitutionalize the practice, that the state's criminalization violated the Due Process Clause of the Fourteenth Amendment "which protects against state action the right to privacy, including a woman's qualified right to terminate her pregnancy."[25] In announcing its decision, the Supreme Court did two things that have been often forgotten or swept under the rug of legal history: First, the court made plain that the decision is not a license for abortion on demand since that right is "qualified" and that there are competing claims on life itself that deal with the woman's life and integrity, and at the same time, a fetus, a "potential human life" that the state has every right to protect.[26] At no place in the decision does the court announce an unbridled, unchecked and unregulated right to abortion, and in fact, the court erects a trimester system to give some guidance on how that right might be exercised. In doing so, the court accepts and propounds a wide array of theories regarding viability and the durational quality of a pregnancy from conception to the later stages of infant development whereby the state has a "compelling interest" in oversight.[27] The court makes eloquently plain:

> With respect to the States's important and legitimate interest on potential life, the "compelling point" is at viability. This is so because the fetus then presumably has the capacity of meaningful life outside the mother's womb. State regulation protective of fetal life after viability thus has logical and biological considerations.[28]

So unequivocal is the court's conclusion on the latter stage of fetal development that it further announces that it is even proper for the state to forbid or "proscribe abortion during that period."[29]

The lead up to Roe was long in the making, especially when considering its predecessor case on birth control—*Griswold v. Connecticut*[30]—the inventor of the right to privacy in matters unenumerated or ever envisioned by the framers. Nowhere is the right to birth-control pills part of our long and traditional landscape, at least in a constitutional sense, and most legal scholars at that time still showed slight deference to the Ninth Amendment that reserved rights to the states when federal constitutionalism neither explicitly or implicitly ever construed the claim of privacy. In the court's dissent, Justice Rehnquist lays out the argument, "To reach its result, the Court necessarily has to find within the scope of the Fourteenth Amendment a right that was apparently completely unknown to the drafters of the Amendment."[31]

And when the court justifies its inventiveness by reliance on "penumbras"—ghost like phantasms of a right—that naturally occur in an alternative legal universe, the claims for privacy rights, in a constitutional sense, could only proliferate. After that door was left ajar, it was only a matter of time before our Supreme Court would be as creative as it could be regarding what is a fundamental right protected by an invented legal argument. For the court to wade into such an ethical thicket, with crosscurrents of opinions and religious, spiritual and moral differences already pretty marked, makes Roe even more perplexing. Roe's Justice Blackmun recognizes the complexity of the matter when he comments in the first paragraphs of the decision:

> We forthwith acknowledge our awareness of the sensitive and emotional nature of the abortion controversy, of the vigorous opposing views, even among physicians, and of the deep and seemingly absolute convictions that the subject inspires. One's philosophy, one's experiences, one's exposure to the raw edges of human existence, one's religious training, one's attitudes toward life and family and their values, and the moral standards one establishes and seeks to observe, are all likely to influence and to color one's thinking and conclusions about abortion.[32]

Justice Blackmun then ironically, and most curiously, indicates that the task before this court is a resolution "free of emotion and predilection,"[33] yet in very close sentences immediately gets into completely irrelevant content riddled with emotion, by his discussion on "population growth, pollution, poverty and racial overtones,"[34] as if these criteria possess some sort of legitimate place in this legal rationale. With this sort of proclamation, the justice tips a hand and a mind already laboring under variables of no import to constitutional analysis.

Despite these legal gymnastics, it is clear that the court, engaged in a radical paradigm shift in the matter of constitutional protections, may have still echoed a semblance of natural law jurisprudence. Notions of fetal life, viability, potential and actual human life, tradition and history, common practice, self-preservation and the maintenance of life as a natural and inherent good, all encompass the natural law jurisprudence witnessed for nearly 2,500 years in the West. Any close reading of Roe perceives a court wishing to decide with an appreciation of what preceded its announcement, not a severing of our legal past or tradition by leaping into a brave, new, and uncharted world, but by some strange ambition to find continuity in the past with the present. Roe, Justice Rehnquist notes in his dissent, "commands his respect" due to its efforts to deal with this "troubling question" using both "extensive historical fact and a wealth of legal scholarship."[35]

What makes Roe all the more befuddling is how earnestly it treats the past, the history of abortion, the tradition of the nation-states regulating it and how crucial and integrative are the views of theologians, philosophers and scientists in its overall reasoning. This appeal to history, a sort of long view of how life operates and unravels, is clearly a natural law quality. For millennia, those who have urged a natural law thesis have relied upon human operations as an edifier for what is natural. In other words, Cicero's call for a microscopic examination of how human beings engage one another over time and space.[36] His great claim that law and life is the same in Athens, Rome or Sparta makes the point.[37]

Aquinas concludes precisely in the same way when he states that the natural law is "common to all nations" and the law of nature "the same for all."[38] Hence, the idea of historical precedent and reality always tugs at natural law advocates, for what has been done with regularity over the timeline of history tells us something about its regularity and propriety. Not all things have withstood the test of time, but certain forms of human behavior that elevate the human person have a certain permanency or perennial quality to it. So, when Justice Blackmun begins at the beginning of recorded philosophical history, he does so because the past often edifies the present and even predicts the future. One gets that sense from Blackmun as he courses through the various time periods and thinkers having something to do with the abortion issues.

History and tradition in Roe v. Wade: *A natural law inclination without natural law application*

From the time of the Greeks and Romans, abortion posed challenges at varying levels. That opinions and conclusions varied is not in dispute. Roe references the Greco-Roman gynecologist, Soranos of Ephesus (c. 98–138 A.D.), who discussed abortion in "terms of two main genres of abortifacients," *phthorion*, "which destroys what has been conceived," and *ekbolion*, "which expels what has been conceived."[39] Soranos, while generally finding abortion a faulty practice, did allow for it to occur when the life of the mother was at stake.[40] Roe additionally cites the Hippocratic Oath itself as context for its decision when the oath condemns the practice of abortion. Hippocrates, the "Father of Medicine" (460–377 BC), provides no justification for the act of abortion. The oath explicitly holds, "I will give no deadly medicine to any one if asked, nor suggest any such counsel; and in like manner I will not give to a woman a pessary to produce abortion."[41]

Even a cursory reading of the oath displays its general correlation between life maintenance, life sustenance and the role of a physician in assuring a life ethic.[42] While there are many curiosities in *Roe v. Wade*, the historical march through the greatest philosophical and theological traditions on the question of human life, viability, animation and ensoulment does little to justify its eventual conclusion. When Roe states, acknowledging that most zealous followers of the Hippocratic Oath were the Pythagoreans, a group that deduced that the "embryo was animate from the moment of conception, and abortion meant destruction of a living being," how does that reference support a claim for legalized abortion?[43]

Even the court's scrutiny of the Plato and Aristotle delivers a cautious agreement that abortion may be wise for various political or familial planning reasons and at the same time, the court correctly notes that abortion would be condemned by both thinkers "prior to viability."[44] However, while Aristotle could never be characterized as "pro-life" in the modern sense of the term, his insightful potentiality–actuality argument regarding human existence provides a solid and formidable backdrop for those urging the illegality of abortion at all phases of human development.[45] The position of Catholic-Christian philosophy on abortion takes up this mantle.

Justice Blackmun's historical analysis gives greater weight to the prohibition of abortion than its sanction. From Christian tradition forward, the question of humanity becomes inexorably tied to the form and vivification of that person by ensoulment—being more than a mere physical being without sensory powers, appetites or intellectual operations. Put another way, when does a person become a person or as Roe poses, "These disciplines variously approached the question in terms of the point at which the embryo or fetus became 'formed' or recognizably human, or in terms of when a 'person' came into being, that is, infused with a 'soul' or 'animated.'"[46]

Roe's excursion into the philosophical dimension even evaluates the concept of "mediate animation"—a measurable point between actual conception and the live birth where the life of the fetus becomes entitled to full-fledged protection.[47] Both Aristotle and Aquinas concluded that point be around 40–80 days or so and in both cases, the charge of abortion as a form of homicide would not be justified.[48] What Roe fails to address is the Thomist condemnation of abortion in all cases, except to save the life of the mother. Even in the pre-animated phase of development, Thomas never supports the practice of abortion since it is utterly contrary to the natural law and a "mortal sin" punishable by eternal damnation.[49] In the same vein, the Roe opinion builds on the animation argument by referencing the "quickening" theory whereby the fetus, its movement and reaction being detected, takes on the human form. Here the Roe court again cites St. Thomas Aquinas as part of its historical jurisprudence, noting,

> Due to continued uncertainty about the precise time when animation occurred, to the lack of any empirical basis for the 40–80 day view, and perhaps to Aquinas' definition of movement as one of the two first principles of life, Bracton focused upon quickening as the critical point. The significance of quickening was echoed by later common law scholars and found its way into the received common law in this country.[50]

Hence, the common law tradition of this Republic, Roe mentions, was largely negative on abortion, citing not only great jurists like Bracton and Coke but also the diversity of English laws that prohibited abortion in most forms until the 1960s in England.[51] In the American statutory experience, since the foundation of the nation, the trend has not been toward liberalization of abortion practice. While prosecutions were rare for the act, most legislative designs made pre-quickening acts misdemeanors and later phases felonies.[52] By the Civil War, the view on abortion had further solidified to a negative posture on its practice. Roe cites the American Medical Association's (AMA's) 1857 view on the practice and it pulls no punches at all.

> The Committee would advise that this body, representing, as it does, the physicians of the land, publicly express its abhorrence of the unnatural and how rapidly increasing crime of abortion; that it avow its true nature, as no simple offence against public morality and decency, no mere misdemeanor, no attempt upon the life of the mother, but the wanton and murderous destruction of her child [...] [And] Resolved, That while physicians have long been united in condemning the act of producing abortion, at every period of gestation, except as necessary for preserving the life of either mother or child, it has become the duty of this Association, in view of the prevalence and increasing frequency of the crime, publicly to enter an earnest and solemn protest against such unwarrantable destruction of human life.[53]

Over time, the AMA's regular and consistent protection of the unborn and its general reticence for the abortion right claim withered away under public pressure and a purposeful disengagement from this complex moral dilemma. In its place, it merely became one among many other medical procedures and recognized "that this trend will continue."[54]

By the time of Roe, the American legal landscape had solidified its general opposition to the practice of abortion. With 36 states proscribing the practice, the justices in Roe entered into an atmosphere lacking all consensus or even remote unanimity. The list of states outlawing abortion in 1970 are found at Table 1.[55]

Indeed, it is a safe observation that the majority of the American populace found abortion an unacceptable and troublesome practice. Justice Rehnquist remarked in his dissent on this chasm between what was decided and the current cultural climate upon which that decision was hurled. "Even today, where society's views are changing, the very existence of the debate is evident that the 'right' to an abortion is not so universally accepted as the appellant would have us believe."[56]

Table 1 Jurisdictions having enacted abortion laws prior to the adoption of the Fourteenth Amendment in 1868.

1. Alabama	Ala. Acts, c. 6, 2 (1840).
2. Arizona	Howell Code, c. 10, 45 (1865).
3. Arkansas	Ark. Rev. Stat., c. 44, div. III, Art. II, 6 (1838).
4. California	Cal. Sess. Laws, c. 99, 45, p. 233 (1849-1850).
5. Colorado (Terr.)	Colo. Gen. Laws of Terr. of Colo., 1st Sess., 42, pp. 296-297 (1861).
6. Connecticut	Conn. Stat., Tit. 20, 14, 16 (1821). By 1868, this statute had been replaced by another abortion law. Conn. Pub. Acts, c. 71, 1, 2, p. 65 (1860).
7. Florida	Fla. Acts 1st Sess., c. 1637, subc. 3, 10, 11, subc. 8, 9, 10, 11 (1868), as amended, now Fla. Stat. Ann. 782.09, 782.10, 797.01, 797.02, 782.16 (1965).
8. Georgia	Ga. Pen. Code, 4th Div., 20 (1833).
9. Kingdom of Hawaii	Hawaii Pen. Code, c. 12, 1, 2, 3 (1850).
10. Idaho (Terr.)	Idaho (Terr.) Laws, Crimes and Punishments 33, 34, 42, pp. 441, 443 (1863).
11. Illinois	Ill. Rev. Criminal Code 40, 41, 46, pp. 130, 131 (1827). By 1868, this statute had been replaced by a subsequent enactment. Ill. Pub. Laws 1, 2, 3, p. 89 (1867).
12. Indiana	Ind. Rev. Stat. 1, 3, p. 224 (1838). By 1868 this statute had been superseded by a subsequent enactment. Ind. Laws, c. LXXXI, 2 (1859).
13. Iowa (Terr.)	Iowa (Terr.) Stat., 1st Legis., 1st Sess., 18, p. 145 (1838). By 1868, this statute had been superseded by a subsequent enactment. Iowa (Terr.) Rev. Stat., c. 49, 10, 13 (1843).
14. Kansas (Terr.)	Kan. (Terr.) Stat., c. 48, 9, 10, 39 (1855). By 1868, this statute had been superseded by a subsequent enactment. Kan. (Terr.) Laws, c. 28, 9, 10, 37 (1859).
15. Louisiana	La. Rev. Stat., Crimes and Offenses 24, p. 138 (1856).
16. Maine	Me. Rev. Stat., c. 160, 11, 12, 13, 14 (1840).
17. Maryland	Md. Laws, c. 179, 2, p. 315 (1868).
18. Massachusetts	Mass. Acts & Resolves, c. 27 (1845).
19. Michigan	Mich. Rev. Stat., c. 153, 32, 33, 34, p. 662 (1846). [410 U.S. 113, 176]
20. Minnesota	Minn. (Terr.) Rev. Stat., c. 100, 10, 11, p. 493 (1851).
21. Mississippi	Miss. Code, c. 64, 8, 9, p. 958 (1848).
22. Missouri	Mo. Rev. Stat., Art. II, 9, 10, 36, pp. 168, 172 (1835).
23. Montana (Terr.)	Mont. (Terr.) Laws, Criminal Practice Acts 41, p. 184 (1864).
24. Nevada (Terr.)	Nev. (Terr.) Laws, c. 28, 42, p. 63 (1861).
25. New Hampshire	N. H. Laws, c. 743, 1, p. 708 (1848).
26. New Jersey	N. J. Laws, p. 266 (1849).
27. New York	N. Y. Rev. Stat., pt. 4, c. 1, Tit. 2, 8, 9, pp. 12-13 (1828). By 1868, this statute had been superseded. N. Y. Laws, c. 260, 1-6, pp. 285-286 (1845); N. Y. Laws, c. 22, 1, p. 19 (1846).

Table 1 (*cont.*)

28. Ohio	Ohio Gen. Stat. 111 (1), 112 (2), p. 252 (1841).
29. Oregon	Ore. Gen. Laws, Crim. Code, c. 43, 509, p. 528 (1845-1864).
30. Pennsylvania	Pa. Laws No. 374, 87, 88, 89 (1860).
31. Texas	Tex. Gen. Stat. Dig., c. VII, Arts. 531-536, p. 524 (Oldham & White 1859).
32. Vermont	Vt. Acts No. 33, 1 (1846). By 1868, this statute had been amended. Vt. Acts No. 57, 1, 3 (1867).
33. Virginia	Va. Acts, Tit. II, c. 3, 9, p. 96 (1848).
34. Washington (Terr.)	Wash. (Terr.) Stats., c. II, 37, 38, p. 81 (1854).
35. West Virginia	See Va. Acts., Tit. II, c. 3, 9, p. 96 (1848); W. Va. Const., Art. XI, par. 8 (1863).
36. Wisconsin	Wis. Rev. Stat., c. 133, 10, 11 (1849). By 1868, this statute had been superseded. Wis. Rev. Stat., c. 164, 10, 11; c. 169, 58, 59 (1858).

And Roe's judicial fiat—that antagonism to such a large swath of the general population—an almost contemptuous view that all those opinions and conclusions are to be replaced by the Olympian wisdom of the majority opinion is just another telling reason Roe can never avoid all the angst it creates. For Roe, aside from everything else that has been laid out, proceeds in contravention to so much that cannot be denied. In science, its interpretation and conclusions border on the infantile; in philosophy and theology—its conclusion recites the near universal suspicion and trouble with the practice, over two millennia—then sweeps these considerations aside as nuisance and the public and moral opinion of so many well-intentioned citizens whose views are not valued but instead heavily marginalized. In Roe we see all the earmarks of a bad, almost incoherent, legal decision that does little to resolve the problem, soothe the citizenry or avoid chaotic responses. In fact, that is about the only truly effective thing that Roe does; it stirs the pot of animosity without pause. It has not, as Antonin Scalia opined in *Planned Parenthood v. Casey*,[57] produced the vaunted "Pax Roena."[58]

Roe v. Wade *and the natural law: Potentiality, actuality, personhood and self-preservation*

Critics of the Roe decision often demonize its path and reasoning. For those wholly convinced on the merits of a pro-life position, and for those equally at home in a natural law jurisprudence, it is easy to reach that conclusion long in advance of a close reading. Part of this text's purpose is to manifest how natural law jurisprudence, despite its steady and gradual fall from interpretative prominence, and the erroneous claim it left the intellectual arena long ago, seems to course its way through court decisions even until the present. While it is difficult to fathom how Roe's conclusion could ever be consistent with natural law principles, it is equally cumbersome, if not impossible, to overlook the language of the natural law throughout the majority opinion. When Justice Rehnquist dissented, he did so with an intellectual respect, although deeply troubled by the court's willingness to invent new and unfounded legal rationales in the realm of privacy, fundamental rights, unenumerated protections and disregard for states' resolution of this dilemma. Part of that respect might emanate from, though never fully provable, the majority opinion's willingness to argue in the language of natural law concepts or principles. Why else would Justice Blackmun repeatedly reference the idea of life in both potential and actual terms? What other explanation can there be for authoritative philosophical and theological journey traced from the early Greeks and Romans? What other purpose would multiple references to the Angelic Doctor of Roman Catholicism be? Justice Blackmun emphatically divides up the interests of mother and the "other life" at stake instead of vanquishing the fetus at all costs and under every circumstance. The majority opinion unreservedly announces,

> The pregnant woman cannot be isolated in her privacy. She carries an embryo, and later, a fetus, if one accepts the medical definitions of the developing young in the human uterus. [...] Texas urges that, apart from the Fourteenth Amendment, life begins at conception and is present throughout pregnancy, and that therefore, the State has a compelling interest in protecting that life from conception and after conception. We need not resolve the difficult question of when life begins.[59]

Here, Justice Blackmun lays out the fundamental natural conundrum and moral challenge—admitting to life at dual levels—and then at the same time, while metaphysically framing the abortion issue in terms of human life, runs from the challenge of making any firm decision. The court admits to its lack of competence yet feels competent enough to avoid finding truth on this matter. Strangely, Blackmun remarks, "When those trained in the disciplines of medicine, philosophy and theology are unable to arrive at any consensus, the judiciary, at this point in the development of man's knowledge, is not in a position to speculate as to the answer."[60]

The court, however, is inconsistently comfortable reaching the very opposite conclusion. Thus, on the one hand, it rattles its readers with musings about potentiality in the human life; it erects a legal rationale based on two millennia of abortion findings—the bulk of which has been unfriendly to the practice—and then simultaneously, despite its confessed ignorance of life's continuum, announce a practice that assures destruction of the human person. In many respects, Roe is a case straddling the classical view of human life with a more sterile, mechanical and self-interested world based on individual claims of harm or injury. There is no effort beyond raising proper questions, queries central to natural law reasoning, such as: when does life begin; what is human life; what makes us human; is potential life in need of protection or given the Aristotelian–Thomistic dogma of potentiality–actuality, how can this court simply refuse to go beyond the mere raising of questions. Why bother laboring on about "quickening" or "mediate animation" or the state's "compelling interest" to protect these dual beings if the court's mind is set on some legal theory that poses the troublesome thicket then hides behind a privacy veil? The majority opinion could not be clearer when they comment: "The Constitution does not explicitly mention any right to privacy."[61]

As each line of Roe is analyzed, the reader is left in utter confusion, not about the most fundamental questions human life poses but why the court seems to disregard its own profound musings about what it confronts. Roe, despite contrary opinion and modern media spin and manipulation, is not about abortion on demand. And, it is not about the eradication of fetal life from the equation. Roe is poignantly clear about this when it states,

> On the basis of elements such as these, appellant and some amici argue that the woman's right is absolute and she is entitled to terminate her pregnancy at whatever time, in whatever way, and for whatever reason she alone chooses. With this we do not agree.[62]

In this context we discover a view, even in Roe, on the potentiality and actuality of the human person and with corresponding rights and obligations that measure and rule the abortion practice. Nothing is more central to natural law reasoning than life itself—its preservation and flourishing, its maintenance and sustenance and its assurance that each human being can achieve the good or goods intended for it. Self-preservation is fully natural in both a biological and a theological sense and the Roe court explicitly mentions the distinction. Why else would Roe confirm the right of any state to regulate the abortion practice past points of viability? Abortion on demand—the current clamor from abortion advocates—sweeps aside these natural restrictions and singularizes the right in the woman's right to choose. Roe never reaches a conclusion even close to that errant judgment. The Roe decision holds:

> We repeat, however, that the State does have an important and legitimate interest in preserving and protecting the health of the pregnant

woman, whether she is be a resident of the State or a nonresident who seeks medical consultation and treatment there, and that it has still *another* important and legitimate interest in protecting the potentiality of human life. These interests are separate and distinct. Each grows in substantiality as the woman approaches term and, at a point during pregnancy, each becomes "compelling."[63]

Found within its own summary, the Roe court reemphasizes this dual life reality, which today has been blotted out of the conversation. The court declares, "For the stage subsequent to viability, the State in promoting its interest in the potentiality of human life, may if it chooses, regulate, and even proscribe abortion except where it is necessary, in appropriate medical judgment, for the preservation of the life or health of the mother."[64]

For example, the court understands the existence of life, in need of regulation and protection, at some *compelling point*,[65] and then gives its imprimatur in any state's decision to protect that life. The majority states, "State regulation of fetal life after viability thus has logical and biological considerations. If the state is interested in protecting fetal life after viability it may go so far as to proscribe abortion during that period, except when it is necessary to preserve the life or health of the mother."[66]

Where the Texas statute falters, according to Roe, is not that it seeks to regulate or forbid abortion at some point along the way—even though it recognizes the "life-saving" exception—it is that it attempts to do it from the point of conception onward. This Roe concludes "sweeps too broadly."[67]

Hence, while acknowledging the existence of human life at some stage in the process, it attempts to objectify that stage of humanity or personhood by adopting a trimester system with varying degrees of permissibility. Aside from this faulty mechanical construct of measurement, and its horrid almost immature view of fetal and human development, the court felt it not only obliged to deliver said rule but to act like it had the competence to issue it. Viability is even more concerning because it strikes at the very heart of the natural law, that tenet that rightfully dwells on maintenance and self-preservation as each being attempts to reach its fullest and richest potential. Abortion and viability rests side by side as justification or rationale, for a viable human person, a living being, cannot be killed or murdered. So fundamental is this conclusion in the natural law that every being seeks the good proper to its end and proper operation. A viable, living infant, in the womb or delivered, possesses not only the right to live but also rights that inure to the benefit of that person by operation of law and our constitutional Republic. The Roe court is well aware of this argument when it deals with "personhood" and extraordinary implications of granting that status to any fetus at any point on its artificial continuum. The court understands the dynamic when it observes,

> The appellee and certain amici argue that the fetus is a "person" within the language and meaning of the 14th Amendment. In support of this, they outline at length and in detail the well-known facts of fetal development. If this suggestion of personhood is established, the appellant's (ROE) case, of course collapses, for the fetus' right to life would then be specifically guaranteed by the Amendment.[68]

In its findings, Roe never explicitly concludes when personhood emerges, except to make the argument that courts have generally not granted identity status to a fetus. The court further remarks that personhood, in the language of the Constitution itself, refers to a person as being "born or naturalized" in the United States. Here, Roe displays its almost ancient understanding of fetal and human development, having no real sense or understanding of how viability standards in the world of premature birth and delivery have destroyed their notion of viability. Today's viability is vastly different than experienced or understood 50 years ago. Yet this court bandies about the language of personhood and viable life while at the same time exhorts the right regulatory schema to protect it. Indeed, if in fact, the "personhood" argument takes hold, the entire Roe substructure implodes on its massive illogic. Roe falters in other ways on the question of viability and personhood because it admits that it cannot discern the precise period for its illumination, so to speak. However, it is willing to grant that there is a range of views on the topic, and that only one will eventually be tolerable under its ruling. In a most general sense, viability, Roe announces, is when a fetus "is, potentially able to live outside the mother's womb, albeit with artificial aid."[69]

In contemporary medical practice, it is not uncommon for a fetus to be delivered at a period or month once undreamt of and then advancing successfully to full adulthood. While Roe promotes 28 weeks as a measure for viability, contemporary medicine would beg to differ. And while reasonable people may disagree on the day of conception being the starting point for viability, even though all would agree on that life's potentiality, the point of viability can certainly be well in advance of 28 weeks. The court does reference these various schools often influenced by deeply held religious beliefs such as Judaism and Roman Catholicism.[70]

In its final analysis of viability and personhood, Roe decides that this recognition cannot be granted to the "unborn" or before "live birth."[71] This conclusion finds exceptions of all sorts in the law, Roe points out, from the appointment of a guardian ad litem to protection of the interests of a developing fetus to the propriety of a wrongful death claim based on medical malpractice. From a similar vantagepoint, if a life is capable of existing under the court's own definition of viability—either born with or without assistance, the premature infant, aided by mechanical methods—as all preemies are, does this not qualify for personhood?

There is a sort of illogic in Roe that cannot be fully explained, and this has often been cited as one of many reasons for why Roe never settled anything, especially complicated ideas like personhood. So, on the one hand, Roe concludes at some stage in some continuum of human development there is viability while on the other, that which is viable is human in both a potential and actual sense. As a result of this very basic conclusion, that being has every right to protection and preservation as a competing life with the woman entrusted with that fetus. Finally, it is not arbitrary for any state to protect that life even to the point of proscribing abortion, as long as the life of the mother is not at stake, particularly in the last of the trimester terms. For at this stage, development is closest to birth itself and the regulatory oversight can be its most intense. Justice Rehnquist's dissent observes that he does not even know if the plaintiff in this case has reached that third part of the trimester system and only seems to know that the appellant was a "pregnant woman."[72]

As in so many other facets of the case, the court's own justices cannot even really place the appellant within its invented trimester timeline. This lack of awareness, coupled with an inventive spirit about unenumerated rights, an expansion of a privacy doctrine that lacks any explicit basis constitutionally as well as a disregard of a heavy majority of American jurisdictions, citizens, religious denominations and philosophical and theological traditions place Roe in a perpetual state of legal upheaval. The majority opinion borders on inconsistencies almost impossible to fully delineate, but a few major ones include an historical account of more than 2,000 years that largely rejects abortion; a statutory history and collective view of some level of criminalization; an acknowledgment of points of viability and the right of state to regulate; a lack of scientific neonatal science; a rejection of right of that being that reaches viability to self-preserve under natural law principles, all of which are squashed by a "right" to privacy that framers never envisioned or likely would ever anticipate. Roe remains in turbulent seas for these and many other reasons.

Doe v. Bolton, 410 U.S. 179 (1973)

From Roe forward a series of cases will largely challenge or seek to test the court's majority ruling. That Roe did not make peace is not arguable and since its pronouncement the country has yet to reconcile a place where various and differing viewpoints can be comfortably exercised. Hence, the bulk of case law in this genealogy will challenge abortion on the regulatory frontier and this new legal reality began almost instantaneously. In *Doe v. Bolton*,[73] an almost companion case announced within days of Roe harkens for less procedural regulation than the Georgia law dictates. A close reading of Doe indicates its very different flavor, for now abortion, despite its infancy as a legal right and practice, comes across as so settled. When Georgia seeks to regulate abortion by an insistence on qualified and accredited facilities, as well as a review by an abortion committee at said facility, the climate of oversight appears to trouble the court. The Act stated in part,

CHAPTER 26-12. ABORTION.

26–1201. Criminal Abortion. Except as otherwise provided in section 26–1202, a person commits criminal abortion when he administers any medicine, drug or other substance whatever to any woman or when he uses any instrument or other means whatever upon any woman with intent to produce a miscarriage or abortion.

26–1202. Exception. (a) Section 26–1201 shall not apply to an abortion performed by a physician duly licensed to practice medicine and surgery pursuant to Chapter 84–9 or 84-12 of the Code of Georgia of 1933, as amended, based upon his best clinical judgment that an abortion is necessary because:

(1) A continuation of the pregnancy would endanger the life of the pregnant woman or would seriously and permanently injure her health; or
(2) The fetus would very likely be born with a grave, permanent, and irremediable mental or physical defect; or
(3) The pregnancy resulted from forcible or statutory rape.
    (b) No abortion is authorized or shall be performed under this section unless each of the following conditions is met:
(1) The pregnant woman requesting the abortion certifies in writing under oath and subject to the penalties of false swearing to the physician who proposes to perform the abortion that she is a bona fide legal resident of the State of Georgia.
(2) The physician certifies that he believes the woman is a bona fide resident of this State and that he has no information which should lead him to believe otherwise.
(3) Such physician's judgment is reduced to writing and concurred in by at least two other physicians duly licensed to practice medicine

and surgery pursuant to Chapter 84–9 of the Code of Georgia of 1933, as amended, who certify in writing that, based upon their separate personal medical examinations of the pregnant woman, the abortion is, in their judgment, necessary because of one or more of the reasons enumerated above.

(4) Such abortion is performed in a hospital licensed by the State Board of Health and accredited by the Joint Commission on Accreditation of Hospitals.

(5) The performance of the abortion has been approved in advance by a committee of the medical staff of the hospital in which the operation is to be performed. This committee must be one established and maintained in accordance with the standards promulgated by the Joint Commission on the Accreditation of Hospitals, and its approval must be by a majority vote of a membership of not less than three members of the hospital's staff; the physician proposing to perform the operation may not be counted as a member of the committee for this purpose.[74]

Even though it reaffirms that the "right" to an abortion is not absolute,[75] the committee structure that reviewed the request undercut the free exercise of that right rooted in privacy and Fourteenth Amendment principles announced in Roe. These requirements, the court argued, "chilled and deterred" exercise of that right.[76]

As to viability and potentiality, Doe is a decision that appears to have quickly forgotten Roe's various cautions about the trimester and the right of the state to regulate for potential life as those later stages emerge. In reaffirming the "privacy right," Doe's opinion seems to liberalize the potentiality argument, that is, making potentiality less of a reason for state interference. In a concurring opinion, Justice Douglas takes aim at the potentiality–actuality argument and indicates his reticence to wade into this sort of metaphysical argument.

To say that life is present at conception is to give recognition to the potential, rather than the actual. The unfertilized egg has life, and if fertilized, it takes on human proportions. But the law deals in reality, not obscurity—the known, rather than the unknown. When sperm meets egg, life may eventually form but quite often does not. The law does not deal in speculation.[77]

Another unfortunate by-product of the Roe lineage is the type of illogic so clearly evident in this musing by Justice Douglas. Life, for him, is speculation rather than reality, a conclusion that any observer of nature and natural order would find puzzling. At no place in the Roe doctrine are protections extended to sperm or an egg, for these two biological realities lack human form in and of themselves. It is a given that these two processes are equally independent and potentially codependent on one another. In the former instance, abortion legalities and subtleties are completely irrelevant. In the latter category, where unification occurs, and nature and the natural order and its laws conclude, forms the basis for a human being. No speculation exists in this latter category. Now whether that unification has achieved sufficiency in the human form and development may be an arguable question, but Justice Douglas displays an errant view of this fundamental biological process.

It is exquisitely clear that Justice Douglas tends to disfavor the presumption of life or any humanity in the developmental fetus. Gone from Doe is any real mention or attention to the trimester scheme. In its place, the question of life and the preservation of that life has been replaced by an amorphous pondering on the nature of privacy, especially when the very Act he objects to calls for a physician–patient review, resting upon the "best clinical judgment" upheld by this very court.[78] Seeing the legal problem through another prism is something quite evident in the concurring opinion of Justice Douglas who often argues like a social commentator rather than jurist. For Douglas and others, abortion is strictly a personal matter like "marriage, divorce, procreation, contraception and the education and upbringing of children."[79] At other places, he poses the recurring argument of "freedom of choice" as if this standard was a legal arbiter. Such relative measures can never provide the moral anchor needed in complex, ethical dilemmas, and history has shown this sort of legal reasoning generally falters. For both Roe and Doe adopt all types of almost pompous assumptions about potential child-bearers, such as a poor woman, given the fact that they are poor, may make abortion more preferable in their circumstance, or that racism causes impoverished communities to depend upon the practice. Doe improperly assumes that in order to properly care for offspring—a bona fide natural law principle espoused in nearly all natural law circles—that abortion will assist in achieving that end by caring and elevating our affection for our offspring. The Doe court cannot even hide its elitism by citing let alone granting any credence to the appellant's argument that to restrict abortion access, under every regulatory measure posed by the State of Georgia may "be physically and emotionally damaging to Doe to bring a child into her poor, 'fatherless' family."[80] In a twisted way, the care of offspring and familial argument, a natural law tenet, gets contorted to provide a rationale for the right to an abortion that is free and unrestricted from unnecessary regulation. The factual background of the appellant portrays the correlation between abortion and the hard-luck story.

> Her husband had recently abandoned her and she was forced to live with her indigent parents and their eight children. [...] She had been a mental patient at the State Hospital. She had been advised that an

abortion could be performed on her with less danger to her health than if she gave birth to the child she was carrying. She would be unable to care for or support the new child.[81]

In Doe, and other abortion cases, the law submits to these story lines—as if there never will be any other alternatives to the practice, nor can these elite jurists ever anticipate that someone might adopt—or some charity would assist, or that a church down the road might support her in this time of need. Doe advocates for abortion rights not because there is some explicit right at any page corner of our founding documents but because it wants these hard luck stories to be remedied. In this way, the legal rationale is no better than a soap opera, and clearly attentiveness to natural law principles like self-preservation and care of offspring either disregarded or touted for all the wrong reasons.

Doe also more emphatically deals with those conditions that justify abortion in the latter phases of fetal development despite the Roe trimester system. In that last phase, the "life of the mother" could always justify a lawful abortion but creeping into this analysis is the term "health of the mother" that appears to have few boundaries. The court cites the context in the most liberal terms, "in light of all factors—physical, emotional, psychological, and the woman's age—{all} relevant to the wellbeing of the patient. All these factors may relate to health."[82]

In his dissenting opinion, Justice Byron White cuts right to this expansion or elastic interpretation of the "life of the mother" standard, which now seems nothing more than a ruse upon a close reading of Doe. For Justice White, regardless of when and for what reason, the language of the majority opinion allows literally any rationale for the abortion right, especially since a physician oversees and evaluates the basis for that exercise.

At the heart of the controversy in these cases are those recurring pregnancies that pose no danger whatsoever to the life or health of the mother but are, nevertheless, unwanted for any one or more of a variety of reasons—convenience, family planning, economics, dislike of children, the embarrassment of illegitimacy, and so on. The common claim before us is that, for any one of such reasons, or for no reason at all, and without asserting or claiming any threat to life or health, any woman is entitled to an abortion at her request if she is able to find a medical advisor willing to undertake the procedure.[83]

Hence, the value of life, under this critique, loses its favor under a system that listens to any claim based on a myriad of rationales. What is clear, Justice White argues, is that potential life of the fetus takes secondary status to the "convenience, whim, or caprice of the putative mother."[84]

For advocates of the Doe result, it is difficult to reconcile its fullest influence with a Roe decision that captures all the limelight. In a way, Doe is the silent case that slips under the wall and opens every point of entry. And for many jurists, including Justice Byron White, the court's decision is almost magical in light of law and jurisprudence. Doe, Justice White muses, "simply fashions and announces a new constitutional test for pregnant mothers and, with scarcely any reason or authority for its action, invests that right with sufficient substance to override most existing state abortion statutes."[85] White additionally concludes that Doe "constitutionally disentitled" 50 states that may have had rules on the subject matter and that sort of judicial fiat "an improvident and extravagant exercise."[86]

For natural law jurisprudence, the majority simply avoids in matters of self-preservation and viability and then imposes a perverse hint that the poor need abortion because the poor are incapable of caring for their offspring. The dissent correctly chides the majority that potential life is properly regulated under the Roe doctrine.

Thornburgh v. American College of Obstetricians and Gynecologists, 476 U.S. 747 (1986)

While there were relatively minor challenges to the Supreme Court on the abortion issue, none of those require exceptional consideration here. Many of the modifications dealt with public funding,[87] the invalidation of various procedural requirements[88] and question of consent from parent or spouse.[89] In the decade after Roe's issuance, the legal approach had been cautious to say the least. While it is no mystery that Roe caused and continues to cause great upheaval in the population—a condition quite apparent in the recent objections to the nomination of Supreme Court candidate Brett Kavanaugh—whole scale challenge to Roe's validity is yet to be witnessed. While proponents may have wished that end, the legal landscape and the general firmness of the court's opinion would make the action likely unsuccessful.

Because of this, the challengers to the validity of abortion under the Roe doctrine would chip away at accessibility, procedural requirements, alternatives to abortion and medical education relating to the practice.

In 1986, the Pennsylvania legislature passed the Abortion Control Act.[90] The Act was multidimensional covering some uncharted territory. First, the Act sought to provide educational information on the medical implications, the risks and alternatives to the abortion decision. Second, the Act encouraged outside providers to inform the patient that entities and organizations would support a decision not to abort and provide a path to delivery. In addition, the Act called upon the attending physician to verify that the abortion was not being carried out in a viability setting and to report said findings in an official document. If determined viable, the attending physician must take added steps to protect that fetus by choosing medical procedures, including the presence of a second doctor, that assure that viability continues. Each and every statutory construction was held to be inconsistent with Roe and nothing more than "poorly disguised elements of discouragement for the abortion decision."[91] All of these efforts, the court declared, "chills the performance of a late abortion."[92]

In general, the majority opinion in Thornburgh, authored by Roe's Justice Blackmun, continues to defensively protect the abortion practice not in light of its consistency with Roe but with new and improved ways of denying the very language that Roe dictates about viability and life itself. Justice Blackmun reduces these regulatory efforts as an effort to "intimidate women into continuing pregnancies."[93] If Roe's premise rests on the "pro-choice" doctrine, the court's rationale seems to be a curious way of discerning a learned choice since suggestions of alternatives to abortion are unconstitutional.

As for the regulation regarding "informed consent," the Court, despite the natural intrusiveness and complexity of abortion practice, would rather its participants not understand the medical, emotional and physical dynamics of the abortion procedure. In literally every form of medical procedure, from an ingrown toenail to a heart transplant, the doctrine of "informed consent" applies. Yet any effort to apply in the abortion setting is better described as a sort of bullying and the court appears to prefer an unenlightened and completely undiscerning patient who simply trusts others in this affair. Anything else posed to the patient might rattle their decision making. Woe to those who lay out the possible medical complications, the state of fetal development and the potential for alternatives to abortion such as adoption or support from groups that will assist in carrying to term. All of these intrusions, according to the court, impede the abortion. In its place, the court is calling for a patient choosing in a vacuum of ignorance. The court, citing a previous precedent,[94] concludes that the informed consent requirement has one express purpose, that is to "persuade her to withhold it all together."[95] Knowing about these things, the court strains to deduce, is the "antithesis of informed consent."[96]

Not to outdo itself, the court also concludes that any journey through the various intervals of fetal development equally gets in the way of an informed and free decision because, according to Thornburgh, it is always better to know nothing than to know something. It is always better to remain in a world where potential human life merely remains a mass of un-agglutinated cells—always better to never differentiate the timing and development at stages. This type of information, the court wistfully concludes, will only "increase a patient's anxiety."[97]

Viability and self-preservation

If Thornburgh touches historic natural law tenets, the coverage will be about viability and the self-preservation of life. This line of reasoning touches most abortion cases especially since the Roe court identified two lives at stake depending upon trimester and human development principles. In Thornburgh, the question of viability is not merely the stuff of guesses but a scientific evaluation by both the attending physician performing the abortion and a second doctor whose sole task was to protect the life of any baby born viable during the abortion process. Section 3210(b) reads,

> Every person who performs or induces an abortion after an unborn child has been determined to be viable shall exercise that degree of professional skill, care and diligence which such person would be required to exercise in order to preserve the life and health of any unborn child intended to be born and not aborted and the abortion technique employed shall be that which would provide the best opportunity for the unborn child to be aborted alive unless, in the good faith judgment of the physician, that method or technique would present a significantly greater medical risk to the life or health of the pregnant woman than would another available method or technique and the physician reports the basis for his judgment. The potential psychological or emotional impact on the mother of the unborn child's survival shall not be deemed a medical risk to the mother. Any person who intentionally, knowingly or recklessly violates the provisions of this subsection commits a felony of the third degree.[98]

Section 3210(c) reads,

> Any person who intends to perform an abortion the method chosen for which, in his good faith judgment, does not preclude the possibility of the child surviving the abortion, shall arrange for the attendance, in the same room in which the abortion is to be completed, of a second physician. Immediately after the complete expulsion or extraction of the child, the second physician shall take control of the child and shall provide immediate medical care for the child, taking all reasonable steps necessary, in his judgment, to preserve the child's life and health. Any person who intentionally, knowingly or recklessly violates the provisions of this subsection commits a felony of the third degree.[99]

That second physician was also to make recommendations on how and in what manner the abortion was to be performed to assure the greatest chance of survival for the viable fetus. Thornburgh's majority opinion negates these requirements as calling for a "trade-off" to the detriment of maternal health as to fetal life.[100] The court here is not talking about the "life of the mother" but something else altogether, holding that to have such regulatory steps become a burden to the person seeking to exercise the right to an abortion. Under Roe, that right is neither absolute nor unconditional but instead must be measured against the backdrop of viability and personhood in the fetus. The court seems to disregard this dual compelling interest, a question of life and its self-preservation when it concludes that these restrictions "are here for chilling the performance of a late term abortion."[101] In holding that these sorts of determinations of viability and in later stage potential or even actual human life to be unconstitutional, the court seems to abandon the Roe measure of competing life interests in late stage or viable fetus settings. In fact, the court's concurring opinion by Justice Stevens runs past the viability argument as if it never had any relevance in the Roe conclusion. He remarks,

> Again, I recognize that a powerful theological argument can be made for that position, but I believe our jurisdiction is limited to the evaluation of secular state interests. [...] Nor is it an answer to argue that life, and that "there is no non-arbitrary line separating a fetus from a child, or indeed, an adult human being." For, unless the religious view that a fetus is a "person" is adopted [...] three is a fundamental and well-recognized difference between a fetus and a human being. [...] And if distinctions may be drawn between a fetus and a human being in terms of the state interest in their protection—even though the fetus represents one of "those who will be citizens"—it seems to me quite odd to argue that distinctions may not also be drawn between the state interest in protecting the freshly fertilized egg and the state interest in protected the 9-month gestated, fully sentient fetus on the eve of birth.[102]

This commentary is strangely at odds with the Roe trimester system—for here the Pennsylvania legislature seeks to devise a means or a method of measuring viability—when in question, not at the "fertilized, fresh egg stage" but at a point of true viability, and the court flattens the attempt as unconstitutional. Chief Justice Burger, an original supporter of *Roe v. Wade*, is taken aback by this aggressive disregard for the viability principles enunciated in Roe. He declared, "In short, every member of the Roe Court rejected the idea of abortion on demand. The Court's opinion today, however, plainly undermines that important principle and, I regretfully conclude that some of the concerns of the dissenting Justices in Roe, as well as the concerns I expressed in my separate opinion, have now been realized."[103]

Justice Burger reiterates with emphatic clarity the Roe premise that a viable fetal life has a compelling place in the analysis of abortion rights and with its pronouncement "abandons that standard and renders the solemnly stated concerns of the 1973 Roe opinion for the interests of the state's mere shallow rhetoric."[104]

This seeming ignorance of the competing interests at viability was targeted by Justice Byron White who passionately argued that the majority opinion is "not even consistent with its decision in Roe v. Wade."[105] In so holding in this manner, White concludes, any regulation that inhibits abortion—at any phase or term of viability—would be naturally unconstitutional, adding further that no court has ever "disavowed that concession"[106] or understanding of the compelling interest of a viable fetus. Justice White could not be clearer on this score: "The Court's ruling today that any tradeoff between the woman's health and fetal survival is impermissible is not only inconsistent with Roe's recognition of a compelling state interest in viable fetal life, it directly contradicts one of the essential holdings of Roe—that is, that the State may forbid all post-viability except when necessary to protect the life or health of the pregnant woman."[107]

With the court's finding that any effort to detect or measure viability violative of the Constitution and a protocol to protect a scientifically determined, viable fetus labeled legally suspect, Roe's lineage has jumped off its own DNA. Roe's legacy, according to Justice White, in opinions as issued today, manifests an extraordinary "insecurity."[108] The descendants of Roe now appear, in less than two decades, unrecognizable, a reality now all that surprising for a case based on invented rights, indescript privacy protection rooted and a general disregard of the explicit language of the Roe ruling. Then again, Justice White, like so many other critics of *Roe v. Wade*, could never really ever achieve legal legitimacy because its very foundation is built on "something out of nothing."[109]

Care of offspring

Another tenet of natural law reasoning is closely connected with the idea of self-preservation and viability, namely the natural instinct for either parent to care for their offspring. Human history as well as the natural order make this tendency plain. For the most part, and in most cases, actual as well as prospective parents and child-bearers seek to protect offspring from harm or injury. Part of the reason abortion is such a traumatic event is its intrusion on our natural operations, an interference with the natural cycle of childbirth and development. Whether pro-life or pro-choice, both sides of the equation can agree on the invasive nature of the procedure and why most advocates, either way, do not see the actual experience as a positive one. It may be necessary for a variety of reasons rationalized by the party seeking it, although it is unlikely anyone willingly desires the experience.

What is adequately clear is that regulatory efforts on abortion often directly deal with the care of the offspring principle. For example, the idea of consent for a minor's abortion from the parents or other adult in supervision gives respect to a parent's right to know and approve for a minor child. Or the idea that educating a mother carrying a fetus may or may not know the developmental stages that involve the abortion process. Educating parents, both actual and prospective, about the medical risks, the emotional studies and the stages of fetal development are all examples of the care of offspring standard.

In Thornburgh, the Commonwealth of Pennsylvania tackled a bevy of offspring questions but more particularly that the patient become an "informed consent" guarantor by learning about the gestational life cycle of the infant carried. In addition, the patient had to be educated on the various medical risks to both self and the baby carried before any abortion could occur. Next, the abortion candidate had to be advised that there were alternatives to abortion, from support groups when carrying to full term, to adoption, and the availability of help with prenatal care.[110] All of these factors played a central role in determining the constitutionality of these restrictions in light of Roe. For the majority in Thornburgh, these elements could be lumped together as "undue burdens" on a specified right. Protecting that life, according to the majority opinion, is nothing more than an imposition of a "value preference"[111] rather than a good faith effort to care for actual or potential offspring.

Under natural law principles, the care of offspring is fundamental to human operations. And that care extends to the mother as well whereby enlightened information about fetal development and gestational stages, and identifiable medical risks in the process, has been declared unconstitutional under the ruling. Chief Justice Burger expresses total perplexity when he deduces,

> Yet today the Court astonishingly goes so far as to say that the State may not even required that the woman contemplating an abortion be provided with medical information concerning the risks inherent in the medical procedure she is about to undergo. [...] Can anyone doubt that doctors routinely give similar information concerning risks in countless procedures having far less impact on life and health, both physical and emotional than an abortion, and risk a malpractice lawsuit if they fail to do so?[112]

Thornburgh also remands back to the lower court further consideration of the minor consent requirement and avoids its conclusion on what Burger sees as an easy call. But as courts reject the requirement that parents know their children are about to undergo the abortion regimen, the likely easiest of all regulations that should be upheld, the Thornburgh decision, cannot reach a consensus on this requirement. It is a sign, Justice Burger opines, of how far "the distance traveled since Roe."[113]

Webster v. Reproductive Health Systems, 492 U.S. 490 (1989)

As the Roe lineage continues its tortured evolution, against the backdrop of flawed science and legal analysis, the chaos caused by the decision manifests quite keenly in Webster. While the Thornburgh decision struck down provisions that sought to regulate the abortion process, Webster is really the first decision where every justice seems to be having second thoughts about Roe or at least intense pleas for adherence to the Roe ruling. For what Roe says and what the world experienced were two distinct universes. Webster seems to insist that advocates and cases try to remember the language of Roe, and as such, much of the case deals with matters of viability, personhood and the right of the state to protect fetal life if at a suitable gestational age.

From its very foundation, Missouri legislators posited in the Preamble of the restrictive legislation that "each human life begins at conception" and that "unborn children have protectable interests in life, health and well-being."[114] The Act declared,

> Before a physician performs an abortion on a woman he has reason to believe is carrying an unborn child of twenty or more weeks gestational age, the physician shall first determine if the unborn child is viable by using and exercising that degree of care, skill, and proficiency commonly exercised by the ordinarily skillful, careful, and prudent physician engaged in similar practice under the same or similar conditions. In making this determination of viability, the physician shall perform or cause to be performed such medical examinations and tests as are necessary to make a finding of the gestational age, weight, and lung maturity of the unborn child and shall enter such findings and determination of viability in the medical record of the mother.[115]

Since the Preamble merely affirms the state's overall approach to the value of life, the court never formally ruled on its language nor its application. However, it made plain Missouri has every right to so declare since its pronouncement would not impact abortion availability or access.

Other matters, bearing on viability, namely the requirement of viability determinations before actual abortions and whether or not state funding for abortions at state hospitals can be restricted, become central to the majority opinion's analysis. While there are a plethora of opinion subtleties and nuances, it is clear that even Roe's original author, Justice Blackmun, finds merit in part of the regulatory framework. In response to the viability check, Blackmun bristles at the court's general rejection of the trimester system and chides the majority for its "deceptive," "tortured" and "feigned restraint."[116] Simultaneously, Blackmun reaffirms a central tenet of Roe regarding the power of the state to measure abortion rights in light of a competing life interest, namely the fetus. Blackmun concludes,

> No one contests that, under the Roe framework, the State, in order to promote its interest in potential human life, may regulate and even proscribe nontherapeutic abortions once the fetus becomes viable.[117] If, as the plurality appears to hold, the testing provision simply requires a physician to use appropriate and medically sound tests to determine whether the fetus is actually viable when the estimated gestational age is greater than 20 weeks (and therefore within what the District Court found to be the margin of error for viability,[118] then I see little or no conflict with Roe. Nothing in Roe, or any of its progeny, holds that a State may not effectuate its compelling interest in the potential life of a viable fetus by seeking to ensure that no viable fetus is mistakenly aborted because of the inherent lack of precision in estimates of gestational age. A requirement that a physician make a finding of viability, one way or the other, for every fetus that falls within the range of possible viability does no more than preserve the State's recognized authority.[119]

Viability, personhood and self-preservation

As natural law analysis dictates, a being's natural penchant for its preservation and flourishing, that is seeking its own good as well as the greater and greatest goods achievable, generally drives human operations. To preserve oneself is to assure the maintenance and sustenance of the human person. The Webster decision expends a significant amount of its time addressing viability and self-preservation and—employing the Roe doctrine affirms emphatically the right of the state to regulate abortion in light of a competing and compelling life— at a point in which viability is demonstrable. The Missouri law that called for a viability analysis of each fetus met with qualified acceptance and resistance in the Webster decision. As Roe edifies, viability is not a slide rule or mathematical determination but dependent on a host of developmental variables. The Act chose the 20-week measure as that compelling point of viability but given this period not being part of the last period in the trimester, but instead the second phase, arguments on constitutionality of the restriction surrounded the "mandatory" nature of the testing. This, according to abortion rights advocates, would be contrary to the power of the state in the second part of the trimester calendar and better reserved for the third phase. In essence, there is a "presumption of viability" in the 20-week period. That line between viability and nonviability cannot be resolved in a trimester system, and because of this, the majority rules the trimester system ineffectual in that determination. The majority rules,

> The Roe framework is hardly consistent with the notion of a Constitution like ours that is cast in general terms and usually speaks in general principles. The framework's key elements—trimesters and viability—are not found in the Constitution's text, and since the bounds of the inquiry are essentially indeterminate, the result has a been a web of legal rules that have become increasingly intricate, resembling a code of regulations, rather than a body of constitutional doctrine. There is also no reason why the State's compelling interest in protecting potential human life should not extend throughout the pregnancy, rather coming into existence only at the point of viability. Thus the Roe trimester framework should be abandoned.[120]

In its place, the court finds a reasoned alternative posed in the Act whereby a trained physician, a duly trained and reasonably skilled physician, performs "medical examinations and tests as are necessary to make a finding of the gestational age, weight and lung maturity of the unborn child and shall enter such findings and determination of viability into the medical record of the mother."[121] In upholding the viability determination, the court simply adheres to the Roe mandate that allows a state to regulate abortion after a finding of viability and "even proscribe"[122] abortion, as long as the life of the mother exception remains.[123]

In Webster, instead of a trimester calendar, the decision of viability is best left to the attending physician whose "degree of care, skill and proficiency"[124] make for a more suitable alternative than Roe's imprecise timeline. Justice Sandra Day O'Connor confirms in her concurring opinion when she writes that no "decision of this Court has held that the State may not directly promote in potential life when viability is possible."[125] Given the critical importance of viability in most abortion cases, Missouri's attempts to provide guidelines or erect some method to measure or get close to measuring the compelling point of viability, the majority opinion upholds the viability testing regimen. This is not done as a universal proposition but as a test in the latter stages of the developmental cycle, although not even this technique for measuring viability after Webster abandons the Roe trimester. In its place, the Webster court relies on the judgment and skill of the attending physician who knows viability when he or she encounters it; it is, as Justice O'Connor notes, "that requiring the performance of examinations and tests" consistent with the viability principles long enunciated by precedent and such requirements do "not impose an undue burden."[126]

Justice Scalia emphatically affirms the right of any state to determine viability and indicates that has been our proper jurisprudence since Roe. He comments,

> No one contests, that under the Roe framework, the State, in order to promote its interest in potential human life, may regulate and even proscribe nontherapeutic abortions once the fetus become viable. [...] Nothing in Roe, or any of its progeny, holds that a State may not effectuate its compelling interest in the potential life of a viable fetus by seeking to ensure that no viable fetus is mistakenly aborted because of the inherent lack of precision in estimates of gestational age.[127]

Hence, a physician's review of any close call on a timeline, something quite impossible under the nebulous trimester system, provides an accurate and scientific system for the measurement. Scalia goes farther in his critique of the overall finding in Webster, essentially calling upon the court to stop the "masquerades"[128] of defective trimesters with a more urgent plea for a more textual vision of the Constitution, to revisit the alleged "right to privacy" and the tendency of the contemporary court to utilize "judge-made methods for evaluating and measuring the strength and scope of constitutional right."[129]

There is little doubt that viability and personhood, as well as the corresponding natural right to self-preservation, weigh on the minds of nearly every participant in the Webster decision. Indeed, even Justice Blackmun, curiously although not surprisingly relies upon St. Thomas Aquinas to buttress all arguments against "life begins at conception." For, as noted earlier, Thomas, as Aristotle, discerns full personhood by animation—a formed fetus—generally a state after 40–80 days.[130] In that time frame, the unformed, unanimated fetus does not achieve full human qualities and hence the argument by Thomas is that the state may not properly charge homicide. However, this caution on using the criminal justice system is by no means an approval of the practice for abortion at all stages is an egregious act in contravention to the natural order and the natural law and punishable as a "mortal sin" and eternal damnation.[131]

Blackmun, like so many others thinking they are capable of discerning the natural law theory of St. Thomas, leaves this bit of information out every time. In his misguided interpretation, Blackmun holds,

> There can be no interest in protecting the newly fertilized egg from physical pain or mental anguish, because the capacity for such suffering

does not yet exist; respecting a developed fetus, however that interest in valid. If fact, if one prescinds the theological concept of ensoulment— or one accept St. Thomas Aquinas' view that ensoulment does not occur for at least 40 days—a State has no greater secular interest in protecting the potential life of an embryo that is still "seed" than in protecting the potential life of a sperm or an unfertilized ovum.[132]

One certain conclusion that can be derived from Webster is its continuing analysis of neonatal and fetal development. While judges proclaim their desire to stay out of those sorts of ruminations, some never hesitate giving their "scientific" conclusions.

Planned Parenthood of Southeastern Pennsylvania v. Casey, 505 U.S. 833 (1992)

Nearly two decades after Roe, the Supreme Court as well as a host of state and federal appeals courts still labor under the Roe conclusions and the legal landscape is anything but tranquil. In *Planned Parenthood v. Casey*, the majority author, Justice Sandra Day O'Connor commenced her opinion by stating, "Liberty finds no refuge in a jurisprudence of doubt. Yet 19 years after our holding that the Constitution protects a woman's right to terminate her pregnancy in its early states, that definition of liberty is still questioned."[133] For some legal commentators, Casey represents a shift to the liberty interest over the once dominant "right to privacy" arguments that built the Roe empire. How this occurs befuddles analysts but poor reasoning in legal decisions generally leads to even poorer rationales that seek to prop up a questionable case.[134]

There are a host of explanations for this unsettled state—some already mentioned, such as a lack of legal precision in the standards upon which the decision rests; the theological and philosophical divide on this troublesome question and as Justice Scalia so keenly points out when stating, "The Constitution says absolutely nothing about it, and the longstanding traditions of American society have permitted it be legally proscribed."[135] Critics of *Planned Parenthood v. Casey* are not in short supply and some of the critics have labeled the decision one of the worst in the history of American constitutional law. Professor Michael Paulsen sees little value in Casey and sternly criticizes its method.

> Casey creates an essentially unrestricted, substantive legal right of some human beings to kill-murder, really, since the power is plenary and requires no serious justification for its exercise-other human beings, at a rate of approximately a million and a half a year. On this view, Casey

affirms and embraces human genocide in the United States of a dimension exceeding, in the decade that has just past, that of the Rwandan genocide, the Nazi Holocaust, Stalin's purges, and Pol Pot's killing fields, combined.[136]

To be blunt, Roe has resolved very little in the realm of consensus and legal, moral and ethical resolution. The "emptiness of the reasoned judgment"[137] coupled with the naturally divisive nature of the subject matter and practice was not resolved by Roe but instead, "it did more than anything else nourish it, by elevating it to the national level where it infinitely more difficult to resolve. [...] Profound disagreement existed among our citizens over the issue."[138] Scalia harkens the Roe quest for settling the matter. Seeking out a "Peace of Westphalia" which he labels "nothing less than Orwellian."[139] Roe is nothing more than a "perpetuation of that disruption.[140]

Part of what makes Planned Parenthood so compelling, especially in terms of natural law theory, is that it is a raucous call, by some, especially Scalia, Thomas and White, to end the madness and overrule Roe. Aside from the radicality of the approach, there is growing awareness that Roe is unfixable despite protestations otherwise. Scalia poetically refers to Roe justices as the "Imperial Judiciary"[141] those "unelected, life tenured judges—leading a Volk who will be "tested by following."[142]

In Planned Parenthood there is an outward revolt by select justices calling for a return to first principles based on life, personhood, the resistance to a faulty legal logic that can no longer be conceptually supported—and the mindless standing "by an erroneous constitutional decision" to assure the "court's legitimacy."[143] Even the argument that Roe's weak "doctrinal footings" have yet to be replaced by something better by making Roe "obsolete"[144] manifests the turmoil and "perpetual chaos" associated with this divisive decision. Some have even argued that the demise of Roe, as originally announced, may happen by a sort of slow gradualism, and a review of the cases up to and including Casey at least edifies more tolerance to regulatory oversight and control.[145]

Even though the court cannot muster the votes to overrule its precedent in Roe, the court does display an increasing tolerance for reasonable and rational regulations in the world of abortion. These same regulatory challenges may, given the current composition of the court, have been decided differently, but for this time, the partial approval of restrictions was quite significant. To be sure, the court has altered some of its previous conclusions. For example, the court considers a Pennsylvania statute that covers territory discussed in some earlier cases and comes up with differing results on the question of Minor–Parental Consent, Informed Consent for Abortion patients. In the matter of spousal consent, the results are mixed and not majoritarian. However, the emphasis in Planned Parenthood shows this steady toleration of state regulations. While Justice Anthony Kennedy's majority opinion can be more prose than vigorous legal reasoning, it is fair to conclude that the court's authors are trying to maintain Roe while holding fast to some suspect legal reasoning. Kennedy is often accused of moral subjectivism in his opinion to uphold post-Roe regulations on abortion. His legal ambiguity is quite stunning in his "mystery of life passage."

> Our law affords constitutional protection to personal decisions relating to marriage, procreation, contraception, family relationships, child rearing, and education. Carey v. Population Services International.[146] Our cases recognize the right of the individual, married or single, to be free from unwarranted governmental intrusion into matters so fundamentally affecting a person as the decision whether to bear or beget a child.[147] Our precedents "have respected the private realm of family life which the state cannot enter."[148] These matters, involving the most intimate and personal choices a person may make in a lifetime, choices central to personal dignity and autonomy, are central to the liberty protected by the Fourteenth Amendment. At the heart of liberty is the right to define one's own concept of existence, of meaning, of the universe, and of the mystery of human life. Beliefs about these matters could not define the attributes of personhood were they formed under compulsion of the State.[149]

Admittedly Kennedy's mystery of human life is made all the more mysterious by such legal language.

What crops up more clearly in Planned Parenthood, as to natural law dynamics, still includes viability, personhood and self-preservation but then expends considerable energy within the familial environment, for example, the nature of parental consent and spousal participation in the decision making. Indeed the court's family dimension of Planned Parenthood is quite striking and aside from the self-preservation principle of the natural law, nothing is more intimately bound to human life than that of the human family. Planned Parenthood went beyond the litigants alone when making its judgment for it was wise enough to discern how the decision to have any abortion is not one made in isolation or vacuum. As Justice O'Connor's rightfully observes that abortion is an act "fraught with consequences for others."[150]

The complexity of the decision influences much beyond the advocate clamoring for this right or that right. Planned Parenthood makes plain that the abortion decision is usually a familial decision.

Viability, personhood and self-preservation

One of subtle characteristics of *Planned Parenthood v. Casey* is the ease at which the viability problem is stated and the perfunctory way in which the court reiterates the role viability plays in the assessment of regulations involving abortion.[151] From its earliest paragraphs, it states that the decision is a

> [c]onfirmation of the State's power to restrict abortions after fetal viability, if the law contains exceptions which endanger a woman's life or health. And third is the principle that the State has legitimate interests from the outset of pregnancy in protecting the health of the woman and the life of the fetus that may become a child. These principles do not contradict one another; and we adhere to each.[152]

The court continuously reiterates the right of the state to regulate at that compelling point in fetal development—viability whereby the opinion accepts the lack of rigor in a timeline. Whether it be 20, 23, 24, or 28 weeks, the variety of which it considers normative, the "soundness or unsoundness" of that judgment is not pinned to a perfect calculation.[153] If the court seeks elasticity in that determination, it appears to achieve that. The court further concludes, "And there is no line other than viability which is more workable. To be sure, as we have said, there may be some medical developments that affect the precise line of viability, but this is an imprecision within tolerable limits given that the medical community and all those who must apply its discoveries will continue to explore the matter."[154] All this being said, the right of the state to regulate at the point of viability should not always be construed as an "undue burden" but instead a full recognition that "not all regulations must be deemed unwarranted."[155]

The various proposed requirements of the Pennsylvania legislature may or may not impede the right to choose before viability. The questions posed in Planned Parenthood always seem to come back to the matter of viability and knowledge of an abortion's impact on both the client and the fetus. For example,

> Does the dissemination of information on gestational timelines and fetal developments violate the Roe Doctrine? Response: No
>
> Does the Requirement that the client sign an Informed Consent document after reviewing relevant literature violate the right to an abortion? Response: No
>
> Do regulations subsequent to viability automatically cause an undue burden on the party seeking an abortion? Response: No

Is it proper for the State to proscribe abortion in post-viability cases? Response: Yes

Planned Parenthood v. Casey unequivocally affirms the competing interests of a viable human life that resides within the carrying mother. These are distinct yet compatible interests that need, in accordance with Roe, to be never severed from one another but considered in a unified way. This press for the preservation of a viable fetus likely made way for abortion decisions to be made on the basis of "informed consent," a factor worthy of further consideration.

Informed consent, self-preservation and viability

While efforts to inform patients about the medical and developmental reality of the fetal life and corresponding abortions have been attempted in other cases[156] and with mixed results, Planned Parenthood's majority were quite comfortable with the Pennsylvania method of informed consent. In a nutshell, the Act called for the following:

- A 24-hour waiting period to consider disseminated information
- Health risks on both abortion and actual childbirth
- Probable gestational age of the unborn child
- Description of the fetus and its development
- Medical assistance for childbirth—if needed and by what agencies
- Child services that provide alternatives to abortion[157]

While portions of the Act relating to spousal consent were struck down as undue impediments under Roe, the provisions as to informed consent were fully supported by the majority. In this context, we witness another effort to advance the potentiality and actuality of life as well as a sense of personhood, which are fully consistent with natural law principles. While one cannot directly connect natural law thinking, why else would these provisions really matter except that the life of the viable fetus does matter in terms of its self-preservation? Add to this the very clear possibility that the informed consent doctrine may in fact stop a once decided person from proceeding with that abortion after full consideration of the consequences to the medical procedure. As noted in earlier cases, there has been this subliminal tendency, or even express for that matter, to hope that abortion candidates simply remain ignorant of abortion process and procedure. This is completely inconsistent with consent notions present in literally every imaginable medical procedure. Knowledge is not something a patient should avoid but embrace. The majority opinion properly concludes that every candidate for abortion cannot separate oneself from the very end of the abortion—the fetus—and sensibly deduce that "most women considering an abortion would deem the impact on the fetus relevant."[158]

To fail to do these basic things in advance of any abortion, any medical procedure, is to leave a patient in a sort of factual darkness that in turn fails to lead to enlightened decisions. Informed consent mitigates suffering from some later consequence, such as the court points out, "devastating psychological consequences" because "her decision was not fully informed."[159]

In declaring these processes being of no substantial or undue burden, the majority affirms the need for intelligent decision making in the matter of fetal life—a far cry from earlier calls for abortion on demand at any stage and at any time. In a sort of curious way, Roe provides the defense mechanism to assure at least some level of self-preservation and fetal personhood. Roe's language has always been tentative about latter stages of fetal development while the more rabid "abortion on demand" cannot brook any regulation until the last day and the last hour. Infanticide is not off-limits for some of abortion's most radical supporters. In these sorts of cases, we witness not an ethic of self-preservation or viability but instead a zealous singular myopia—where the right to choose has no boundaries, no limitations and no regulatory schema that can ever be justified. Roe never envisioned a land so wasted on this side of the question. And as the progeny of cases proceed, the court is increasingly striking a tone that allows restrictions once verboten to emerge with caution.[160]

These sentiments are also gleaned from the majority opinion who no longer see abortion as some clinical, sanitized action without ripples of influence on family, the person seeking the abortion and the family experiencing it. This case is no longer the sterile world of people and medical procedures. As Justice O'Connor poses so poignantly,

> [T]hough the abortion decision may originate within the zone of conscience and belief, it is more than a philosophic exercise. […] It is an act fraught with consequences for others: for the woman who must live with the implications of her decision; for the persons who must perform and assist in the procedure; for the spouse, family, and society which must confront the knowledge that these procedures exist, procedures some deem nothing short of an act of violence against innocent human life."[161]

Family and care of offspring

Natural law jurisprudence reflects the primary and secondary precepts of what constitutes the natural law. Within the abortion realm, questions involving life and viability, self-preservation and the maintenance and flourishing of being to its fullest capacity remain fixtures in natural law analysis. Side by side with these tenets rest the matter of family and care of offspring—both of which are fundamental measures of compliance with natural law thinking. For a family to be compatible with the natural law, it must advance and solidify the nature and role of family in a collective, communal environment. Family is the central component of any thriving and worthwhile civilization. Children, offspring, maintain the continuity of any society or culture and provide the bond of family. By nature, we are inclined to both things—family and children. Any law that undercuts or negatively impacts family, undermines its stability and integrity, is bound to be contrary to the natural law.

In *Planned Parenthood v. Casey*, the majority opinion appears well aware of how abortion protocol and process can impact family and children. Aside from the obvious destruction of potential and even actual children, this principle of the natural law looks to how the practice might structurally influence the family operation. In particular, the court fathoms two dilemmas: first, the right of parental consent in the case of a minor seeking an abortion, and second, the right of a spouse, a husband to be both informed and consent thereto.

Minor's consent

The matter of parental authority, the role of a minor in the patterns of family decision making and the capacity of youth to make learned and enlightened decisions in most affairs, is something that *Planned Parenthood v. Casey* appears to appreciate. In common law terms and surely basic legal tradition, unemancipated minors can neither contract nor make decisions for themselves without some consent or voucher from an adult parent or guardian. The provisions of the Pennsylvania Act at 3206 include:

> Except in the case of a medical emergency or except as provided in this section, if a pregnant woman is less than 18 years of age and not emancipated, or if she has been adjudged an incompetent under 20 Pa. C. S. § 5511 (relating to petition and hearing; examination by court-appointed physician), a physician shall not perform an abortion upon her unless, in the case of a woman who is less than 18 years of age, he first obtains the informed consent both of the pregnant woman and of one of her parents; or, in the case of a woman who is incompetent, he first obtains the informed consent of her guardian. In deciding whether to grant such consent, a pregnant woman's parent or guardian shall consider only their child's or ward's best interests. In the case of a pregnancy that is the result of incest, where the father is a party to the incestuous act, the pregnant woman need only obtain the consent of her mother.[162]

Nothing herein rests in radical contrast to how parental consent controls in most instances of a minor's life. On top of this, the law provides for a medical emergency exception and even a "judicial bypass" option, which may be justified given the specific relationship and circumstances of the minor and her parents.[163] In upholding the parental consent provisions, the majority seems to recognize the impact of subverting the process natural in families when serious decisions must take place. Justice Scalia, citing Justice Potter Stewart,[164] comments, "There can be little doubt that the State furthers a constitutionally permissible end by encouraging unmarried pregnant minor to seek the help and advice of her parents in making the very important decision whether or not to bear a child. We thus conclude that Pennsylvania's parental consent requirement should be upheld."[165] Justice Rehnquist affirms that this sort of requirement is a legitimate concern and "legitimate interest" for its youthful citizens.[166] The majority opinion, despite some obvious differences in outlook, upholds the minor's consent requirement since "minors benefit from consultation with their parents and that children will often not realize that their parents have their best interests at heart."[167]

Although the consent requirement receives a majority vote, the path chosen by this court and the many others before it, after Roe, is one that will never be satisfactory according to Justice Scalia. For in minor's consent, or spousal consent, of whatever the regulation may be for the moment, the court continues its attempt to bring legal peace to the question at hand. This ambition has become both a factual and legal impossibility under the Roe foundation since its very undergirding is entirely rooted in a nebula of theories—all of which are nonexplicit in the Constitution. In the final analysis, Scalia argues, we have chosen a "social consensus" and "political pressure" as tests for that resolution and a "new mode of constitutional adjudication that not upon text or traditional practice to determine the law."[168] In its place, the court asks the litigants and the arbiters to make a "reasoned judgment"—even though what is reasonable seems to depend upon the whim, the caprice, the pressure applied to political and social realities.[169]

This is, by most measures, an undependable strategy to discern and apply constitutional rights. In essence, the question of family, minors and consent is not a constitutional one—but one best left to legal tradition, to the states and, yes, even to natural law jurisprudence where the assumption is that family is sacrosanct and in need of stability. To allow third-party abortion providers to usurp the role of parent undercuts family integrity—and allows the state to replace, without permission, the values that the family in question may vehemently disagree with. It is not the state that serves in the parental role but rather the parents who bore or who care for these offspring. Under every level and gradation of natural law jurisprudence, the state's efforts to vanquish parental rights is an affront to this basic natural law right of the family and its members. As Justice Scalia offers up, "We should get out of this area, where we have no right to be and where we do neither ourselves or the country any good by remaining."[170]

Spousal consent

The majority opinion rejected efforts at spousal consent under the Pennsylvania Act. Section 3209 reads in part,

> In order to further the Commonwealth's interest in promoting the integrity of the marital relationship and to protect a spouse's interests in having children within marriage and in protecting the prenatal life of that spouse's child, no physician shall perform an abortion on a married woman, except as provided in subsections (b) and (c), unless he or she has received a signed statement, which need not be notarized, from the woman upon whom the abortion is to be performed, that she has notified her spouse that she is about to undergo an abortion. The statement shall bear a notice that any false statement made therein is punishable by law.[171]

Identical concerns regarding family integrity, respect for the marital pact and the assumption that husbands are often the best counselors in such situations are readily gleaned factors in the court's decision. And in the case of this particular Pennsylvania statute—the essence of its content is not about pure, unbridled consent but instead "notification"—the spouse must certify that the other spouse was given notice unless she qualifies for the well-delineated exceptions. However, the slim majority are less persuaded by these rationales than whether or not the requirement imposes a significant undue burden on the party seeking an abortion. And here the court appears unwilling to count the husband as a party central to the abortion decision, and admittedly there may be many, many good reasons posed for that exclusion, such as sexual and physical abuse, estrangement and psychological abuse. The majority holds, "In a well-functioning marriage, spouses discuss important intimate decisions such as whether to bear a child. But there are millions of women in this country who are the victims of regular physical and psychological abuse at the hands of their husbands."[172]

The court expends considerable energy on the negative, to be sure "devastating forms"[173] of abuse in its many forms as rationale for its strike down. Given these realities, the court construes the spousal consent requirement as the type of obstacle properly labeled "undue" and claims that this sort of consent is an "effective veto."[174] In short, the spousal notification requirement imposes a "substantial obstacle" for a "significant number of women who fear for their safety and the safety of their children."[175] The court's majority opinion also makes a direct point on the common law tradition relating to the husband spouse by declaring that input or consent in this matter would be a "troubling degree of authority over his wife."[176] The court seems to care little for the distinction between required "consent" and simple "notification," yet that distinction makes a major difference in the statute's alleged heavy hand. While the court seems well-intentioned, its conclusion imputes a negative oversight or partnership rather than a marital state, a family of husband and wife—working in unity as partners toward common goals. In this divisive view of the marital state, the court appears to fall prey to generalizations— that "many notified husbands will prevent abortions through physical force, psychological coercion, and other types of threats."[177] As a matter of legal policy, substituting the family decision-making process with a legal standard never works as intended and by corollary, a major intrusion into the operation of a nuclear family. The majority finds that spousal consent may be "consonant with the common law status of married women but repugnant to our present understanding of marriage and of the nature of rights secured by the Constitution."[178] Is it repugnant to think that the abortion decision be shared and consultative? Is the marriage foundation better supported by unilateral secrecy and hidden choices? Is not marriage a unified institution rather than one separated by decisions on troubling questions? How does the court think spouses will react in all cases? To hold that a loving spouse—not the abusive model so often referred to—has no say, no input and absolutely no rights within the confines of a marital state seems an aggressive disenfranchisement of half of the marital partnership. Does the court assume that men, husbands, are mindless tyrants with little interest other than the dominion over their spouse? One cannot help seeing the spouse's helpless state—the conquered second-tier status that male spouses are immediately relegated to in the court's opinion. And this broad, beyond sweeping disenfranchisement of an entire spouse from any participation in the abortion decision cannot uplift the family or the marriage. For in the majority's eyes, the spouse becomes the burden, the obstacle in every case, not just those with mitigating and extenuating circumstances, all of which are fully outlined in the proposed code provisions. The Pennsylvania law already accounts for the many legitimate fears and circumstances that make spousal consent most difficult. Instead of accepting the wisdom of Pennsylvania, the court substitutes its judgment for both the legislative process and the spouse who historically and factually is part of the dilemma.

In Planned Parenthood, the husband is utterly demoted as an equal partner from even the procreative end. As Justice Rehnquist argues in the dissent on this matter,

> The question before us is therefore whether the spousal notification requirement rationally furthers any legitimate state interests? We conclude that it does. First, a husband's interests in procreation within marriage and in the potential life of his unborn child are certainly substantial ones. [...] By providing that a husband will usually know of his spouse's intent to have an abortion, the provision makes it more likely that the husband will participate in deciding the fate of his unborn child, a possibility that might otherwise have been denied him.[179]

The dissenting view on spousal notification finds implausible the majority view that the marital relationship cannot handle the stresses and strains of this complex matter, or to gain spousal input is bound to sow "marital discord."[180]

Relationships between husbands and wives, in the familial, marital state, are underpinnings of a natural law jurisprudence that has long recognized the integrity of that union and just as long been reticent to meddle in those intimate affairs. When abortion is added to the mix, the court's usual restraint is cast to the wayside and in doing so elevates an unenumerated right based on a nonexplicit legal standard that garners more legal substance than the matrimonial state can rightfully assume. In the end, the dissent cannot abide by a policy that sees husbands and wives as coequals or as even possibly loving and respectful of one another. For this majority, it is argued, there are only two scenarios where husband–wife relationships are properly described, "So perfect that this type of truthful and important communication will take place as a matter of course; So imperfect, that upon notice, the husband will react selfishly, violently, or contrary to the best interests of his wife."[181]

What is strikingly clear is how draconian the majority view is regarding the rights of the spouse who need not consent but merely be notified. From many fronts, the decision tends to favor viability as not only a legal conception but also a scientific reality, and in this sense, the Planned Parenthood case manifests a shift toward a more demanding recognition of viable life. In natural law circles, self-preservation of this viable life takes on a more prominent role. As to the matter of family and care of offspring, the results are mixed. The finding that parental consent is essential and critically important to family life demonstrates that the court recognizes the right of parents in matters involving children, and this natural caring cannot be simply swept away by undue burden or obstacle analysis. As for spousal consent, or in this case spousal notice, the court, outside of a few dissenters, cannot maintain the integrity of family for very long. Here the male father figure is reduced to mere observer rather than a marital partner—who has every natural right to at least know this event may occur. Even though the statute provides a series of exceptions that eliminate the notice requirement, especially in cases of abuse and violence, the court relegates one parent to a de minimis status.

Stenberg v. Carhart, 530 U.S. 914 (2000)

Less than a decade later, the court will confront another abortion controversy of major significance regarding "partial birth abortion"—a largely controversial practice reserved for later-term abortions. It is not so much the fact that abortions occur, as the nightmare of the medical practice itself is to carry out these abortions under a series of medical euphemisms. In particular, to abort more developed fetuses requires far more invasive methods than witnessed in the first part of the Roe trimester.

In the third part of that trimester, a fetus has full human form and cannot be extracted readily. Hence, the procedure, known as D & E, standing for Dilation and Extraction, medically invades the uterus to "pull out" an existing fetus. In the process of that procedure, it is normative for limbs, arms and other appendages to be torn from the torso. As Dr. Carhart attests, at the end of the procedure, the medical team is left with a "tray full of pieces."[182]

The second procedure, colloquially named, "partial birth abortion" and the intact dilation and extraction (D & X) procedure, dilates and induces the cervix to open to a larger circumference so that the physician might have access to that fetus. Here, the fetus is turned round so that the head remains in the canal, "partially delivered into the vagina,"[183] leading to the illusion and reality that partial birth has occurred, and once assured that the head has yet to be delivered, the physician either crushes the skull of the fetus with forceps or other artifice or drills a hole in the skull to extract the brain. In this way, the fetus is delivered partially, due to its size and development, only to be killed or exterminated. The court's majority opinion crafted by Justice Breyer relays the intricacies of this procedure with dispassion and sterility by design.

The intact D & E proceeds in one of two ways, depending on the presentation of the fetus. If the fetus presents head first (a vertex presentation), the doctor collapses the skill; and the doctor then extracts the entire fetus through the cervix. If the fetus presents feet first (a breech presentation), the doctor pulls the fetal body through the cervix, collapses the skull and extracts the fetus through the cervix.[184] It is a medical methodology "so horrible" says Justice Scalia that the most "clinical description of it evokes a shudder of revulsion."[185] In both cases, Nebraska lawmakers sought to end these practices as being barbaric yet also inconsistent with the viability standards enunciated in Roe and other cases. Pertinent parts of the statute relating to this practice include:

> No partial birth abortion shall be performed in this state, unless such procedure is necessary to save the life of the mother whose life is endangered by a physical disorder, physical illness, or physical injury, including a life-endangering physical condition caused by or arising from the pregnancy itself.[186]

The statute defines "partial birth abortion" as

> an abortion procedure in which the person performing the abortion partially delivers vaginally a living unborn child before killing the unborn child and completing the delivery.[187]

It further defines "partially delivers vaginally a living unborn child before killing the unborn child" to mean

> deliberately and intentionally delivering into the vagina a living unborn child, or a substantial portion thereof, for the purpose of performing a procedure that the person performing such procedure knows will kill the unborn child and does kill the unborn child.[188]

Under general natural law principles relating to self-preservation and the care of offspring, as well as a destruction of the natural procreative process, it is difficult to envision a case more strikingly instructional. In partial birth abortion practice, the fetus is neither an undeveloped postconception mass nor even a creature quickening under a medieval model. Any evaluation of the methods used and employed by the physician assumes something more developed is at stake. How that reconciles with the competing post-viability dogma allegedly part of the Roe doctrine escapes logic. In the majority opinion, the court even mixes and matches procedures—for why would it matter? D & E and D & X are used interchangeably, but the target of these practices remains consistent—a fetus too big to simply suction out or pharmacologically end by other means. Both procedures imply, impute and correctly need a more aggressive method of extraction—and not because that fetus lacks form and materiality but because it possesses those characteristics so obviously. Hence, it is a safe bet to argue that these fetuses reside in a subsequent to viability framework deserving and rightfully demanding some protection as a competing life with the mother carrying that fetus.

Be that as it may, the Stenberg majority seems to disregard that portion of the Roe legacy and then pontificates on other infractions. The rationale for upholding partial birth abortion rests on two theories: first, that the law does not provide a "health exception" for the mother; second, since the law forbids the method, it imposes an undue burden on the right to choose.[189] Even more bizarrely, the Stenberg Court claims that this law has no concern about viable life but only the restrictiveness of the abortionist's methods. Under any reasonable interpretation of the statute's aim and overall purpose, that conclusion seems incongruous but like so much in the upside-down world of abortion jurisprudence—the endgame of maintaining abortion matters more than either the facts or the law. To be sure, the majority avoids the ugliness of it all by centering its attention on process over substance. Not to outdo itself, the majority opinion justifies its legal finding by a perverse theory, namely that the skull crushing and limb tearing piece by piece is the "safest procedure."[190] Because of our concern for women's health, the majority indicates, it is unconstitutional to ban either practice.

Self-preservation, viability and personhood

Stenberg is riddled with natural law nuances and issues. From the very idea that viable life deserves protection under our jurisprudence to the actual delivery—albeit partially—of a demonstrably viable human being, to a third trimester being given rightful protection under Roe—these are not beings unformed and undeveloped. These beings, as the natural law dictates to seek the good, seek what is best for sustenance and maintenance and seek to live rather than perish. Any medical protocol that thwarts these most basic inclinations does so in contravention to the natural law. And reaching this deduction, the court seems to argue that the likelihood of mix up and timing relative to fetal development causes this law to forbid earlier abortions in a previable status. On that score, it is difficult to envision a physician clamoring to use D & E or D & X when simple vacuum aspiration works in the earliest of fetal stages. The protocols considered by the Stenberg court are by nature intrusive, invasive and far more extreme for any early pregnancy. Even in the dissenting opinion of Justice Stevens, joined by Justice Ginsburg, the trek toward illogic continues without much reservation. The dissenters label the practices "gruesome" noting, "But one need not even approach this view today to conclude that Nebraska's law must fall. For the notion that either of these two equally gruesome procedures performed at this late stage of gestation is more akin to infanticide than the other, or that the State further any legitimate interest by banning one but not the other, is simply irrational."[191]

Stenberg's contortions to reach a result can only be described as inexplicable. On the one hand, the majority opinion reaffirms the Roe doctrine on competing life interests in subsequent viability cases while on the other hand rejects any effort to regulate or oversee the medical procedures that clearly affront the life of a viable fetus. To reach this conclusion, the court had to deny a host of things including, but not limited to, the concept of viability as properly enunciated in precedent; the recognition that both abortion protocols are for later-term, not earlier-term, abortions; and a rejection of state statutes that properly apply these doctrines. Justice O'Connor concludes that the restrictions are unconstitutional because the "health of the mother" is not provided for as an exception. However, the statute excepts any mothers whose "life is endangered by physical disorders, physical illness or physical injury."[192] A reasonable reading of the language does not preclude health considerations but emphatically delineates them.

In addition, the majority opinion seems incapable of finding any permissible restriction on the method for abortion practice. If in fact, the potential life, the viable life has a competing and rightful interest to protection under Roe and its progeny, why should the method employed to abort the fetus not matter in some cases? The majority contorts this argument by claiming that it is best for the health of the mother that partial birth abortion be an acceptable protocol. As a result of this position, the viable life really has no place in abortion analysis. Whether tearing limb by limb or forcing a fully viable fetus into breech so that the head is not delivered, and then to be crushed or evacuated, the court minimizes the technique as if there is no other life interest. While the majority indicates that medical protocols cannot be up to the "unfettered discretion"[193] of the physician alone, what type of protocol might allow the court to consider a competing interest in life? If we accept that D & E and D & X are done in the latter stages of fetal development, how can the method chosen become so quickly irrelevant in this constitutional morass? The court's own majority opinion describes in ironic and exquisite detail the life interest at stake and how either method can trouble the conscience:

> The statute forbids "deliberately and intentionally delivering into the vagina a living unborn child, or a substantial portion thereof, for the purpose of performing a procedure that the person performing such procedure knows will kill the unborn child." We do not understand how one could distinguish, using this language, between D&E (where a foot or arm is drawn through the cervix) and D&X (where the body up to the head is drawn through the cervix). Evidence before the trial court makes clear that D&E will often involve a physician pulling a "substantial portion" of a still living fetus, say, an arm or leg, into the vagina prior

to the death of the fetus. Indeed D&E involves dismemberment that commonly occurs only when the fetus meets resistance that restricts the motion of the fetus: "The dismemberment occurs between the traction of [...] [the] instrument and the counter-traction of the internal os of the cervix."[194]

Nor does the majority wish to confront or deal with the obvious two-stage process of the D & X whereby the still living fetus is partially delivered while preferably leaving the head in the vagina, at step one. While at step two, the fetus must be put to death by either a crushed skull or an evacuated brain. That Nebraska wishes to ban this procedure does not tread on abortion rights by undue burden but by enacting this law gives recognition to and prominence for that competing life under Roe analysis.

Under every reasonable standard of viable life, the majority appears drawn to other criteria than that set out clearly and explicitly in Roe. In the final analysis, *Stenberg v. Carhart* sanctions any abortion method, for it cannot take umbrage with this protocol, it is likely impossible to find any medical approach that would offend the sensibilities of the average physician or citizen. Everyone, who has any sense of proportion, finds the methods employed here to be less than civilized. Even Justice Ginsburg indicates that these types of abortions are "distressing and susceptible to gruesome description."[195] That this sort of reality shows susceptibility to being gruesome misses the point since the procedure by its very nature speaks to its gruesomeness. The extremes to which this court will go to protect these practices reach the heights of misplaced ethics when the court sympathizes with those physicians performing these practices who live in fear of "prosecution, conviction, and imprisonment."[196]

The dissenters in Stenberg zero in on not only the barbarity of the medical procedure but also its target—the viable, later-stage fetus and its rightful place in abortion analysis. In essence, it is not enough to simply say that any abortion procedure must allow for the life and health of the mother. What is equally compelling, Justice Scalia argues, is that the decision permits an abortionist to believe "that this live-birth method of destroying the child might be safer for the woman."[197] Scalia's dissent cannot be described as gentle or political for in Stenberg he sees abortion jurisprudence imploding on its own illogic. The majority opinion, simply and succinctly, approved a "method of killing a human child"[198] and at the same time prohibited the states from "banning this visibly brutal means of eliminating our half-born posterity."[199] From its first days, Roe has unleashed a sling of irrational arguments for why abortion is rooted in an imaginary constitutional principle, Scalia argues, and Roe's progeny, up to and including *Planned Parenthood v. Casey* is nothing more than an "explication of the inexplicable."[200] In Stenberg, abortion jurisprudence exposes all of its natural shortcomings and theoretical weaknesses making Scalia question why the court persists in this direction when "neither constitutional text nor accepted tradition, can resolve that contention and controversy rather than be consumed by it."[201]

From Justice Kennedy's perspective, his dissent reflects his distaste not only for a failure to follow Roe and its lineage but also for the court's general tendency to sanitize the brutality of the practices confirmed as constitutional. Kennedy pens that the court has crafted a "new method for ending human life."[202] So driven toward the recognition of fetal life in these protocols that Kennedy lists the word games and nomenclature that make the practices more palatable. Kennedy specifies "transcervical procedures, folsmotic dilators, instrumental disarticulation, and paracervical block" as examples of terms that minimize the obvious brutality of these practices.[203] However, these words cannot minimize or mitigate the real essence of these practices. In Kennedy's dissent he highlights the testimony of the chief defendant, abortion doctor Carhart, who when describing the various methods makes plain the physical disassembly. Using terms that equate pulling out a fetus to "pulling the cat's tail," or "dragging a string across the floor, you'll just keep dragging,"[204] the defendant in this case displays a cold, calculating vision of what viability is; what life connotes and what value and dignity there is in a post-viable, yet to be born, child. Dr. Carhart's testimony is fully cited by Justice Kennedy,

> As described by Dr. Carhart, the D&E procedure requires the abortionist to use instruments to grasp a portion (such as a foot or hand) of a developed and living fetus and drag the grasped portion out of the uterus into the vagina. Dr. Carhart uses the traction created by the opening between the uterus and vagina to dismember the fetus, tearing the grasped portion away from the remainder of the body. The traction between the uterus and vagina is essential to the procedure because attempting to abort a fetus without using that traction is described by Dr. Carhart as "pulling the cat's tail" or "drag[ging] a string across the floor, you'll just keep dragging it. It's not until something grabs the other end that you are going to develop traction." The fetus, in many cases, dies just as a human adult or child would: It bleeds to death as it is torn limb from limb. The fetus can be alive at the beginning of the dismemberment process and can survive for a time while its limbs are being torn off. Dr. Carhart agreed that "[w]hen you pull out a piece of the fetus, let's say, an arm or a leg and remove that, at the time just prior to removal of the portion of the fetus, [...] the fetus [is] alive." Dr. Carhart has observed fetal heartbeat via ultrasound with "extensive parts of the fetus removed," and testified that mere dismemberment of a limb does

not always cause death because he knows of a physician who removed the arm of a fetus only to have the fetus go on to be born "as a living child with one arm." At the conclusion of a D&E abortion no intact fetus remains. In Dr. Carhart's words, the abortionist is left with "a tray full of pieces."[205]

And when describing the D & X procedure, Dr. Carhart never flinches or waivers in his full-fledged scientific description of what he does on a regular basis. Aside from turning the fetus around to assure the head remains in the birth canal, that second step will call for some sort of cranial crushing or evacuation of the brain matter. Kennedy precisely lays out the procedure:

> The abortionist then inserts a suction tube and vacuums out the developing brain and other matter found within the skull. The process of making the size of the fetus' head smaller is given the clinically neutral term "reduction procedure."[206] Brain death does not occur until after the skull invasion, and, according to Dr. Carhart, the heart of the fetus may continue to beat for minutes after the contents of the skull are vacuumed out.[207] The abortionist next completes the delivery of a dead fetus, intact except for the damage to the head and the missing contents of the skull.[208]

Justice Kennedy's consternation and simmering concern does not end here for he cannot reconcile how the previous abortion decisions, which compare and contrast competing life interests in subsequent viability settings, can be so disregarded, especially in light of the *Planned Parenthood v. Casey* decision. In *Casey*, the court fully endorsed a state interest, a rationale for regulatory oversight of the abortion process particularly in clear viability cases. Kennedy properly deduces,

> Casey is premised on the States having an important constitutional role in defining their interests in the abortion debate. It is only with this principle in mind that Nebraska's interests must be given proper weight. The State's brief describes its interests as including concern for the life of the unborn and "for the partially-born," in preserving the integrity of the medical profession, in "erecting a barrier to infanticide."[209]

Justice Kennedy's defense and preservation of life and the acknowledgment that fetal life always rests within the legal continuum, rather than separate from it, represents the best qualities of natural law reasoning. As in other cases, the discussion never explicitly lists the natural law as part of the decision, although the arguments advancing and preserving human life cannot be mistaken for anything other than natural law jurisprudence. When Kennedy asserts that states may take sides in the abortion debate and come down on the side of life, even life of the unborn, he affirms the fundamental natural law tenet of life and its maintenance. A state has every right to assure its medical providers act in accordance with some level of medical propriety or ethic, to be "healers, sustained by a compassionate and rigorous ethic and cognizant of the dignity and value of human life, even life which cannot survive without the assistance of others."[210]

Historical critics of Justice Kennedy often cite his malleable legal principles regarding tough moral and ethical dilemmas but his Stenberg dissent demonstrates his zeal to protect the life of the unborn. The current clamor and shouts regarding his replacement, Justice Brett Kavanaugh being extreme when compared to the "moderate" and reasonable Kennedy, fail to read the strong language of Kennedy's dissent in Stenberg, the clearly pro-life language seeking to preserve human life and to care for live birth offspring. Ambiguity does not find a home in his analysis when he claims that these abortion protocols are "dehumanizing" and nothing more than a "commandeering" of the live birth process "until the skull is pierced."[211] Even pro-choice advocates, Kennedy argues, cannot defend the indefensible and can only conclude "that both procedures are subject to the most severe moral condemnation, condemnation reserved for the most repulsive human conduct."[212]

Kennedy also dispenses with the alleged lack of a "health exception" noting that not even the American College of Obstetrician and Gynecologists could enumerate any circumstances in which D & X would be the singular option for protecting the life or health of the mother.[213] A similar conclusion was reached by the expert panel of the AMA.[214] In essence, the dissenters cannot abide by a medical protocol that is not exclusive to the exception requirement, there being viable alternatives, nor that this extreme practice be "part of standard medical practice."[215] In the final analysis, the majority opinion, Kennedy argues, has ignored the will of Nebraskans and substituted its judgment for the Nebraska legislature and "sweeps the law away."[216] It has displayed no deference to differences, so much so that not even these egregious medical procedures can be barred at the state line, and manifests little respect for the idea that "medical procedures must be governed by moral principles having their foundation in the intrinsic value of human life, including the life of the unborn,"[217] and in the end stands for the proposition that a process so "abhorrent" and even properly described as the "most serious of crimes against human life."[218] The majority, Justice Kennedy claims, "closes its eyes to these profound concerns."[219]

The final dissent of Stenberg, authored by Justice Clarence Thomas, joined by Justice Scalia, attends to the natural law questions of viability and life, self-preservation and care of potential and actual offspring. Early in their dissent, these medical protocols are essentially characterized as "hard to distinguish from infanticide."[220] The process of D & E and D & X, despite the "majority's sanitized description," is "so gruesome that its use can be traumatic even for the physicians and medical staff who perform it."[221]

The graphic depictions posed by Justice Thomas are not for the sake of rattling nerves as much as he wishes his reader to see reality of what unfolds. In other words, it is not possible to rule on the propriety of the process without a full understanding of its step-by-step mechanics. To say the descriptions are unsettling is to understate the severity. Justice Thomas speaks of grabbing "fetal extremities," tearing off "pieces of the fetus," "removal of the brain and other intracranial contents," "crush the skull," "tear or perforate the skull" and "cervical entrapment of the head."[222]

All of these graphic accounts cannot whitewash the brutal methods employed to complete the abortion for in these late-stage fetal states, there is simply no way to perform neatly and cleanly. Given the advanced viability state, the physician has little other choice than to either pull apart a living fetus or to falsely deliver in order that that the brain might be neutralized. Nothing of this reality escapes Justice Thomas who has difficulty reconciling a practice so hideous, so grotesque that some constitutional right trumps its control or regulation. He appreciates the irony of technique that requires delivery in order that death be exacted. He comments,

> In other words, even if one assumes, arguendo, that dismemberment—the act of grasping a fetal arm or leg and pulling until it comes off, leaving the remaining part of the fetal body still in the uterus—is a kind of "delivery," it does not take place "before" the death causing procedure or "for the purpose of performing" the death-causing procedure; it *is* the death-causing procedure. Under the majority's view, D&E is covered by the statute because when the doctor pulls on a fetal foot until it tears off he has "delivered" a substantial portion of the unborn child and has performed a procedure known to cause death. But, significantly, the physician has not "delivered" the child *before* performing the death-causing procedure or "for the purpose of" performing the death-causing procedure; the dismemberment "delivery" is itself the act that causes the fetus' death.[223]

In the D & X, the methodology employed could not be more antagonistic to the nature of life, to any reasoned measure of viability and to our sense and sensibility as to what constitutes human life. Under natural law principles, each being seeks its natural and proper good, its preservation and flourishing, its continued existence and maintenance. The process utilized in these abortion settings not only undermines the natural order, it annihilates life as we understand it. Justice Thomas finds no majority rationale that is defensible in light of human life and why the state of Nebraska correctly seeks to end the practice. When the majority descends into semantics about whether partial birth abortion really occurs, Justice Thomas explains in profoundly exquisite detail how a D & X is in fact a delivery with death as the endgame, a technique that "dehumanizes the fetus and trivializes human life."[224] At no place in the Thomas dissent can the horrid nature of D & X be captured than in the cited testimony of a nurse who witnessed this procedure.

> The baby's little fingers were clasping and unclasping, and his little feet were kicking. Then the doctor stuck the scissors in the back of his head, and the baby's arms jerked out, like a startle reaction, like a flinch, like a baby does when he thinks he is going to fall.
>
> The doctor opened up the scissors, stuck a high-powered suction tube into the opening, and sucked the baby's brains out. Now the baby went completely limp.[225]

From there one can only wonder how states lack the authority to regulate the procedure in question, how a forbiddance of the practice negates Roe or undercuts Casey. For Justice Thomas, to descend into these sorts of legal machinations borders on the inane for in "a civilized society, the answer is too obvious, and contrary arguments too offensive to merit further discussion."[226] In Stenberg, any semblance of the Casey doctrine, which permitted a "profound respect for fetal life," has evaporated.[227]

Gonzales v. Carhart, 550 U.S. 124 (2007)

That Dr. Carhart would somehow disappear from the legal landscape was surely not to be. In many ways, he has become the most identifiable target for those seeking to end his advocated practice of D & E and D & X. Carhart would always remain a zealous advocate for these procedures and could describe these experiences as if there were no implications involving the preservation of life or measure of viability. He and others displaced their persons from the very acts committed, a sort of detachment that manifests a blank, overly clinical view of life itself. One physician, witnessed in the earlier Carhart case, makes a return and repeat visit to this court explaining the procedures with an amoral precision.

At this point, the right-handed surgeon slides the fingers of the left [hand] along the back of the fetus and "hooks" the shoulders of the fetus with the index and ring fingers (palm down).

While maintaining this tension, lifting the cervix and applying traction to the shoulders with the fingers of the left hand, the surgeon takes a pair of blunt curved Metzenbaum scissors in the right hand. He carefully advances the tip, curved down, along the spine and under his middle finger until he feels it contact the base of the skull under the tip of his middle finger.

The surgeon then forces the scissors into the base of the skull or into the foramen magnum. Having safely entered the skull, he spreads the scissors to enlarge the opening.

The surgeon removes the scissors and introduces a suction catheter into this hole and evacuates the skull contents. With the catheter still in place, he applies traction to the fetus, removing it completely from the patient.[228]

In reaction to these methods as well as a continuing public objection, in many quarters to a toleration and legitimization of D & E and D & X, the US Congress attempted to legislate a remedy. Crushing skulls, evacuating brain matter and severing limbs to assure passage through the body rightfully tug at the moral and national conscience and are just as compelling for those who must labor under these circumstances, especially nurses and support staff. The majority court weighs and evaluates whether recently enacted federal legislation, seeking to control and minimize these protocols, can withstand constitutional muster. In passing 18 U.S.C. section 1531, the legislative intent and deliberate purpose of the Act was made clear: "a moral, medical, and ethical consensus exists that the practice of performing a partial-birth abortion [...] is a gruesome and inhumane procedure that is never medically necessary and should be prohibited."[229]

The Act states in part:

(a) Any physician who, in or affecting interstate or foreign commerce, knowingly performs a partial-birth abortion and thereby kills a human fetus shall be fined under this title or imprisoned not more than 2 years, or both. This subsection does not apply to a partial-birth abortion that is necessary to save the life of a mother whose life is endangered by a physical disorder, physical illness, or physical injury, including a life-endangering physical condition caused by or arising from the pregnancy itself. This subsection takes effect 1 day after the enactment.

(b) As used in this section—
  (1) the term 'partial-birth abortion' means an abortion in which the person performing the abortion—
    (A) deliberately and intentionally vaginally delivers a living fetus until, in the case of a head-first presentation, the entire fetal head is outside the body of the mother, or, in the case of breech presentation, any part of the fetal trunk past the navel is outside the body of the mother, for the purpose of performing an overt act that the person knows will kill the partially delivered living fetus; and
    (B) performs the overt act, other than completion of delivery, that kills the partially delivered living fetus; and
  (2) the term "physician" means a doctor of medicine or osteopathy legally authorized to practice medicine and surgery by the State in which the doctor performs such activity, or any other individual legally authorized by the State to perform abortions: Provided, however, That any individual who is not a physician or not otherwise legally authorized by the State to perform abortions, but who nevertheless directly performs a partial-birth abortion, shall be subject to the provisions of this section.[230]

As in Stenberg, the lower courts rejected the Act due to its constitutional flaws of a "health exception" and its breadth as to most D & E procedures, particularly the distinction between intact versus "torn apart" fetuses. How the latter critique has any constitutional ambience escape most readers, although the court notes that there is a lack of evidence to prove that the life or health of the mother cannot be accommodated through alternative means.

In authoring the majority opinion, Justice Kennedy continues his firm reliance on the Roe-Casey lineage, which plainly and unequivocally concludes that the state has a "substantial interest in preserving and promoting fetal life."[231] Post-viability fetal life garners not a secondary, peripheral status in the matter of self-preservation but surely something of a higher order than popular opinion espouses. The Act differs from the Nebraska provisions in diverse ways and overcomes the previous critiques which overturned the state oversight of D & X methods. First, the act precisely describes the abortion physician "vaginally delivers a living fetus."[232] Second, liability under the act depends upon specifically delineated "anatomical markers" such as the head being outside the mother or the "fetal trunk past the navel outside the body of the mother."[233] If these markers are not measured, the Act does not apply. Third, the physician must perform an "overt act, other than completion of delivery, that kills the partially delivered living fetus."[234] Finally, the Act requires a high level of intentionality, rather than an event caused by normal medical measurements that can be imprecise. In order for the Act to apply, the physician must "deliberately and intentionally," not by inadvertence or medical error, commit an overt act that results in the termination of the fetus. When compared to the Nebraska Act, the US Code lays out some objective measures to assure the maintenance of viable life. Justice Kennedy compares and contrasts the difference with clarity:

> The identification of specific anatomical landmarks to which the fetus must be partially delivered also differentiates the Act from the statute at issue in Stenberg.[235] The Court in Stenberg interpreted "substantial portion" of the fetus to include an arm or a leg. The Act's anatomical landmarks, by contrast, clarify that the removal of a small portion of the fetus is not prohibited. The landmarks also require the fetus to be delivered so that it is partially "outside the body of the mother."[236] To come within the ambit of the Nebraska statute, on the other hand, a substantial portion of the fetus only had to be delivered into the vagina; no part of the fetus had to be outside the body of the mother before a doctor could face criminal sanctions.[237]

Hence, for the majority, the federal law does not cause an undue burden nor pose as a substantial obstacle to any woman seeking an abortion within the historic guidelines. The Act in question "proscribes a method of abortion in which a fetus is killed just inches before the completion of the birth process."[238] The majority also purposely cited some legislative history gleaned from the Congressional Record that pulls no punches on the brutality of the abortion method. Congress, by passage of the Act, restricts this "brutal and inhumane procedure."[239] Failure to ban the process will "further coarsen society to the humanity of not only newborns but all vulnerable and innocent human life, making it increasingly difficult to protect such life."[240] The court then goes even further when it remarks that the "procedure itself [is] laden with the power to devalue human life."[241]

Family and care of offspring

Another natural law current derived in the majority opinion relates to two issues: the natural bond of a mother with an unborn child; and, second, the impact the abortion decision has upon the family unit. For in the majority's view, abortion is not a singular decision made by a singular party. While Roe and its lineage speak of competing rights in a woman's right to choose and the viability determination of any fetus triggering a competing life, the Gonzales decision expends considerable energy on the relationship between mother and the unborn child. At this stage of fetal development, when these processes occur, it is difficult to envision any mother so devoid of relational feelings at some level. The majority opinion makes this plain when it states, "Respect for human life finds an ultimate expression in the bond of love the mother has for her child. The Act recognizes this reality as well. Whether to have an abortion requires a difficult and painful moral decision."[242]

In Gonzales, the court treats the choosing mother as more than a mere automaton, who fully displaces herself from the full consequence and ramifications of the abortion act. It is never that clean nor that easy. For under natural law principles, the care of offspring, the love of family, is not something learned as much as one is already disposed toward. The term "maternal instinct" says much about what is natural to every childbearer. And while the dissenters scathingly critique this type of human observation, it is never something that can be stripped away from the human person, especially the mother of any child. The majority has put a real face on the participants, a human face that deals with all the complexities and nuances of choice, not like a placard or billboard carried in a march, but internally moving and choosing something that forever and inexorably changes life as encountered. Part of that recognition is the court's extraordinary insight that many proponents of these practices do not want to get into the details of how it unfolds and how some "doctors prefer not to disclose precise details of the means that will be used, confining themselves to the required statement of risks the procedure entails."[243] Indeed, if full and unequivocal disclosure took place with regularity, it is a safe bet that more patients would opt out of the process. No mother wishes an unborn fetus she is carrying to be torn limb from limb or pulled out just far enough so that a doctor partially delivers and crushes the skull or evacuates the brain to insure death. The majority holds that any state that feels compelled to fill in those details should be able to do so under the viability standards the court has long agreed to. The court holds that its interest in that viable life and the "grave choice" to end it should permissibly allow the state to advise the mother of the act's implications.[244]

While abortion advocates prefer the equation of abortion with any medical procedure—whether an appendectomy or a glaucoma operation—that position disregards, as previous decisions have concluded, that abortion is "fraught with emotional consequence."[245] Indeed, from its very earliest of considerations, the mulling over the abortion choice is far different than having a tooth pulled. Mothers and families know this with intense clarity and the courts have an obligation to paint a picture that is not sanitized or sterile but one in which all the facts are divulged and on the table. The costs of abortion can be significant, especially the emotional ones, from the outset, to the operating table, and to the end of one's life, as long as memory allows. Some women, though surely not all, come to stages of regret, subsequent second-guessing and an overall reconsideration of choice and circumstances like a show running perpetually in one's mind. No one with any understanding of human psychology can think the decision has no life beyond the day of choice. Gonzales, in its appeal to mothers, their natural care of love for children and offspring, seems to get these dynamics better than previous decisions. The court goes far when it raises the specter of "regret" over choice, especially when the actor was not informed or who subconsciously did not want to really know the reality of these later-term abortions. The court held,

> It is self-evident that a mother who comes to regret her choice to abort must struggle with grief more anguished and sorrow more profound when she learns, only after the event, what she once did not know; that she allowed a doctor to pierce the skull and vacuum the fast-developing brain of her unborn child, a child assuming a human form.[246]

Any rational person, engaging the full panoply of events, circumstances and protocols called for in these later-term abortions, knows how close potential life is to actual and how in some cases, depending on time and calendar, there may be a viable human being, fully formed and fully capable of either independent living or with some assistance. Every abortion patient must weigh and evaluate that knowledge in order to make any reasoned choice. Otherwise, the choice made is not merely about abortion but whether or not that choice "perverts a process during which life is brought into the world."[247]

Gonzales makes plain that the state has legitimate interests in educating women and family members about the full ramifications of D & E and D & X. That also includes an evaluation on whether or not there are alternatives to these practices that accomplish the same ends sought but do so with less barbarity. Doctors do not have "unfettered choice in the course of their medical practice,"[248] and if permitted, the physician would supplant the judgment of the patient, the mother as well as the family whose serious examination of these processes can only occur if fully aware of the options. Using doctors as shields to the brutality of the protocol or medical regimen undercuts maternal choice and leaves family members in a darkened state, a reality that no natural law thinker finds acceptable.

At the dissent, authored by Justice Ginsburg, the retort appears less legal, less ethical and clearly less aware of the act's moral dimensions nor is there any sign remotely related to natural law jurisprudence. In fact, Justice Ginsburg takes exception to including or evaluating "moral concerns" in the court's conclusions.[249] In fact, the dissent tends to be highly political and driven by arguments rooted in social justice, feminist and gender theory. A "woman's autonomy" that power to "determine her life's course" appears to drive the alleged legal reasoning. One of the better examples of this tendency, and which explicitly disassociates itself from traditional family or maternal arguments, is as follows:

> Those views, this Court made clear in Casey, "are no longer consistent with our understanding of the family, the individual, or the Constitution."[250] Women, it is now acknowledged, have the talent, capacity, and right "to participate equally in the economic and social life of the Nation."[251] Their ability to realize their full potential, the Court recognized, is intimately connected to "their ability to control their reproductive lives."[252] Thus, legal challenges to undue restrictions on abortion procedures do not seek to vindicate some generalized notion of privacy; rather, they center on a woman's autonomy to determine her life's course, and thus to enjoy equal citizenship stature.[253]

Any effort to equate emotional ramifications associated with abortion choice triggers a particular distress on her part. Referring to this finding as a "shibboleth," Ginsburg finds discussion of this sort nonempirical, lacking any "reliable evidence"[254] and not much more than stereotypical concerning gender. The "fragile emotional state" and the "bond of love" provide little illumination in this matter.[255] For Ginsburg and other choice advocates, those types of arguments are the result of stereotypical thinking about gender roles and an effort to undercut and destroy "autonomous choice."[256]

Ginsburg manifests a general hostility toward any reasonable efforts to regulate and oversee these late-term abortion processes calling the majority analysis "bewildering," "flimsy and transparent" justification that cannot be supported.[257] At its best, the dissenting opinion reiterates the Roe doctrine but does so without much regard for the competing life or interest. In the final analysis, the question of abortion is not about natural law jurisprudence and more driven toward social, political and gender-based arguments.

Summary and Conclusion

The evolution of abortion law and individual rights has been by most measures perpetually unsettling. If the law's chief aim is the rule and measure of both individuals and the collective, and to carry out purpose with certitude and general agreement, the abortion decisions have miserably and almost pathetically failed in that aim. Ever since the Roe decision was pronounced, the legal world has been one of tumult; the society in division and the resolutions posed erratically and sometimes even incoherently decided. Another part of the Roe legacy that seems to never be consolable relates to its legal justification. Critics, on both the left and right, have long argued that Roe was a legal case that might have been best left to the individual states to decide, for that is precisely how life was previous to Roe. The majority of states outlawed abortion, and under our constitutional framework, that is perfectly acceptable. However, abortion advocates could not rest easy and wanted a national legal pronouncement that swept aside all those states that felt otherwise. This is but the first of many rotted foundational beams in Roe. The second relates to "privacy," that imaginary right—as imaginary in Griswold as it is in Glucksberg—a judicial invention concocted in a legal laboratory whose text cannot be discovered and whose precedent cannot be accurately fathomed. Privacy is a major component in a living, breathing constitution rather than a fixed document. Yet privacy can hardly be grasped for any significant time frame since it is a relative legal concept rather than a more permanent version. This reality also leads to the unsettled and very unstable nature of Roe and its progeny.

Even despite these flaws, Roe posed some legal principles that are often swept under the rug that sometimes slows the process of liberalization and access up. For example,

> Roe recognized and acknowledged fetal life, development of the human person and the potentiality of life.
>
> Roe issued a proclamation that would vary depending on timing, guided by a trimester system that was woefully infantile on fetal medicine.
>
> Roe left unfettered choice in the first part of that trimester system.
>
> Roe allowed for some restrictions in the second part, but much would depend on fetal stage.
>
> Roe issued a conclusion that potential human life, viable life, the last part of the trimester system could be properly regulated, and even proscribed, as long as exceptions existed for the life of the mother. The issue of "health" less descript.
>
> Roe recognized the complexities inherent in the abortion decision, traced Western tradition, cited natural law thinkers like Aquinas, Plato and Aristotle in the matter.
>
> Roe always objected to the principle of Abortion on Demand.

From Roe forward, the court began to grapple with efforts to control or regulate abortion, commencing soon after the decision. This chapter traces some of the more pertinent decisions that impacted Roe. What can be said with clarity and certitude is that all of these decisions sought change in the abortion landscape; all of these decisions were legislative and statutory efforts to thwart Roe's general and sweeping application. Efforts since Roe have been to restrict, and in some cases these efforts being declared obstacles or undue burdens; others have been fully endorsed and approved by the Supreme Court. Some permissible examples are the following:

- Informed consent
- Educational materials
- 24-hour waiting period
- Recognition of viability
- Illegality of partial birth abortion unless medically necessary
- Alternatives to abortion information

In a way, the adoption of these qualifications to the abortion decision assures that abortion is never an unbridled right but a complete recognition, as Roe and every other abortion case have long recognized, that the state has a "legitimate interest in potential human life." Roe was unequivocally clear about that. On the other hand, many parts and precepts in Roe seem to dissipate in later abortion jurisprudence, as *Planned Parenthood v. Casey* opined, that since Roe courts have "undervalued the State's interest in potential life."[258]

Since the Roe doctrine was promulgated, the court has had to continuously revisit and give oversight to abortion policy and practice, something better left to the communities at the state level. As Justice Scalia argued over and over, this is a place we ought not be nor do we have any right to be.

What seems even more challenging for the Supreme Court is how it can avoid the role and place of natural law jurisprudence in nearly every abortion decision. It may seem quaint, but it is likely true that if the court adhered a bit more determinedly to natural law jurisprudence, the problem of abortion would likely never be a problem, legal or factual. For the natural law thinker, abortion cannot be justified under any circumstances unless the "life" of the mother is at stake. Abortion strikes at the very heart of natural law precepts and tenets. That observation is unavoidably and inescapably true. In abortion, the self-preservation instinct is simply annihilated. In abortion, potentiality can never be actuality—a thwarting of the natural order—the nature of being itself. In abortion, the natural instinct to procreate is defeated. In abortion the care of offspring, the love of children and the maternal inclination of the child bearer are all undermined. Finally, the act of abortion cannot be described as any form of human flourishing, human fulfillment, human attainment of an end or maintenance of life itself. While there are many, a plethora of arguments based on expediency, utility, feminism, social movements and individual conscience, abortion can never be justified under the theory of natural law.

Notes

1. *Roe v. Wade*, 410 U.S. 113 (1973).
2. See Mary Zeigler, "Beyond Backlash: Legal History, Polarization, and Roe v. Wade," *Washington & Lee Law Review*, 71, no. 2 (2014): 969.
3. Cass Sunstein, "Civil Rights Legislation in the 1990s: Three Civil Rights Fallacies," *California Law Review*, 79, no. 3 (1991): 766.
4. Ruth Bader Ginsburg, "Some Thoughts on Autonomy and Equality in Relation to Roe v. Wade," *North Carolina Law Review*, 63, no. 2 (1985): 381–83; Mary Ziegler, "The Possibility of Compromise: Anti-Abortion Moderates after Row v. Wade," *Chicago-Kent Law Review*, 87, no. 2 (2012): 572.
5. Richard Posner, *Law, Pragmatism, and Democracy* (Cambridge: Harvard University Press, 2003), 125
6. Ibid. 254.
7. Ziegler, "Beyond Backlash," 976.
8. Ginsburg, "Some Thoughts," 381–82.
9. See "Justice Scalia on Federalism and Separation of Powers: 2016 National Lawyers Convention," *Regent University Law Review*, 30, no. 1 (2017): 57.
10. See Aziza Ahmed, "Medical Evidence and Expertise in Abortion Jurisprudence," *American Journal of Law & Medicine*, 41, no. 1 (2015): 85.
11. Richard S. Myers, "Re-Reading Roe v. Wade," *Washington & Lee Law Review*, 1, no. 2 (2014): 1031.
12. Ibid., 1032.
13. Andrea Picciotti-Bayer, "Why Science Strengthens the Pro-Life Argument," *Real Clear Politics*, January 16, 2019, https://www.realclearpolitics.com/articles/2019/01/16/why_science_strengthens_the_pro-life_argument_139181.html.
14. Myers, "Re-Reading Roe," 1025–39.
15. See Ginsburg, "Some Thoughts"; Meredith Heagney, "Justice Ruth Bader Ginsburg Offers Critique of Roe v. Wade during Law School Visit," May 15, 2013, https://www.law.uchicago.edu/news/justice-ruth-bader-ginsburg-offers-critique-roe-v-wade-during-law-school-visit.
16. Yvonne Lindgren, "The Doctor Requirement: Griswold, Privacy, and At-Home Reproductive Care," *Constitutional Commentary*, 32, no. 2 (2017): 341–75.
17. *Roe v. Wade*, 150.
18. St. Thomas Aquinas, *The Summa Theologica*, trans. Fathers of the English Dominican Province, vol. 1 (New York: Benzinger, 1947), Q65, Art. 8, 1472; Ibid., Q118-119 I, 575–78; Ibid., Q90 et seq; Ibid., Q64, Art. 6, 1470; St. Thomas Aquinas, *Summa Contra Gentiles*, 2nd ed., trans. Vernon Bourke (Garden City: Hanover House, 1956; Notre Dame, IN: University of Notre Dame Press, 1975), 88–89; See also Thomas Andrew Simond, "Aquinas and Early Term Abortion," *Linacre Quarterly*, 61, no. 3 (August 1994): 10; John Haldane and Patrick Lee, "Aquinas on Human Ensoulment, Abortion and the Value of Life," *Philosophy*, 78, no. 4 (2003): 255–78.
19. See Colin Dwyer, "Norma McCorvey, Roe of Landmark Roe v. Wade Ruling on Abortion, Dies at 69," *The Two-Way: NPR*, February 18, 2017, at

https://www.npr.org/sections/thetwo-way/2017/02/18/515972447/norma-mccorvey-roe-of-landmark-roe-v-wade-ruling-on-abortion-dies-at-69.
20 See Norma McCorvey and Gary Thomas, *Won by Love: Norma McCorvey, Jane Roe of Roe V. Wade, Speaks Out for the Unborn as She Shares Her New Conviction for Life* (Nashville, TN: Thomas Nelson, 1998).
21 Amy Lai, "Beyond Overruling Roe v. Wade: David Hollenbach's Idea of Intellectual Solidarity and Two Women Scholars of the Catholic Social Thought Tradition," *Journal of Church and State*, 57, no. 4 (2014): 707, 715.
22 Mary Zeigler, "Women's Rights on the Right: The History and Stakes of Modern Pro-Life Feminism," *Berkeley Journal of Gender, Law and Justice*, 28, no. 2 (2013): 268.
23 Professor Mary Zeigler examines this neglect and how the academic sector utterly disregards the pro-life woman in "Women's Rights on the Right: The History and Stakes of Modern Pro-Life Feminism," *Berkeley Journal of Gender, Law and Justice*, 28, no. 2 (2013): 268; Reva B. Siegel, "The Right's Reasons: Constitutional Conflict and the Spread of Woman-Protective Pro-Life Argument," *Duke Law Journal*, 57, no. 6 (2008): 1641; Keith Cassidy, "The Right to Life Movement: Sources, Development, and Strategies," in *The Politics of Abortion and Birth Control in Historical Perspective*, ed., Donald Critchlow (University Park: Penn State University Press, 1996), 141, 144–47.
24 *Texas Penal Code*, Arts. 1191–1194, 1196, at 429–36 (1961).
25 *Roe v. Wade*, 410 U.S. 113, 114 (1973).
26 See the full discussion of Roe at 147–64.
27 Roe, 163–64.
28 Ibid., 163.
29 Ibid., 164.
30 *Griswold v. Connecticut*, 381 U.S. 479 (1965).
31 Roe, 176.
32 Ibid., 116.
33 Ibid.
34 Ibid.
35 Ibid., 171.
36 See Charles P. Nemeth, *A Comparative Analysis of Cicero and Aquinas: Nature and the Natural Law* (London: Bloomsbury, 2017).
37 Cicero, *De Re Publica and De Legibus*, trans. Clinton Walker Keyes (Cambridge: Harvard University Press, 1988), 389.
38 *Aquinas Theologica*, Benzinger, II-II, Q 94, Corpus.
39 Soranos, "Gynecology," in *Corpus Medicorum Graecorum* ed. J. Ilberg, 1.19.60 (London; Berlin, 1927).
40 John T. Noonan, Jr., "Abortion and the Catholic Church: A Summary History," *Natural Law Forum*, 12, no. 1 (1967): 87.
41 Ludwig Edelstein, *The Hippocratic Oath: Text, Translation, and Interpretation* (Baltimore, MD: Johns Hopkins Press, 1943), 3.
42 Noonan, "Abortion and the Catholic Church," 86.
43 Roe, 132.
44 Ibid., 131.
45 Lynn M. Morgan, "The Potentiality Principle from Aristotle to Abortion," *Current Anthropology*, 54, supp. 7 (2013): 15–25.
46 *Roe v. Wade*, 134.
47 Ibid., 133

48 Ibid., 134; see also Nemeth, *Cicero and Aquinas*, 137.
49 Nemeth, *Cicero and Aquinas*, 139; St. Thomas, *Summa*, I, Q. 79, Art. 8.
50 Roe, 134.
51 Roe, 136.
52 Roe, 138.
53 American Medical Association, *The Transactions of the American Medical Association* (Philadelphia: Collins, 1859), 75, 77; See also John Hart, "The American Medical Association: Former Defender of Unborn Babies," *Catholic Social Science Review*, 19 (2014): 287–94.
54 American Medical Association, "Proceedings of the House of Delegates," (1967): 40–51.
55 Roe, 178, n. 1.
56 Ibid. 142.
57 *Planned Parenthood v. Casey*, 505 U.S. 833 (1992).
58 See Ibid.; Jeffrey M. Shaman, "Justice Scalia and the Art of Rhetoric," *Constitutional Commentary*, 28, no. 2 (2012): 287–92.
59 Roe, 159.
60 Ibid.
61 Ibid., 153.
62 Ibid.
63 Ibid., 162–63.
64 Ibid., 164–65.
65 Ibid., 164.
66 Ibid., 164–65.
67 Ibid., 165.
68 Ibid., 156–57.
69 Ibid., 161.
70 Ibid.
71 Ibid., 162.
72 Ibid., 171.
73 *Doe v. Bolton*, 410 U.S. 179 (1973).
74 Chapter 26-12, Criminal Code of Georgia.
75 Doe, 189.
76 Ibid., 187.
77 Ibid., 217.
78 Ibid., 191–92.
79 Ibid., 212.
80 Ibid., 191.
81 Ibid., 186.
82 Ibid., 192.
83 Ibid., 221.
84 Ibid., 221.
85 Ibid., 221–22.
86 Ibid., 222.
87 *Harris v. McCrae*, 448 U.S. 297 (1980); *Maher v. Roe*, 432 U.S. 464 (1979).
88 *Planned Parenthood v. Danforth*, 428 U.S. 52 (1976).
89 *H. L. v. Matheson*, 450 U.S. 398 (1981); *City of Akron v. Akron Center for Reproductive Health*, 426 U.S. 416 (1983).

90 18 Pa. Cons. Stat. §3201 et seq. (1982).
91 *Thornburgh v. American College of Obstetricians and Gynecologists*, 476 U.S. 747, 749 (1986).
92 Ibid., 749.
93 Ibid., 759.
94 *Planned Parenthood of Central Missouri v. Danforth*, 428 U.S. 52, 444 (1976).
95 Danforth, 444.
96 Thornburgh, 765.
97 Ibid., 764.
98 18 Pa. Con. Stat. Ann. §3210(b) (1982).
99 Ibid., §3210(c).
100 Thornburgh, 768–69
101 Ibid., 772.
102 Ibid., 779.
103 Ibid., 783.
104 Ibid., 784.
105 Ibid., 808.
106 Ibid.
107 Ibid., 809.
108 Ibid., 813.
109 Ibid., 814.
110 Ibid., 761.
111 Ibid., 782.
112 Ibid., 783.
113 Ibid., 784.
114 Mo. Rev. Stat. §1.205.2 (1986).
115 Ibid., § 188.029.
116 *Webster v. Reproductive Health Systems*, 492 U.S. 538–539 (1989).
117 Roe, 164–65.
118 Webster, 515–16.
119 Ibid., 544–45.
120 Ibid., 494.
121 Ibid., 513.
122 Ibid., 516.
123 Ibid.
124 Ibid., 526.
125 Ibid., 528.
126 Ibid., 530.
127 Ibid., 544.
128 Ibid., 546.
129 Ibid., 548.
130 Aquinas, *Theologica*, Benzinger, I, Q 118–119, 575–78.
131 Ibid., Q90 et seq.
132 Webster, 569.
133 *Planned Parenthood of Southeastern Pennsylvania v. Casey*, 505 U.S. 833, 844 (1992).
134 See Mattei Ion Radu, "Incompatible Theories: Natural Law and Substantive Due Process," *Villanova Law Review*, 54, no. 2 (2009): 247, http://digitalcommons.law.villanova.edu/vlr/vol54/iss2/2.
135 *Planned Parenthood*, 841.

136 Michael Stokes Paulsen, "The Worst Constitutional Decision of All Time," *Notre Dame Law Review*, 78, no. 4 (2003): 995, 997, http://scholarship.law.nd.edu/ndlr/vol78/iss4/2.
137 Ibid., 983.
138 Ibid., 995.
139 Ibid.
140 Ibid.
141 Ibid., 996.
142 Ibid.
143 Ibid.
144 Ibid., 860.
145 See Niraj Thakker, "Undue Burden with a Bite: Shielding Reproductive Rights from the Jaws of Politics," *University of Florida Journal of Law & Public Policy*, 28, no. 3 (2017): 431–74.
146 431 U.S., 685.
147 *Eisenstadt v. Baird*, supra, 405 U.S., 453 (1972) (emphasis in original).
148 *Prince v. Massachusetts*, 321 U.S. 158, 166 (1944).
149 *Planned Parenthood*, 833.
150 Ibid., 852.
151 Ibid.
152 Ibid., 846.
153 Ibid., 836.
154 Ibid., 870.
155 Ibid., 876.
156 See *Thornburgh v. American College of Obstetricians and Gynecologists*, 476 U.S. 747 (1986).
157 18 Pa. Cons. Stat. Ann. §3205 (1990).
158 *Planned Parenthood*, 882.
159 Ibid.
160 Ibid., 885.
161 Ibid., 852.
162 18 Pa. Con. Stat. Ann. §3206(a)
163 *Planned Parenthood*, 1002.
164 Danforth, 428 U.S. 52 (1976).
165 *Planned Parenthood*, 971.
166 Ibid., 841.
167 Ibid., 895.
168 Ibid., 1000.
169 Ibid.
170 Ibid., 1002.
171 18 Pa. Con. Stat. Ann. 3209(a)
172 *Planned Parenthood*, 893.
173 Ibid.
174 Ibid., 897.
175 Ibid., 894.
176 Ibid., 898.
177 Ibid., 972.
178 Ibid., 838.
179 Ibid., 974.

180 Ibid., 975.
181 Ibid.
182 *Stenberg v. Carhart*, 530 U.S. 914, 959 (2000).
183 Ibid., 975.
184 Ibid., 924.
185 Ibid., 953.
186 Neb. Rev. Stat. Ann. § 28–328(1) (Supp. 1999).
187 Ibid., § 28–326(9).
188 Ibid.
189 Stenberg, 950.
190 Ibid., 927.
191 Ibid., 946
192 Neb. Stat. § 28–328(1).
193 Stenberg, 938.
194 Ibid., 939.
195 Ibid., 951.
196 Ibid., 918.
197 Ibid., 954.
198 Ibid., 953.
199 Ibid.
200 Ibid., 954.
201 Ibid., 956.
202 Ibid., 958.
203 Ibid.
204 Ibid.
205 Ibid., 958–59.
206 11 F. Supp. 2d 1099, 1106 (Neb. 1998).
207 Ibid., App. 58.
208 Stenberg, 960.
209 Ibid., 961.
210 Ibid., 962.
211 Ibid.
212 Ibid.
213 Ibid., 921.
214 Ibid., 924.
215 Ibid., 966.
216 Ibid., 979.
217 Ibid., 964.
218 Ibid., 979.
219 Ibid.
220 Ibid., 982.
221 Ibid., 983.
222 Ibid., 987–88.
223 Ibid., 991–92.
224 Ibid., 1006.
225 Ibid., 1007, H.R. 1833 Hearing 18, statement of Brenda Pratt Shafer.
226 Ibid., 1008.
227 Ibid., 1020.

228 H.R. Rep. No. 108–58, p.3 (2003).
229 *Gonzales v. Carhart*, 550 U.S. 124 (2007), majority slip op., 10.
230 18 USC §1531 (2000 ed., Supp. IV).
231 Gonzales, majority slip op., 17.
232 18 USC §1532 (b) (1) (A) (2003).
233 Ibid.
234 Ibid.
235 Ibid., §1531(b)(1)(A) (2000 ed., Supp. IV).
236 Ibid.
237 Gonzales, majority slip op., 22–23.
238 Ibid., 26.
239 Ibid.
240 Ibid.
241 Ibid., 28.
242 Ibid., 28.
243 Ibid., 29.
244 Ibid., 29.
245 Ibid., 29; See also *Planned Parenthood*.
246 Ibid., 29.
247 Ibid., 30.
248 Ibid., 33.
249 Ibid., 15.
250 *Planned Parenthood*, 897.
251 Ibid., 856.
252 Ibid.
253 Gonzales, Ginsburg dissent slip op., 4.
254 Ibid.
255 Ibid., 17.
256 Ibid.
257 Ibid., 12–13.
258 *Planned Parenthood*, 871.

Chapter 4

NATURAL LAW AND THE SUPREME COURT: SEXUALITY, SEXUAL ATTRACTION AND PROCREATION

Another clear-cut tenet of the natural law relates to sexual attraction. This drive, this inclination, to be attracted to the opposite gender is firmly rooted in natural law tradition and just as cemented in Western legal tradition until very, very recently. Since the time of the Romans and Greeks, the question of sexuality and proper attraction has been mulled over, and while there surely are historical variations, customs and habits slightly more tolerant than the natural law command, it is fair to argue that for most cultures, most societies, the question of sexual attraction has been largely settled—the self-evident opposite sexual attraction. For natural law thinkers, the observable world alone provides strong evidence for the inclination. Up until and including the early 2000s, the question of sexual orientation was not hotly debated—a fact quite obvious in the Supreme Court's *Bowers. v. Hardwick*[1] decision upholding the right of states to criminalize nonheterosexual behavior. Only in Justice Blackmun's Hardwick dissent do we see this dismissive attitude about history, tradition, custom and moral norms generally agreed for to so conclude represents an "obsessive focus in homosexual activity."[2] The comment here avoids historical and traditional reality in the judgment of sodomy for this nation's legal heritage, and indeed the West itself, has long challenged the acceptability of the behavior. Rather, Bowers upholds the natural law tradition when dealing with homosexuality. Even in its academic commentary, the court cited historical codifications that often employed harsh and even dramatically negative tone, such as "abomination" or an "act contrary to nature" or "grave error against the natural order." Chief Justice Burger, in a concurring opinion, appreciates this historical viewpoint and how Western jurisprudence has been long rooted in this prohibition.

Blackstone described "the infamous crime against nature" as an offense of "deeper malignity" than rape, a heinous act "the very mention of which is a disgrace to human nature," and "a crime not fit to be named."[3] The common law of England, including its prohibition of sodomy, became the received law of Georgia and the other colonies. In 1816, the Georgia legislature passed the statute at issue here, and that statute has been continuously in force in one form or another since that time. To hold that the act of homosexual sodomy is somehow protected as a fundamental right would be to cast aside millennia of moral teaching.[4]

In fact, a great deal of discourse involving consensual sodomy was quite naturalistic rather than moralistic—a type of biogenic inquiry into the suitability of conduct.[5] The Supreme Court often trends toward that sort of evaluation as well in its earlier examinations and then moves to intimacy and privacy arguments as more meaningful rationales for justification.

Tied to this analysis comes another natural law precept—the natural desire and inclination to procreate. Procreation is an essential building block for any nuclear family and if sexual attraction bore no relationship between the act and its ultimate end or purpose, namely procreation, it would only be a matter of time before extinction. Within these two principles lies an ethical thicket that has been intensely reviewed and debated in all corners of the republic.

While the court, over these last decades, expends less energy on the "attraction" component, it has not hesitated to consider legal and constitutional questions involving homosexual activity. The same court displays no willingness to consider the question of homosexual action with the reality that procreation cannot be achieved due to obvious biological restrictions. To argue that homosexual sexual activity can result in procreation is at best delusional magic. Thus, on two fronts, the traditional sexual attraction model and the procreative end of that sexual attraction, homosexuality will falter under natural law scrutiny.

The court's most recent decision since *Lawrence v. Texas*[6] hopes to defuse the debate and provide a "national" resolution, although as in abortion, the diverse viewpoints that exist on this subject matter make that a pipedream. For those standing fast to traditional moral evaluations are sure to suffer the slings and arrows for questioning the legitimacy of homosexual activity and the stinging rebukes as well as a hurl of labels and phobias for those adjudging otherwise. For most of Western tradition, any sexual attraction not based on a male–female construct was declared unlawful human activity and even labeled a form of deviancy.[7]

Nearly every state, throughout most of our national history, declared same-sex sodomy to be contrary to the law of nature—to be contrary to the law of God and to be contrary to better interests in family and children. These proscriptions were not imaginary but heartfelt and emphatically sincere and often the product of deeply held religious beliefs that were either based on scriptural evidence or magisterial teaching.

The US Supreme Court case load dealing with these troublesome questions was not as set in stone as most modern readers and interpreters would believe. In its own way, the process of reformulating once rock hard principles on the law of sodomy, sexual attraction of the same sex, same-sex marriage and other legal dynamics has taken its own good time. Depending upon your point of view, the process of change, acceptance and even outright tolerance did not happen overnight. Many might argue that change needed another forum—not the US Supreme Court but the legislative process reflecting the values, wishes and views of the population served. Of course, these arguments were made in and about Roe too. What can be said without much disagreement is that both lines of judicial determination have done little to foster peace and tranquility on a population so acutely divided on both issues—abortion and homosexuality.

Bowers v. Hardwick, 478 U.S. 186 (1986)

Earlier cases on the question of same-sex sexual attraction and corresponding sexual activity were cases of first instance and, in a way, cases that surprised the general population and the overall citizenry. In Hardwick, the court displays a natural hesitancy to substitute its judgment for the will of state legislatures. Here the court is dealing with a few questions, though the one most poignant for natural law analysis relates to consensual sodomy. The court is not dealing with a case of criminality in the form of forced activity but in its place dealing with willing players. The Georgia statute defines even consensual sodomy as criminal in and by design. The Georgia law stated in part:

(a) A person commits the offense of sodomy when he performs or submits to any sexual act involving the sex organs of one person and the mouth or anus of another.
(b) A person convicted of the offense of sodomy shall be punished by imprisonment for not less than one nor more than 20 years.[8]

The statute as defined and adopted during a fully legitimate Georgia legislative session, fully reflective of the will of the citizens of Georgia, is not a legislative anomaly but a common statutory construction for states dealing with this sexual activity. Instead, the statute mirrors the commonly shared view on homosexuality sodomy—a view with extraordinary longevity and general consensus in the many centuries leading up to the present case.

Chief Justice Burger, in a concurring opinion, harkens back to a long history of proscription of the consensual version of sodomy. He notes,

> The proscriptions against sodomy have very "ancient roots." Decisions of individuals relating to homosexual conduct have been subject to state intervention throughout the history of Western civilization. Condemnation of those practices is firmly rooted in Judeo-Christian moral and ethical standards. Homosexual sodomy was a capital crime under Roman law.[9,10]

During the English Reformation, when powers of the ecclesiastical courts were transferred to the king's courts, the first English statute criminalizing sodomy was passed.[11]

In sum, the Bower's case challenges the very core of "ancient roots" posed by Justice Burger—it makes every attempt to rattle the moral cage and shake out the status quo on a selected and well-defined behavior. Its reasoning, which upholds the right of a state and its people to deduce its unacceptability, yet simultaneously allowing another jurisdiction to reach the opposite conclusion, tries its very best to leave the court out of the substitution business—whereby what the people decide should be vanquished by the jurisprudential intelligentsia. In Bowers, the court rules that Georgia has every right to grab onto tradition, Judeo-Christian heritage and even the law of nature itself. When petitioners argue that consensual sodomy should be a "fundamental right" protected by the Constitution under privacy principles, the court cannot brook the chasm between what the Constitution says or not says and what consensual sodomy really means in terms of our own essence, essentiality and dignity as to natural rights. For the majority, the constitutional moorings for finding a fundamental right to engage in a particular sexual practice cannot withstand the weight of any constitutional challenge. The court displays no reticence when it states,

> Precedent aside, however, respondent would have us announce, as the Court of Appeals did, a fundamental right to engage in homosexual sodomy. This we are quite unwilling to do.[12]

Bowers: The law of nature and the natural law

An early feature of the Bowers decision resides in its naturalistic tendency and the complete recognition that Western jurisprudence has long considered the connectivity between natural and unnatural acts, the consistency and constancy of the nature and the natural order and how human agents can act in contravention to that order.[13] The majority court frequently references common law, the treatises of learned scholars like Blackstone and early cases in the republic that could never be typed as friendly to consensual sodomy.[14]

This resistance to sexually normalizing these behaviors was so significant that even heterosexual activity that dealt with oral and anal sexual activity was subsumed into the definition. The court cites a few examples of earlier statutes, like the predecessor law to the statute in question, which defined sodomy as "the carnal knowledge and connection against the order of nature, by man with man, or in the same unnatural manner with woman."[15] The court traces a full legislative history of consensual sodomy laws, which include the following highlights:

- Sodomy was a common law criminal offense.
- Sodomy was forbidden by the laws of the original 13 States.
- In 1868 all but 5 of the 37 States in the Union had criminal sodomy laws.
- Until 1961, all 50 States outlawed sodomy.
- Today, 24 States and the District of Columbia provide criminal penalties for sodomy in private and between consenting adults.

A great many of these statutory constructions targeted the concept of "unnaturalness" in the activity or how consensual sodomy can be properly construed as being in contravention to nature.[16]

The description posed by Virginia edifies the tie to the natural order, the connection to nature's law—even though a careful reading sees the definition as a bit more uncharitable than it should be. But here the gravity of the act connects to the naturalistic measure of the act itself. In natural law reasoning, one of the recurring variables utilized when weighing and evaluating human conduct is its consistency and compatibility with the natural order and the natural function. In this way, the judgment tends to be more biogenic than theological or philosophical. For example, is the human agent utilizing a bodily appendage, an orifice or body part for its intended natural function and purpose? Or does it make sense to measure the propriety of conduct based on whether its aim extends beyond simple pleasure, sensuality or passionate argument or might it be more sensible to discern the conduct's goodness or virtuousness in light of the end sought by acting in a particular way? These queries pose nothing all that inventive or new—for since Aristotle, the question of ethics and specific conduct inevitably weaves its way back to its proper end or goal. Is sexual activity exclusively about the sensual experience or is there something else involved? In natural law reasoning, sexual gratification, merely for its own sake, solely driven by pleasure or excessive hedonism will not be enough—for each sexual act has the potentiality to generate life, procreate and build a nuclear family. While the acts may be intimate and private, their implications extend beyond the act and actor alone. Frankly, the authorship of older sodomy laws, even the consensual versions, understood these arguments well. Thus, it is clear that the terms "unnatural" and "contrary to the law of nature" are much more than an invective or insult but a recognition that human activity need to reach its greatest flourishing and potentiality.

The majority opinion in Bowers understands that the historical realities of Western jurisprudence, the need and necessity for strong and sustained nuclear families generated by a procreative mentality and, finally, the consensus view that nature operates with great similarity shape our conceptions of a sexuality that advances both the individual and the collective. So holding does not intimate any animus toward the dignity and essential rights of every person, homosexual or heterosexual, nor would it be fair to not allow these arguments to be posed at all. Not everyone is going to agree and for a natural law thinker, the encounter with this form of sexual more is tough to reconcile. This difficulty, however, and this noted emphatically, is not in the person, the humanity thereto, rather in particular actions that appear contrary to the law of nature and the natural law.

Add to this the petitioner's argument that this behavior has a constitutional protectionism and the dilemma gets even more troublesome. For even if we assume the acts are contrary to nature and its laws, there is nothing that precludes a state or other governmental authority from disagreeing with that judgment. In fact, most jurisdictions do not have the slightest wish to wade into that territory. At the same time, assigning a constitutional right to a sexual act seems beyond the scope of both the judiciary and the Constitution itself. And the fact, the dissenters argue that the conduct was performed in the privacy of a home, does not make the constitutional application to a particular sexual behavior any more compelling. If courts have no business in the bedroom, then these same entities have no business assigning constitutional protections. And the privacy arguments falter even more dramatically, the court holds:

> And if respondent's submission is limited to the voluntary sexual conduct between consenting adults, it would be difficult, except by fiat, to limit the claimed right to homosexual conduct while leaving exposed to prosecution adultery, incest, and other sexual crimes even though they are committed in the home. We are unwilling to start down that road.[17]

The term "unnatural" has not fully disappeared from the criminal lexicon as is evident by a current Florida criminal statute that holds,

Unnatural and lascivious act.—A person who commits any unnatural and lascivious act with another person commits a misdemeanor of the second degree, punishable as provided in s.775.082 or s. 775.083.[18]

At the same time, it is undeniable that this type of naturalistic measure has fallen into statutory disfavor. And one can certainly argue that this shift in statutory description has lessened the severity of our view regarding behavior. While bestiality and necrophilia may still command the unnatural definition, homosexual behavior has surely shed the imagery. The relationship between biology, the natural order and accepted natural law principles seems to have lost its grip on this codification analysis. It may be perfectly correct to reach said conclusion, but like all things in the law, a radical shift that purges the principles may not be thoughtful enough or rational enough to fully support. Couple this with a general cultural reticence to invade and prosecute such activities, and the uniform hesitancy of our entire legal infrastructure to make this type of adjudication common in any sense, and the thrust is to make what was once "contra gravissima natura" into something far less serious or important as history once described. Clearly, violations of the law of nature, acts contrary to the natural order, as long as between consenting adults, take on a very different meaning in a society properly disposed toward tolerance and charity.[19]

In fact, the court's dissent, authored by Justice Blackmun, is pushing a new narrative—hoping to escape the harsh rhetoric of natural thinking, the tough condemnation of acts in contravention to what nature generally witnesses. He states,

> There can be no assumption that today's majority is "right" and the Amish and others like them are "wrong." A way of life that is odd or even erratic, but interferes with no rights or interests of others, is not to be condemned because it is different.[20]

To be sure being "different" connotes a benign inevitability in human conduct, as if one can never really expect its elimination nor even want that type of result.

From another vantage point, another argument may be plausible in nature and the natural order—that homosexual activity does exist in the animal kingdom—not a rule or universal principle but as a derivation or distinct difference in the natural order. Some creatures in nature can even switch their gender roles, can be bisexual, etc. However, equating the human person with the animal kingdom is neither a truly fair comparison nor necessarily edifying. For a natural law thinker, only the rational creature, in reason, can really discover the natural law. The rest of nature is instinctual or predisposed without any thought or comprehension. Yet, as Cicero so often weighed in his wonderful examination of the law of nature and the natural law, the cosmos itself is driven to meaning in every aspect of its operations.[21] Or, as in both Aristotle and Aquinas, every being in the natural world works toward its preservation and maintenance.[22] In other words, there is much that nature can teach us about how life unravels and plays out. And if nature has instructive differences—more than ever anticipated or fully understood—or if homosexual tendencies are ever discerned in the DNA chain, the natural world and the moral evaluation might be turned on its head. The arguments, in their best light, are far less condemnatory than "unnaturalness."

Bowers: Family, procreation and the natural law

The Bowers holding does not connect the idea of family, marriage and procreation with the conception of consensual sodomy. If not a case of apples and oranges, the majority never connected those dots as it had in numerous cases before—with affirmative conclusions in matters of birth control, the education of children and protection of the procreative power. This lack of joinder is not insignificant, for the majority deems sexual activity as something remarkably critical or constitutional for that matter. Forced sterilization and a denial of a parent to educate his or her child in a Catholic school are radically different cases.[23]

Sitting side by side, with consensual sodomy, the court appears almost bewildered by the comparison. On the one hand, the US Supreme Court has dealt with weighty questions regarding these fundamental rights, for example, procreation and care of offspring by educational school of choice, to name a few, and on the present hand, we encounter a constitutional protection to engage in particular sexual act. In the end, court's dilemma is all about consensual oral and anal sexuality between same-sex partners. In the context of graver questions, like sterilization, forced castration and compulsory public education over parochial education, the present rumination seems almost trivial.

The majority opinion emphatically rejects the comparison with these other fundamental rights when it remarks,

> No connection between family, marriage, or procreation, on the one hand, and homosexual activity, on the other, has been demonstrated, either by the Court of Appeals or by respondent. Moreover, any claim that these cases nevertheless stand for the proposition that any kind of

private sexual conduct between consenting adults is constitutionally insulated from state proscription is unsupportable.[24]

When the court reasons that consensual sodomy may be fundamental, its finding can find no legitimate rationale for this position and does not hesitate to label the argument utterly "unsupportable." This advocacy, the court decides, bears no "resemblance" to these other fundamental rights either under "liberty" or "due process constructions." Any plain reading of the Bowers majority quickly discovers a real hesitancy to go down this new path of sexual activity being constitutionally protected. The court cannot reconcile this new approach to fundamental rights as it declares,

> It is obvious to us that neither of these formulations would extend a fundamental right to homosexuals to engage in acts of consensual sodomy. ... Against this background, to claim that a right to engage in such conduct is "deeply rooted in this Nation's history and tradition" or "implicit in the concept of ordered liberty" is, at best, facetious.[25]

Seven of the court's members employ tough love to the arguments and critique without hesitation by labeling the plea "facetious" without "resemblance" to historic rulings on fundamental questions and an overall question left out of the constitutional realm and better resting at the state level. Just as compellingly, the court is not ready to disregard the moral traditions on a long-held determination regarding sexual activity nor willing to apply constitutional protections to sexual preferences. The court notices how tradition, history and civilizations have dealt with the question.

> To hold that the act of homosexual sodomy is somehow protected as a fundamental right would be to cast aside millennia of moral teaching.
> This is essentially not a question of personal "preferences," but rather of the legislative authority of the State. I find nothing in the Constitution depriving a State of the power to enact the statute challenged here.[26]

Within this framework, the Bowers majority is especially tolerant of those wishing to preserve the historic, heterosexual paradigm and perfectly willing to give deference to those that disagree with the alternative perspective. On the other hand, the court is just as amiable to allow state-by-state determinations of question, cognizant of state-by-state cultural differences on this and other questions involving personal morality and religious expression. Even the dissent by Justice Blackmun and Stevens accepts the theological dynamic, the influence of the greatest natural law thinker, Thomas Aquinas, although that recognition will not translate into authority for the dissenters.

> Society has every right to encourage its individual members to follow particular traditions in expressing affection for one another and in gratifying their personal desires. It, of course, may prohibit an individual from imposing his will on another to satisfy his own selfish interests. It also may prevent an individual from interfering with, or violating, a legally sanctioned and protected relationship, such as marriage. And it may explain the relative advantages and disadvantages of different forms of intimate expression. But when individual married couples are isolated from observation by others, the way in which they voluntarily choose to conduct their intimate relations is a matter for them—not the State—to decide.[27]

As for the idea that sexual practices have protection under the due process clause, the court is equally unimpressed—for these matters of intimate preference are not the stuff of procedural rights just as clearly these same preferences are subject to constitutional oversight. This is all the more obvious when the court knows its task is not to overturn a myriad of jurisdictions that conclude differently nor is it the proper power and function of any court to overturn an entire legislative process that thinks differently than the petitioners. The court holds,

> The law, however, is constantly based on notions of morality, and if all laws representing essentially moral choices are to be invalidated under the Due Process Clause, the courts will be very busy indeed. Even respondent makes no such claim, but insists that majority sentiments about the morality of homosexuality should be declared inadequate. We do not agree, and are unpersuaded that the sodomy laws of some 25 States should be invalidated on this basis.[28]

In the final analysis, Bowers upholds a variety of things: first, the power of legislative determination at the state level because of a lack of constitutional applicability either expressly or implicitly; second, a rejection of sexual acts as a rationale for due process rights; third, an affirmation that history and tradition in moral matters has some bearing on the court's deliberations and finally, a recognition that states have an interest in strengthening the traditional nuclear family, applying long-held and cherished moral norms for the common good and respecting the "natural order" argument—all of these relevant to natural law jurisprudence.

Romer v. Evans, 517 U.S. 620 (1996)

Despite the strong ruling from the court regarding the "constitutionalization" of gay or homosexual rights, the advocates for providing greater legal protections continued their efforts at alleviating any restrictions on said rights. While many states had already implemented widespread protections and reforms in matters involving housing, employment and association, lacking for many was a centralized measure that would guarantee selected rights—whether those rights be codified or constitutionalized. As advocacy continued to spread across various jurisdictions, arguments for nationalized legalization of homosexual conduct unsettled once-staid and very traditional perspectives on sexual norms. As a result, some states set up anticipatory restrictions—as to granting special rights or preferences based on sexual orientation. Other states simply rejected the classification or deduced that constitutional protections were unnecessary in the arena of sexual orientation given all other remedies already on the books in matters of housing, education and the like. In other words, the Colorado Amendment expressly announced that no special, preferential rights would be based on homosexual orientation. In a sense, the argument was that sexual orientation was always external to the human person, not essential to it in the same way race, creed or ethnicity might be, and as a result, it is incumbent upon the state to limit these classifications seeking constitutional protections. The Romer decision does precisely this by popular vote and plebiture—asking the state's citizens to approve a constitutional amendment that rejects legislative efforts to add "sexual orientation" as a discriminatory class. The amendment states in part,

> No Protected Status Based on Homosexual, Lesbian or Bisexual Orientation. Neither the State of Colorado, through any of its branches or departments, nor any of its agencies, political subdivisions, municipalities or school districts, shall enact, adopt or enforce any statute, regulation, ordinance or policy whereby homosexual, lesbian or bisexual orientation, conduct, practices or relationships shall constitute or otherwise be the basis of or entitle any person or class of persons to have or claim any minority status, quota preferences, protected status or claim of discrimination. This Section of the Constitution shall be in all respects self-executing.[29]

What the amendment primarily sought to do was prevent sexual orientation, whether it be bisexual, homosexual or heterosexual, from serving as a basis for a claim of discrimination in the same way race, creed or color might. The amendment passed the muster of Colorado voters. Even though the amendment expressly does not discriminate against any classification, the petitioners asserted its passage and implementation "infringed the fundamental right of gays and lesbians to participate in the political process."[30] Put another way, if the aggrieved parties claim that since they cannot be listed and classified as a discriminatory victim under the amendment, the tendency is to foster discrimination. The logic boggles dissenter Justice Scalia when he observes that the "amendment prohibits 'special treatment' of homosexuals, nothing more."[31] In his view, given the majority opinion, it is impossible to reconcile this reverse imagery of a constitutional right. Here no person is having any particular right violated under traditional civil rights laws and legislation. Here, the legislative gestalt of Colorado voters decides that it need not open up a new panorama of constitutional classifications. Here, the amendment imposes no burden or promotes any type or kind of discriminatory practice against homosexual persons. Yet, the majority construes the unwillingness to list, ad seriatim, the current discrimination laws in Colorado as evidence of discriminatory aim or purpose. Justice Scalia cannot reconcile the illogic:

> The central thesis of the Court's reasoning is that any group is denied equal protection when, to obtain advantage (or, presumably, to avoid disadvantage), it must have recourse to a more general and hence more difficult level of political decision making than others. The world has never heard of such a principle, which is why the Court's opinion is so long on emotive utterance and so short on relevant legal citation. And it seems to me most unlikely that any multilevel democracy can function under such a principle.[32]

The Romer majority makes plain that any effort to "keep off" the list of discriminatory classifications for the homosexual person is itself evidence of discriminatory intent. To be certain, Coloradans may or may not have had that wish but on the amendment's vote, it is clear that Coloradans supported the special preference exclusion. Their reasons may or may not have been prompted by a more traditional view of morality in these matters. Even if we assume that be the case, under natural law reasoning, a citizen may reach that conclusion and should be able to reach it depending upon a long-held moral posture.

Romer: Moral tradition, family and the natural law

Romer tends to be a far more procedural case than witnessed in *Bowers v. Hardwick*[33] where the court showed a great deal more inclination to tackle the moral parameters of homosexuality. In Romer, the court primarily focuses on the equal protection argument—that by refusing to allow a special classification for homosexuals and bisexuals, the state singles out these same groups for discriminatory practice. As noted by Justice Scalia, this argument is a stretch, for the most that could be said is the amendment merely indicates that the state of Colorado will not constitutionally remedy injustices based on sexual orientation. The majority calls this rationale "implausible."[34] On top of this, the state and the court impact nothing. Colorado's legislative process, in matters of housing, education, adoption or any other subject matter, will not tolerate discriminatory practices, although the majority seems to think these protections will evaporate if the Second Amendment is not struck down.[35] For Romer misapplies the protectionist standard by imputing a loss of rights when that same homosexual or bisexual citizen still has every right that every other citizen holds fast too. The rub here is that something more special is being advocated and demanded.

In so many ways, the Romer majority can only inferentially deduce that this omission from the list of constitutionally protected classes implies or imputes some discriminatory motive. Hence, the majority opines that it is essential that gays and lesbians be "enumerated" as a protected class.[36]

However, the court skirts peripherally natural law content by sheer avoidance in the majority view authored by Justice Kennedy and in direct application obvious in the dissenting opinion authored by Justice Scalia. Any party resisting or objecting to homosexuality, under these findings, is given a true secondary status—a view that promoters of this amendment manifest a hatred of the class posed as in need of protection not a well-reasoned moral determination based on natural law principles. Anyone who objects, Justice Kennedy curiously argues, displays the "inevitable inference" that is "born of animosity" toward that group.[37] Justice Scalia does not buy the inference when he holds that the court "has mistaken a Kulturkampf for a fit of spite."[38]

From the Scalia perspective, the Coloradans who enacted this amendment by popular vote and in the majority have every right to make these moral and legal judgments. And the wisdom of the plebiscite consistently reflects the court's 1986 Bowers decision, which kept the gate open to the criminalization of consensual sodomy. So, in one sense, it is perfectly proper to assign criminal definitions and penalties to consensual sodomy but on the other hand utterly discriminatory to not delineate gays and lesbians as part of protected constitutional class. Justice Scalia stingingly critiques the illogic,

> In holding that homosexuality cannot be singled out for disfavorable treatment, the Court contradicts a decision, unchallenged here, pronounced only 10 years ago, and places the prestige of this institution behind the proposition that opposition to homosexuality is as

reprehensible as racial or religious bias. Whether it is or not is precisely the cultural debate that gave rise to the Colorado constitutional amendment (and to the preferential laws against which the amendment was directed). Since the Constitution of the United States says nothing about this subject, it is left to be resolved by normal democratic means, including the democratic adoption of provisions in state constitutions.[39]

Scalia and the dissenting opinion never minces his disdain for those who will not permit any traditional moral examination of the behavior as if a contrary view can only be labeled conduct driven by hatred and bigotry. Coloradans and Americans, under Romer reasoning, are not permitted to hold firm to those moral conclusions, to those natural law traditions and tenets that have guided Western ethical tradition for thousands of years. In this moral thicket, citizens are not even permitted to democratically resolve a particular issue or dilemma and instead must bear the insults of an "elite class" that cannot fathom how anyone could possibly deduce otherwise.[40] The dissenting view cannot reconcile the intellectual inconsistency of this application, calling it "terminal silliness."[41] By denying special protection to a distinct class, the majority has perversely construed the denial as a violation of equal treatment when the special protection sought makes equal treatment a remote possibility.

In light of Bowers, the Romer decision is even more inconsistent with natural law tradition, moral continuity and the historic permissibility of making consensual sodomy a crime. From one vantagepoint, one can criminalize the behavior, while from another perch, one cannot exclude from a favored list the very same parties who might be prosecuted. The level of illogic does not escape the dissenting opinion when Justice Scalia states,

> In Bowers v. Hardwick, 478 U. S. 186 (1986), we held that the Constitution does not prohibit what virtually all States had done from the founding of the Republic until very recent years—making homosexual conduct a crime. That holding is unassailable, except by those who think that the Constitution changes to suit current fashions. But in any event it is a given in the present case: Respondents' briefs did not urge overruling Bowers, and at oral argument respondents' counsel expressly disavowed any intent to seek such overruling, Tr. of Oral Arg. 53. If it is constitutionally permissible for a State to make homosexual conduct criminal, surely it is constitutionally permissible for a State to enact other laws merely disfavoring homosexual conduct.[42]

Any effort to morally scrutinize behavior long held to be "unnatural" can only be driven by "animus" and "animosity toward homosexuality, as thought it has been established as un-American."[43] Romer provides no safe harbor for any thinker wishing to retain a semblance of the nation's moral heritage. In its place, the court force feeds and marches its readers from logic to mere insult. Scalia cannot believe his eyes as he rebukes this effort to strip all moral sanction or differentiation in the matter of homosexuality—even though Bowers is still the law of the land. This alleged "animus" or hatred cannot be presumed to be motivated by a disdain for the dignity of every human person but might properly be an objection to particular conduct. Scalia targets this faulty line of reasoning,

> Surely that is the only sort of "animus" at issue here: moral disapproval of homosexual conduct, the same sort of moral disapproval that produced the centuries-old criminal laws that we held constitutional in Bowers. The Colorado amendment does not, to speak entirely precisely, prohibit giving favored status to people who are homosexuals; they can be favored for many reasons-for example, because they are senior citizens or members of racial minorities. But it prohibits giving them favored status because of their homosexual conduct—that is, it prohibits favored status for homosexuality.[44]

Scalia takes it even further when he declares that the majority accuses the Colorado population of "hate-filled gay-bashing," which he terms "so false as to be comical."[45] Coloradans, like every American citizen, every free being, have the right to retain that "homosexuality is morally wrong and socially harmful."[46] Of course for those having no objections to these behaviors, this "alternative life style,"[47] the court finds a perfect realm and aura of protection, of tolerance and sage-like wisdom. For those who wish to retain the "social disapprobation of homosexuality," the court reserves its special animus. Instead of the vaunted "diversity of opinions" so often touted in a pluralistic society, the court supplants divergent viewpoints with a more dictatorial model that enforces a uniform and unrelenting view of the behavior. The court holds that the democratic processes be damned for such unenlightened Cretans—the citizens of Colorado cannot permissibly think this particular way. Its majoritarian view cannot and will not be accepted despite its inherent democratic process and any effort to "preserve its view of sexual morality statewide" will be considered utterly invalid.[48]

In the end, Romer lacks legal regularity for its pronouncements are hardly legal and more firmly rooted in social movements and political pressure—something generally at odds with natural law thinking. In natural law, the advocate discerns the suitability of human behavior based on consistency with our natural dispositions, predilections and inclinations. Natural law also gauges sexuality in light of its ends or goals—not exclusively grounded in pleasure but always open to the procreative act. In homosexuality, the act of anal or oral sex between same-sex couples cannot achieve those ends. And it is perfectly right, suitable and indeed very lawful for one to challenge the conduct on many levels—note the conduct not the dignity of that person. However, Romer has no room for such thinking—it cannot bring itself to recognize the legitimacy of any disagreement even in the case of a majority population that agrees to disagree with this majority opinion. The arguments here are not about moral propriety, naturalness and even moral tradition but something else tethered to a movement or political interest group. And that group can change by the hour for today's clamor for homosexual righteousness will be tomorrow's fervent advocacy for polygamy. And why not, asked Justice Scalia.

> Polygamists, and those who have a polygamous "orientation," have been "singled out" by these provisions for much more severe treatment than merely denial of favored status; and that treatment can only be changed by achieving amendment of the state constitutions. The Court's disposition today suggests that these provisions are unconstitutional, and that polygamy must be permitted in these States on a state-legislated, or perhaps even local option, basis—unless, of course, polygamists for some reason have fewer constitutional rights than homosexuals.[49]

Romer's dissent relies heavily upon the polygamy comparison for moral objections to polygamy, especially as to family and offspring, part of the natural law first principles, are equally relevant to the arguments on homosexuality. With no express rights to homosexual activity, no lineage or legal history supporting the practice, a continuum of time and states banning the activity since the founding of the republic and aligned arguments regarding the natural order and the natural law, it is difficult to see how it is all swept away in an instant. In this framework, there is nothing to hinder the advancement of polygamy, nor incest, nor bestiality, nor pedophilia—absolutely nothing. How could there be when rights are reconciled by social forces and pressure groups substituting their judgments for the collective and the common good and even more compellingly, a complete disregard for our constitutional law heritage. The court's own *Murphy v. Ramsey*[50] decision, outlawing polygamy, from 1885, should soon be on the chopping block—and especially so when you consider its natural law language.

> [C]ertainly no legislation can be supposed more wholesome and necessary in the founding of a free, self-governing commonwealth, fit to take rank as one of the co-ordinate States of the Union, than that which

seeks to establish it on the basis of the idea of the family, as consisting in and springing from the union for life of one man and one woman in the holy estate of matrimony; the sure foundation of all that is stable and noble in our civilization; the best guaranty of that reverent morality which is the source of all beneficent progress in social and political improvement.[51]

In the next few years, Romer's irrationality will become even more obvious and at the same time, Romer's efforts at social justice will win the day as the court overturns Bowers and replaces it with a decision that will be even more difficult to reconcile, *Lawrence v. Texas*.[52]

Boy Scouts of America v. Dale, 530 U.S. 640 (2000)

While the majority of constitutional advocacy on homosexual rights have centered on the Fourteenth Amendment's equal protection claims, or substantive due process claims, the Dale decision represents a legal challenge based on First Amendment principles, particularly the right of free expression and free association. In Dale, the Boy Scouts of America's (BSA's) policy asserting that homosexuality was a disqualifier for being appointed a leader, such as Assistant Scoutmaster, of any individual who was open and communicative of being gay was considered. In this case, the court considered a long-time scout who had hoped to continue as a leader. James Dale's membership in the BSA was revoked when it became common knowledge that he was a gay activist at Rutgers University. In reaction, Dale filed a legal complaint in the New Jersey Superior Court alleging that the BSA abridged his rights in light of the Public Accommodation Law that forbade usage of any public facility if the organization seeking to use discriminated against any party based on "sexual orientation."[53] The law reads in part:

> All persons shall have the opportunity to obtain employment, and to obtain all the accommodations, advantages, facilities, and privileges of any place of public accommodation, publicly assisted housing accommodation, and other real property without discrimination because of race, creed, color, national origin, ancestry, age, marital status, affectional or sexual orientation, familial status, or sex, subject only to conditions and limitations applicable alike to all persons. This opportunity is recognized as and declared to be a civil right.[54]

At the lower courts of New Jersey, the BSA fared very favorably due to two factors: first, that the BSA was a private entity naturally exempt from the statute's coverage; and second, that holding to their moral conclusion regarding homosexuality was perfectly permissible under the First Amendment right of free expression.[55]

By the time the case weaves its way through the higher courts of New Jersey and to the US Supreme Court, the picture becomes very muddled. The "private nature" of this BSA as an institution appears to have lost its exemption punch and for no good reason since the statute expressly, explicitly delineates its inapplicability to "distinctly private" entities.[56] And the right to correlate moral values and reasoning—so imbued in the BSA mission and formula—to a rejection of homosexual behavior is now considered completely irrelevant and lacking all ethical and moral probity. Here, the Dale majority encounters a lower court decision that simply disregards the express language of a legitimate legal provision and, at the same time, rejects the right to associate and express particular views that do not subsume the legitimacy of homosexuality. It is a presumptuous and even pompous result displaying little, if any, regard for a contrary viewpoint on a troublesome moral and ethical question that lacks universal agreement. For natural law jurisprudence, the Dale Court tackles a specific application in how these tenets and precepts play out in human operations. Dale confronts two sides of an issue—those that find homosexuality normative and as healthy as heterosexuality and those that find the behavior inconsistent with natural operations and in opposition to what the natural order appears to dictate. In fact, the Dale Court tries to reconcile the quandary by blending the free expression—First Amendment right—with the traditional and historic mission of the BSA—which trains and molds young men in order that these same people might grow and evolve in accordance with a particular code. Not surprisingly, the court even cites both the scout oath and the scout law:

Scout Oath
On my honor I will do my best
To do my duty to God and my country
and to obey the Scout Law;
To help other people at all times;
To keep myself physically strong,
mentally awake, and morally straight.
Scout Law
A Scout is:
Trustworthy   Obedient
Loyal   Cheerful
Helpful   Thrifty
Friendly   Brave

Courteous   Clean
Kind   Reverent.[57]

In essence, the BSA promulgates its programs and training by forging a way of life, a way of thought and belief—to "instill values in young people."[58] That oath and that law hope to provide a "positive moral code for living" and to assure "morally straight" and "clean" citizens who benefit from the Scouting habituation. Whether homosexuality acts in opposition is a heady and difficult issue for the majority court, but in the spirit of free speech and free association, and whether one agrees or not, the BSA should have the right to conclude the inconsistency of homosexuality with its own code of living. On the other hand, the BSA as an organization, or its members by vote or agreement, may expand, alter or redefine its traditional definition. As a private entity, it has every right to move in that direction. So for some in favor of the change, sexuality is not central to the matter of being "morally straight," and the question of morality deals more with integrity, honesty and living in a virtuous direction regardless of sexual orientation. Indeed, scouting has altered its own policies on these matters and now considers the definition more expansively. Whether or not this liberalization is consistent with the traditional meaning accorded moral straightness is a matter better left to the organization than by judicial fiat.

Boy Scouts v. Dale: *Tradition, natural order and the natural law*

While the Dale decision lacks express references to the natural law, there is little doubt that the debate concerning homosexuality's consistency with the nature and natural acts courses its way through the opinion. The fact that the court gives weight to the "morally straight" portion of the scout oath and the "clean" category of the law attests to this tendency. Of course, people of good faith and good will can take a completely opposite position but at this time, and at this place, the homosexual lifestyle was held by the BSA to be "inconsistent" with the oath and law.[59] Nor, the court cites, does the BSA hold that homosexuals are suitable "role models" for its Scouting members.[60]

While the dissenting opinion expends far greater energy laying out the evidentiary proof of Scouting's official rejection of the homosexual lifestyle, the majority accepts that view as equally legitimate to those who hold fast to historic evaluation and moral reasoning regarding the practice. To force the BSA to adopt a position contrary to the entity's mission and moral perspective is to abridge a belief system that the BSA has long held. Throughout its history, the BSA has held firm on this finding. What is sought, however by the petitioner, is the condemnation of this traditional position, its eradication and purging under a public accommodations law. To force the question, the majority holds, is to change what the BSA stands for and impose a series of beliefs it cannot brook. The court remarks,

> Dale's presence in the Boy Scouts would, at the very least, force the organization to send a message, both to the youth members and the world, that the Boy Scouts accepts homosexual conduct as a legitimate form of behavior.[61]

Believing in the traditional, natural order analysis regarding sexual behavior, in any form for that matter, for an institution long focused on those traditional values, would become discriminatory if the court sided with Dale. Any credence given such beliefs would be simply crushed by the insistent demand that every person and every entity must agree with a particular behavior or else. The majority's tent is far bigger than the appellant who wish to push out the traditionalist—the moral agent who finds objection in homosexuality. The court declares,

> Here, we have found that the Boy Scouts believes that homosexual conduct is inconsistent with the values it seeks to instill in its youth members; it will not "promote homosexual conduct as a legitimate form of behavior.[62]

For the majority opinion, the traditional, historic perspective remains equally valid to the contrary view. When the BSA espouses that being "morally straight" is a requirement of its members, it proclaims that certain conduct is simply not as straight as other conduct. The whole panorama of nature and the natural order encompasses the notion of moral straightness. The same could be said of clean and cleanliness—ideas that will vary to be sure but the history of scouting indicates its zeal for purity of thought and deed. In historic terms and traditional definition, "unnatural" acts fail to qualify under the cleanliness standard. While this rationale may seem harsh and even uncharitable, that essence of free speech is not that everyone likes the alternative view or the alternative lifestyle for free speech encompasses even that which we may or may not find distasteful. Justice Stevens's dissenting opinion is not convinced there is any correlation between these concepts and homosexuality for "it is plain as the light of day that neither one of these principles—"morally straight" and "clean" says the slightest thing about homosexuality."[63]

The majority court displays a proper balance when it comments,

> The presence of an avowed homosexual and gay rights activist in an assistant scoutmaster's uniform sends a distinctly different message

from the presence of a heterosexual assistant scoutmaster who is on record as disagreeing with Boy Scouts policy. The Boy Scouts has a First Amendment right to choose to send one message but not the other. The fact that the organization does not trumpet its views from the housetops, or that it tolerates dissent within its ranks, does not mean that its views receive no First Amendment protection.[64]

Put another way, the majority view, as crafted by Justice Rehnquist, properly tolerates a diversity of viewpoints under First Amendment principles. Free speech rights are granted not because all agree but precisely because contrary views roam freely in the American experience. The court never deals with the moral propriety of homosexuality, although it easily and readily accepts that the long-standing prohibition of homosexuality in naturalistic and natural law thinking is just as defensible as the contrary conclusion. So much of the contemporary debate on troublesome ethical and moral difficulties tend to be muted due to political correctness and incessant litigation and victimization. This climate is highly corrosive and ruinous to the true nature of free speech. To hold otherwise "compels" the result rather than engages the difference. Justice Rehnquist finalizes the issues by noting,

> We are not, as we must not be, guided by our views of whether the Boy Scouts' teachings with respect to homosexual conduct are right or wrong; public or judicial disapproval of a tenet of an organization's expression does not justify the State's effort to compel the organization to accept members where such acceptance would derogate from the organization's expressive message.[65]

For the dissenting opinion, this tendency to hold dearly to historical definitions regarding homosexuality and the history and philosophy of the BSA appears disjointed. Justice Stevens cannot discover how this long-standing reticence to fully legitimize homosexuality in the world of the BSA makes any sense at all. Amazingly he deduces,

> Whatever values BSA seeks to instill in Scouts, the idea that homosexuality is not "appropriate" appears entirely unconnected to, and is mentioned nowhere in, the myriad of publicly declared values and creeds of the BSA. That idea does not appear to be among any of the principles actually taught to Scouts.[66]

The imaginative dissent of Justice Stevens boldly goes to the outer reaches of the indiscernible when it finds that nothing proves or disproves the BSA's institutional rejection of homosexuality in the shaping of its member. Nothing in the law, the oath, the handbook and the leader's guide expressly condemns or forbids the practice. Justice Stevens selectively forgets so many authorities and BSA sources when he states,

> Moreover, there is simply no evidence that BSA otherwise teaches anything in this area, or that it instructs Scouts on matters involving homosexuality in ways not conveyed in the Boy Scout or Scoutmaster Handbooks. In short, Boy Scouts of America is simply silent on homosexuality. There is no shared goal or collective effort to foster a belief about homosexuality at all—let alone one that is significantly burdened by admitting homosexuals.[67]

After this curious view, Justice Stevens returns to his only remaining argument that hate and phobia drive the decision to restrict members in the BSA. Because "homosexuals are simply so different from the rest of society, that their presence alone—unlike any other individual's—should be singled out for special First Amendment protections."[68] No matter which way the court decides, the fundamental question is whether or not a conclusion that certain sexual activity is outside the boundaries of scouting's moral straightness can be defensible in a constitutional sense. Here the court indicates this be a proper finding. On the other hand, the BSA is perfectly free, as a private entity, to amend its operational policies and the scout oath itself—something it eventually implements.

None of these dissenting arguments clarify or resolve the effort to squelch or restrict free speech in this cumbersome area of law and ethics. Instead, arguments like these impute some sort of malicious intent and invite personal critiques based on moral reasoning that has had a permanency in Western jurisprudence. Four thousand years of moral philosophy and ethical tradition cannot be so easily swept into the dustbin of history. For in natural law analysis, these millennia have edified that truth or falsity of human conduct provided an extraordinary opportunity to see how nature unfolds and operates and allowed us to discover a consistency in human operations.

Lawrence v. Texas, 539 U.S. 558 (2003)

In less than a decade after Bowers, the court will reverse its own precedent in *Bowers v. Hardwick*—an astonishing fact given the personal preferences.[69] The case will never be but more aptly described as a shift of the court because there has been a partial shift in sentiment regarding homosexual rights. *Lawrence v. Texas* condemns its own lineage almost shamelessly. The court cannot envision how it could have been as unenlightened as it was in Bowers when it remarks,

> That statement, we now conclude, discloses the Court's own failure to appreciate the extent of the liberty at stake. To say that the issue in Bowers was simply the right to engage in certain sexual conduct demeans the claim the individual put forward, just as it would demean a married couple were it to be said marriage is simply about the right to have sexual intercourse.[70]

As in Bowers, the court considered a criminal statute that criminalized consensual sodomy. The provision states in part:
The statute defines "deviate sexual intercourse" as follows:

(A) any contact between any part of the genitals of one person and the mouth or anus of another person; or
(B) the penetration of the genitals or the anus of another person with an object.[71]

And with a mighty cutting down of its own logic in Bowers, the Lawrence Court will no longer brook the criminalization of such personal, intimate, and private sexual activity strangely restricted to the "home." For such control is an attack against the amorphous "liberty" dogma that started its twisted history in *Griswold v. Connecticut.*[72]

Liberty, Justice Kennedy poetically and indeterminately writes, controls the legal reasoning from top to bottom in this decision. Parts of the descriptive text are almost incapable of jurisprudential measure such as: "Liberty presumes an autonomy of self that includes freedom of thought, belief, expression, and certain intimate conduct. The instant case involves liberty of the person both in its spatial and more transcendent dimensions."[73]

Aside from residing in a "spatial and transcendent" dimension, the majority opinion fails to even expressly, at least in legal terminology or nomenclature, deny the Bower's finding that consensual sodomy lacks the mettle to be a fundamental right under our Constitution. However, this omission, Justice Scalia argues, "leaves strangely untouched its legal conclusion"[74] regarding the fundamental right claim replacing it with the unrestrained and noncorralable "exercise of their liberty."[75] In liberty, literally anything and any argument may find a suitable home and that is precisely what Lawrence relies upon. Despite the long-standing, jurisprudential decision of most American jurisdictions to outlaw the practice, and despite the fact that the democratic process reserved to the states can and does often make moral decisions that may vary state by state, and despite the fact that this same court can accept some controls in matters involving polygamy and physician-assisted suicide, the Lawrence majority chooses to rest in the nondescript and often imprecise world of liberty as a basis. It is not only the majority's decision to sweep aside generations and millennia of moral determinations by a citizenry that feels strongly enough to legislate against these practices but as Scalia's "imperial judiciary" so prone to do, substitute its judgment for the democratic process. Incredibly, the majority opinion of Justice Kennedy posits that consensual sodomy laws had very little to do with an animus or rejection of homosexuality and more to do with the prohibition of "nonprocreative sexual activity more generally."[76] In other words, the history of Western jurisprudence has misconstrued on the matter of homosexual behavior and the need for tolerance. The fact that most of American and Western jurisprudential history manifests a tendency to restrict rather than permit homosexual behavior is largely a misunderstanding and a view that Justice Kennedy claims is "overstated."[77]

The dissent by Justice Scalia and Thomas exhibits complete bewilderment at how history has been refashioned in almost Orwellian terms and how lacking in defensible legal argument the majority opinion appears. In the end, the Lawrence decision to overrule a precedent is grounded in nothing more than social mores and political pressure.

> Today's opinion is the product of a Court, which is the product of a law-profession culture, that has largely signed on to the so-called homosexual agenda, by which I mean the agenda promoted by some homosexual activists directed at eliminating the moral opprobrium that has traditionally attached to homosexual conduct. It is clear from this that the court has taken sides in the culture war, departing from its role of assuring, as neutral observer, that the democratic rules of engagement are observed.[78]

Lawrence v. Texas: *Nature, moral tradition, procreation and the natural law*

Throughout the Lawrence decision, natural law and law of nature issues crop up periodically. Of common occurrence will be the discussion of how history has played out in this controversy, how states have dealt with the behavior in the past and how intricately bound together are a common morality and the propriety of this type of sexual conduct. Both the majority and dissenting opinions often discuss the past, the legacy and lineage of consensual sodomy laws. Begrudgingly, even the majority opinion accepts that most of our history have imposed restrictions on the behavior. The "condemnation" of the behavior, the majority indicates, is the result of many forces including "religious beliefs, conceptions of right and acceptable behavior, and respect for the traditional family."[79] The majority holds that despite this long-standing tradition and the "profound and deep convictions accepted as ethical and moral principles,"[80] these views are to be fully discounted. At the same time, the court bandies about the term "fundamental liberty" while simultaneously being dismissive of history and tradition. Fundamental rights, the court has often announced, must be "privileges long recognized at common law."[81] Fundamental rights are those deeply embedded in our national heritage and just as "deeply rooted in this Nation's history and tradition."[82]

Under the mantle of "liberty," the idea that intimate, private sexual behavior qualifies as a liberty variable, those traditions are no longer valuable. Employing "immoral and unacceptable" descriptors—as a rational basis for the regulation of behavior—is no longer permissible under this ruling.[83] Justice Scalia's dissent makes this point emphatically:

> State laws against bigamy, same-sex marriage, adult incest, prostitution, masturbation, adultery, fornication, bestiality, and obscenity are likewise sustainable only in light of Bowers' validation of laws based on moral choices. Every single one of these laws is called into question by today's decision; the Court makes no effort to cabin the scope of its decision to exclude them from its holding.[84]

Today, the Lawrence Court sweeps away that tradition without much law or regulatory sophistication and has the unjustifiable boldness to proclaim a lack of a "long-standing history" that forbade or regulated consensual sodomy.[85]

Instead of tradition, the reader of Lawrence is treated to something far more political, as if, as Justice Scalia observes, the court need rule as the "mob" demands.[86] Instead of a natural law tradition, a continuity between our common law principles and the legions of statutory constructions that define homosexuality in criminal, naturalistic contexts, the majority view minimizes the role of history and finds only the contemporary world relevant to its analysis. The court boldly so announces,

> In all events we think that our laws and traditions in the past half century are of most relevance here. These references show an emerging awareness that liberty gives substantial protection to adult persons in deciding how to conduct their private lives in matters pertaining to sex.[87]

It is difficult to fully appreciate the dismissive tone of the court, as if the past could not edify the present—could not aid in any moral determination due to its lack of "relevance." In place of a natural law tradition, the court poses a relativity barometer where the moral propriety of any law could now be measured by what it calls the "emerging recognition" standard. So obtuse is this legal posture that the evaluator shall never be able to grasp the point of emergence or the locus of recognition.[88] Not even utilitarianism grasps at straws like these replacements. To buttress the majority's arguments, the court poses authorities that are equally modern and equally separated from our legal and natural law tradition when it references the European Convention on Human Rights and the member countries, all 45 of the European Commission having the greater insight and tolerance to end these onerous laws of discrimination.[89]

Reliance upon the decisions of the European Commission on Human Rights is just as troubling since that forum lacks any precedential authority or legal influence in matters on the Supreme Court's docket.[90] Yet, this legal meandering is really all the majority authors can depend upon since the American states have largely and historically been free to fashion laws for their constituencies. Federalism appears to halt the advance of "movement" demanding change, so the Europeans provide extraneous proof of how unenlightened the United States has long been. The court says this explicitly when it references Bowers being "rejected elsewhere."[91]

Not to be outdone in its zeal for modern resolutions for age-old ethical problems, the court, after citing the natural protection to any citizen, coincidentally natural law rights, in matters involving "marriage, procreation, contraception, family relationships, child rearing and education,"[92] erects another nondescript and indeterminable standard—the "autonomy of the human person"[93] principle. Justice O'Connor approaches the dilemma by simply asserting that "moral disapproval of a group simply cannot be a legitimate governmental interest"[94]—a proposition so preposterous as to make formal condemnation of any group, whether it be the North American Man/Boy Love Association (NAMBLA) or the Rene Guyon Society, that promotes incest, both protected entities under this specious principle enunciated by the court.

The majority view seems unable to fashion or shape its reasoning and rationale on any well-accepted legal doctrine or principles. It surely cannot claim explicit support in express constitutional documents. Just as assuredly, it is incapable of making an external sexual activity, in the form of consensual sodomy, into some sort of inherent quality involving race, creed or color. Making consensual sodomy a "fundamental" right can never be defended under historic and even contemporary constitutional principles. Rather than resolving the conflict with legal principles that form part of our constitutional landscape, interpreters are subjected to subjective principles incapable of definition. What is the "emerging recognition?" How does the court define "autonomy of the human person?" How can a right, constitutional or otherwise, be based on one's "concept of existence?" By contrast, the natural law tradition provides a meaningful and calculable measure for moral evaluation. Does the behavior under scrutiny reflect the potentiality for human procreation? Does this same conduct mirror the natural inclination for sexual attraction? Is the traditional nuclear family upheld or uplifted by approving these sexual arrangements? In his dissent, Justice Scalia offers up a poignant critique:

> I have never heard of a law that attempted to restrict one's "right to define" certain concepts; and if the passage calls into question the government's power to regulate actions based on one's self-defined "concept of existence, etc.," it is the passage that ate the rule of law.[95]

For the dissenters, the path to overruling its own precedent in *Bowers v. Hardwick*—a case Scalia terms "utterly unassailable"[96]—could not be a logical one. For Bowers properly enunciated a legal position that any fundamental constitutional right had to be based on more than the privacy of one's home or some rule of intimacy. Bowers correctly held that the decision to criminalize consensual sodomy was properly left to the state legislatures— not to an imperial court that imposed its value judgments on the world at large. As Scalia remarks, "Constitutional rights do not spring into existence because some States choose to lessen or eliminate criminal sanctions on certain behaviors."[97] The nebulous and horribly amorphous pronouncement by the majority on "emerging recognition" and "emerging appreciation" for new and novel constitutional rights based on sexual behavior is "so out of accord with our jurisprudence—indeed with the jurisprudence of any society we know."[98]

Obergefell v. Hodges, 135 S.Ct. 2071 (2015)

It was only a matter of time before the Supreme Court would encounter more particularized challenges based on sexual orientation and homosexuality. Once divergent viewpoints had been eradicated by an imperial decision that replaced and vanquished the legislative process so part of federalism, courts could expect an array of challenges based upon equal protection and discriminatory rationales. Justice Scalia labeled the redefinition as "Judicial Putsch" and commented,

> And to allow the policy question of same-sex marriage to be considered and resolved by a select, patrician, highly unrepresentative panel of nine is to violate a principle even more fundamental than no taxation without representation: no social transformation without representation.[99]

The majority makes no attempt to hide their aggressive involvement in the legislative process by using the indiscernible argument that being homosexual and wanting to marry is a "fundamental right." Justice Robert's dissent properly characterizes the decision as an "act of will, not legal judgment" and reminds his colleagues that the court is not a "legislature."[100]

Showing the court's impatience for fast-tracking the move to alter the traditional vision of marriage, Justice Kennedy boldly asserts,

> The dynamic of our constitutional system is that individuals need not await legislative action before asserting a fundamental right. The Nation's courts are open to injured individuals who come to them to vindicate their own direct, personal stake in our basic charter. An individual can invoke a right to constitutional protection when he or she is harmed, even if the broader public disagrees and even if the legislature refuses to act.[101]

On top of this, the majority dispenses with the legislative process while simultaneously claiming it can wait no longer to remedy this vast injustice—forgetting about the majority of states that already legislated on the topic—but not in the direction the court thought wise. Then, too, the court sounds tolerant with those who disagree with its judgment, especially if that view is grounded in "religious conviction,"[102] although that type of disagreement is disagreeable to this court and has to be dismissed.

What history and tradition enunciate on the question has no relevance; what law and jurisprudential standards have applied to domestic relations, which include marriage, no longer have meaning and as the dissenters appreciate more than the majority opinion, that moral view, that notion that some things may or may not be acceptable for some, a few or the many, simply does not matter. For it is "hubris" of sage like judges who know better than the populace.[103]

The concept of traditional marriage held the nation captive for nearly a decade as advocates for same-sex marriage challenged their inability to marry as heterosexual couples have done so for millennia. The dissenters properly advise that this definition has spanned "all those millennia, across all civilizations, 'marriage' referred to only one relationship: the union of a man and woman."[104]

Even less than rigorous defenders of natural law jurisprudence, like former presidents Obama and Clinton had announced their firm and resolute opposition to the idea as late as 2011. Marriage, they and others argued, has long been defined in a certain way with certain parties and no evidence from either history or tradition, law or cultural mores, and surely public opinion would support that claim for redefinition. Indeed, President Clinton signed into law the Defense of Marriage Act (DOMA) that essentially forbade a redefinition declaring that marriage was and is "only a legal union between one man and one woman as husband and wife."[105]

The majority's opinion acknowledges this conclusion be long-standing and without much debate when it states in the first pages of the opinion, "It is fair and necessary to say these references were based on the understanding that marriage is a union between two persons of the opposite sex."[106]

Aside from stating one of more obvious observations any court has ever considered, the court is fully aware that its decision will turn the world on its head for in this jurisprudential dimension, history and tradition only go so far—it is merely "the beginning of these cases." At the same time, the majority, authored by Justice Kennedy, acknowledges the "good faith by reasonable and sincere people" to hold fast to the principle of traditional marital definitions, yet this court is intent on turning this cart upside down.[107] In doing so, the court engages its readership with legal theories and nuances that leave the dissenters in a state of disbelief—for the majority seeks its end without restraint—to redefine the institution of marriage when neither history nor the law makes this a plausible exercise. Marriage, so says the majority, has "ancient origins" that confirm its "centrality" but this state does cause marriage to stand in "isolation from developments in law and society" for the "history of marriage is both one of continuity and change."[108]

Obergefell's majority view is riddled with these sorts of riddles—an almost incomprehensible style completely lacking in legal rigor and advancing, in its place, a social work style of personal humanism that wants everyone to feel cherished. In the end, the court substitutes the historical and legislative vision of American jurisprudence since the days of its founding with an almost saccharine, sugary definition that remains to be elusive for any sort of permanency. Same-sex marriage is a matter of respect rather than law—even the natural version. The court's pronouncement of the characteristics of marriage edifies their misplaced understanding on the true nature of the marital state, gleaned from these words:

> No union is more profound than marriage, for it embodies the highest ideals of love, fidelity, devotion, sacrifice, and family. In forming a marital union, two people become something greater than once they were. As some of the petitioners in these cases demonstrate, marriage embodies a love that may endure even past death. It would misunderstand these men and women to say they disrespect the idea of marriage. Their plea is that they do respect it, respect it so deeply that they seek to find its fulfillment for themselves. Their hope is not to be condemned to live in

loneliness, excluded from one of civilization's oldest institutions. They ask for equal dignity in the eyes of the law. The Constitution grants them that right.[109]

At its heart, the Obergefell decision, as narrow in number as it was, propounds vast social and cultural change without the usual legislative checks and balances at work. In almost horrifying logic, the court cannot even hide its lack of precision because there can be no precision in matter before it other than leaving the matter to the states and their legislative preferences. Justice Scalia characterizes the legal rationale posed by the majority as "a thin veneer of law" and its pontifications nothing more than "mummeries and "showy profundities."[110] The framers never intended a supreme court with such vast legislative authority and power to nullify the legislative processes of the statehouse. Justice Roberts fully recognizes this conceptual displacement so evident in the majority opinion when he dissents,

> If you are among the many Americans—of whatever sexual orientation—who favor expanding same-sex marriage, by all means celebrate today's decision. Celebrate the achievement of a desired goal. Celebrate the opportunity for a new expression of commitment to a partner. Celebrate the availability of new benefits. But do not celebrate the Constitution. It had nothing to do with it.
>
> I respectfully dissent.[111]

Obergefell: Nature, procreation, family and care of offspring and the natural law

Throughout most of the majority opinion, natural law appears an orphan and for that matter, the law as enunciated in rock-hard constitutional principles takes a back seat to a novel approach to legal resolution. While the natural law delivers precepts that are fixed and resolute in select human operations, that steady dependability is utterly lacking in the majority's reasoning. In the place of natural law jurisprudence, the reader encounters a legal relativity that knows no bounds. For example, same-sex marriage has to be considered, as currently under review, because "gays and lesbians" lead "more open and public lives."[112]

In other words, the propriety or suitability of a designated conduct needs to be reviewed in light of what the mass cry might be or whether the numbers rise in participation. If this be not enough to prop up a reality completely at odds with natural law jurisprudence, what of tradition, what of history and what can be gleaned from human operations over the course of millennia. That matters little too as the court announces,

> History and tradition guide and discipline this inquiry but do not set its outer boundaries. That method respects our history and learns from it without allowing the past alone to rule the present.[113]

Hence if history and tradition be right, and if the natural order and nature manifest a practice consistent with its preservation and flourishing, what of it? Even if it is right and correct, does it really even matter? Not to be outdone in this sort of twilight zone of legal analysis, the court holds that it cannot be locked into "assumptions defined by the world and time of which it is part."[114] Here too the court simply purges history, both the good and bad aspects of it, because our world is different—so different we cannot really latch onto any history because we are in the "now." Marriage is as relative as anything else one hopes for and dreams about, according to the majority, and in this state of affairs the natural law's penchant for historical tradition—the idea that some things work for all and in all communities—is thoroughly disassembled. Justice Scalia displays, in his passionate dissent, an almost angry reaction to this sort of legal reasoning to uphold conduct that cannot lie consistently with natural law reasoning. The majority's incomprehensibility in laying out why same-sex marriage is grounded in legal principles completely escapes him. He comments,

> If the opinion is correct that the two clauses "converge in the identification and definition of [a] right," that is only because the majority's likes and dislikes are predictably compatible.) I could go on. The world does not expect logic and precision in poetry or inspirational pop-philosophy; it demands them in the law. The stuff contained in today's opinion has to diminish this Court's reputation for clear thinking and sober analysis.[115]

The majority opinion manifests little hesitancy to new and innovative ways of resolving constitutional legal dilemmas and affirms its complete abandonment of any fixed moral or ethical principles, something crucial to natural law reasoning. For in marriage, the natural law expects that the union between man and women be open to procreation; be partners in the design and shaping of a family and promise to care for not only one another but also those children who are a direct result of that procreative purpose. Scalia further labels the majority opinion as "pretentious as its content egotistic."[116] In his dissent,

Justice Roberts has to remind the majority of this most fundamental purpose of marriage, the building of a stable family with cared for and loved offspring:

> The premises supporting this concept of marriage are so fundamental that they rarely require articulation. The human race must procreate to survive. Procreation occurs through sexual relations between a man and a woman. When sexual relations result in the conception of a child, that child's prospects are generally better if the mother and father stay together rather than going their separate ways. Therefore, for the good of children and society, sexual relations that can lead to procreation should occur only between a man and a woman committed to a lasting bond.[117]

The majority seems even to abandon this most basic definition of the marital state. Justice Kennedy authors another definition—one far more inclusive and far more tolerant of family designs beyond the traditional definition.

> The nature of marriage is that, through its enduring bond, two persons together can find other freedoms, such as expression, intimacy, and spirituality. This is true for all persons, whatever their sexual orientation.[118] There is dignity in the bond between two men or two women who seek to marry and in their autonomy to make such profound choices.[119]

Despite these illusory descriptors, the Obergefell majority drifts back to fundamental natural law principles on occasion. For example, when it lays out the various rationales for marriage, procreation is touted as a basis for marriage, although it need not be required. Contrary to Justice Robert's dissent, where the essentiality of the procreative purpose is highlighted, the majority suggests it to be one of the many reasons why one would marry. The court declares,

> In light of precedent protecting the right of a married couple not to procreate, it cannot be said the Court or the States have conditioned the right to marry on the capacity or commitment to procreate. The constitutional marriage right has many aspects, of which childbearing is only one.[120]

In this sense, the majority posits a marriage theorem that is relative as its reasoning—for whomever wishes this status and for whatever motivations—by mass movement or the clamor of the crowd—it shall be granted. Justice Robert's dissent cuts to the real role of marriage and procreation in not only the rearing of individuals but also assuring the lifeblood of the nation-state. Marriage is more than a social and political preference, he states:

> This universal definition of marriage as the union of a man and a woman is no historical coincidence. Marriage did not come about as a result of a political movement, discovery, disease, war, religious doctrine, or any other moving force of world history—and certainly not as a result of a prehistoric decision to exclude gays and lesbians. It arose in the nature of things to meet a vital need: ensuring that children are conceived by a mother and father committed to raising them in the stable conditions of a lifelong relationship.[121]

Marriage, like the natural law, is grounded in better soil than the mood of the populace and the howlers who demand what everyone else possesses. The marital definition cannot be changed because a group—distinctly different than the original class carrying out its purpose and end, both familially and collectively claims an alleged lack of fairness or equity. Marriage, since recorded history, has taken a shape and form that achieves these goals of procreative reproduction, family bond and structure and the foundational building blocks for any community. Its definition and "core meaning ... has endured."[122]

Those elements have never varied throughout the long history of the marital state. Justice Roberts appreciates this far more than the majority does when he observes,

> In 2009, the legislatures of Vermont, New Hampshire, and the District of Columbia became the first in the Nation to enact laws that revised the definition of marriage to include same-sex couples, while also providing accommodations for religious believers. In 2011, the New York Legislature enacted a similar law. In 2012, voters in Maine did the same, reversing the result of a referendum just three years earlier in which they had upheld the traditional definition of marriage.[123]

The majority view offers some other glints of natural law reasoning when it discusses the role of family in the care of offspring. In the marital state, husband and wife "safeguard{s}children and families and thus draw{s} meaning from related rights of childrearing, procreation and education."[124] In the marital state, the natural law's dictate for the care and education of children is more likely to occur than any other arrangement. At its core marriage promotes and safeguards offspring and hence is for "the good of children and society"[125] and arising "in the nature of things to meet a vital need: ensuring that children are conceived by a mother and father committed to raising them in the stable conditions of a lifelong relationship."[126]

Last, the majority employs the terms "dignity" and "respect" like water under a bridge. With this, there is a natural assumption that certain persons are treated differently than others because that person cannot do all the other can. By corollary, a man could argue that since he cannot get pregnant, the result is discriminatory. In this case, the petitioners make a similar claim—that because they fail to fit the definition of marriage, both historically, legally and naturally, they are not respected. Within the dissent of Justice Thomas, that argument is challenged—especially as any natural law thinker might—for our dignity cannot be bestowed on us by any governmental authority but instead from a transcendency not of this life. Thomas rightfully asserts that "human dignity is innate"[127] and does not come from government. Citing John Locke, Justice Thomas expressly holds that these rights and liberties, so readily bandied about, can never really be tethered to the relative world but must depend on something much higher—such as the "law of nature."

> Locke described men as existing in a state of nature, possessed of the "perfect freedom to order their actions and dispose of their possessions and persons as they think fit, within the bounds of the law of nature, without asking leave, or depending upon the will of any other man."[128]

In that there is true freedom and dignity.

Conclusion

For most of West's history and surely for nearly all of its jurisprudence, from the classical period to the late twentieth century, homosexuality has struggled to achieve a moral acceptability in a universal sense. To be frank, the very opposite has been true over these many centuries—that homosexuality, despite fervent efforts, has not captured the popular culture in many contexts. This is not to say that many sectors are not fully comfortable nor does it intimate that a rejection of homosexuality connotes a rejection or antagonism to that person who practices homosexual acts. Charity and human dignity mandate respect for the actor, although moral inquiry may find that the acts are unacceptable.

The journey since *Bowers v. Hardwick* manifests these competing and sometimes very incongruent features of this debate. On the one hand, the criminalization of consensual sodomy was once considered a normal and highly rational response to a form of deviate sexual activity, while on the other hand, the mood in a keener, contemporary culture was to adopt a posture of nonenforcement or looking the other way due to private nature of the activity. Leaving the law on the books did not necessarily imply any meaningful enforcement. In Bowers, we witness the strains and stresses of state-to-state culture and the proper venting of those differences was to allow state-to-state determinations. It is a brilliant legal strategy that respects both sides of the argument. Bowers was met with incredible opposition most likely because it did not provide a nationalistic resolution of a "rights" plea but still allowed the states to experiment with it. That started to change when the court overruled the Romer plebiscite on special protections due to homosexuality. And in few short years, the powerful precedent that Bowers had been will be overruled by Lawrence, which granted "fundamental rights" status to sexual activity—a grant still in need of study and review. External sexual acts are not so deeply rooted in our nation's history as to ever qualify for that status. The debate on these and other matters reaches a crescendo in Obergefell, which ended any efforts to define marriage in the traditional heterosexual relationship despite a cultural, legal, moral and ethical history that undeniably supported that proposition. In Obergefell, the court's reasoning turns into an emotive mush—feeling through the dilemma more than thinking it through. Justice Kennedy's desire to equalize marital status, while surely kindhearted and good-willed, cannot and will not be remembered for its legal clarity.

In the final analysis, the cases on homosexuality and sodomy perpetually touch natural law jurisprudence. In the first instance, the order of nature, the laws of nature and the natural law itself will always confront or delve into the ends and goals of sexual activity, its openness to procreation, its exclusive stress on pleasure over the generation of children and its conformity to the biological order. Second, the questions of consensual sodomy and homosexuality have been fixtures in the jurisprudence and moral marketplace for nearly all of our legal tradition and our codified systems as well as the common law. By no means is its restriction a novel idea but part and parcel of tradition and the natural order itself. None of the objections can merely be typed as hate or personal animus nor is it fair to claim any disagreement as a sign of contempt or discriminatory motive. Throughout all of these cases, the justices weigh in on these questions by looking to the past, the Judeo-Christian ethic, the dogmatics of Aristotle and Aquinas and the great legal philosophers like Bracton. None of this didactic is engaged in isolation or a moral vacuum. That is precisely why these behaviors will remain a perpetual inhabitant on the natural law landscape. At the same time, charity and respect for the human person should always be at center as the dialogue continues.

Notes

1. 478 U.S. 186 (1986).
2. Bowers, 200.
3. W. Blackstone, Commentaries *215.
4. Oliver Holmes, "The Path of the Law," *Harvard Law Review* 10 (1897): 457, 469.
5. See Charles P. Nemeth, *Aquinas on Crime* (South Bend, IN: St. Augustine's Press, 2008); Charles P. Nemeth, *A Comparative Analysis of Cicero and Aquinas: Nature and the Natural Law* (London: Bloomsbury Academic, 2017).
6. 539 U.S. 558 (2003).
7. Early commentators held firm to the prohibition. See: Blackstone, Commentaries *215.
8. Georgia Code Ann. § 16-6-2 (1984).
9. See Code Theod. 9.7.6; Code Just. 9.9.31.
10. See also Derrick Bailey, *Homosexuality and the Western Christian Tradition* (Harlow: Longmans, Green, 1975); See Paul Johnson, "Buggery and Parliament, 1533–2017" (April 3, 2018). Available at SSRN: https://ssrn.com/abstract=3155522 or http://dx.doi.org/10.2139/ssrn.3155522.
11. 25 Hen. VIII, ch. 6.
12. Bowers, 191.
13. See Nemeth, Cicero and Aquinas; St. Thomas Aquinas, *Summa Theologica*, vol. 1, trans. Fathers of the English Dominican Province (New York: Benzinger Brothers, 1947); Alisdair MacIntrye, *Whose Justice? Whose Rationality?* (South Bend, IN: University of Notre Dame Press, 1988); S. J. Wilson, *The Thought of Cicero* (London: G. Bell, 1964); Marcus Tullius Cicero, *On Old Age and Friendship*, trans. Frank O. Copely (Ann Arbor: University of Michigan Press, 1980); Marcus Tullius Cicero, *On the Good Life*, trans. Michael Grant (New York: Penguin, 1971); Plato, *The Laws of Plato*, ed. Thomas L. Pangle (New York: Basic Books, 1980); Aristotle, *Nicomachean Ethics*, trans. Martin Ostwald (New York: Bobbs-Merrill, 1962); Aristotle, "Politics," in the *Basic Works of Aristotle*, ed. Richard McKeon (New York: Random House, 1941).
14. See Yao Apasu-Gbotsu, Robert J. Arnold, Paul DiBella, Kevin Dorse, Elisa L. Fuller, Steven H. Naturman, Dung Hong Pham, and James B. Putney, "Survey on the Constitutional Right to Privacy in the Context of Homosexual Activity," *University of Miami Law Review*, 40 (1986): 521, 525; See also James J. Rizzo, "The Constitutionality of Sodomy Statutes," *Fordham Law Review*, 45, no. 3 (1976): 553.
15. Ga. Crim. Code § 26–5901 (1933).
16. § 18.1–212. Crimes against nature. If any person shall carnally know in any manner any brute animal, or carnally know any male or female person by the anus or by or with the mouth, or voluntarily submit to such carnal knowledge, he or she shall be guilty of a felony and shall be confined in the penitentiary not less than one year nor more than three years. Ch. 427, [1968] Va. Acts 529 (repealed and reenacted 1975).
17. Bowers, 195–96.
18. 46 Fl. Stat. § 800.02.
19. Bowers, 219, as to the mentality of nonenforcement.
20. Ibid., 206.
21. Cicero, *De Re Publica and De Legibus*, trans. Clinton Walker Keyes (Cambridge: Harvard University Press, 1988).
22. See S. Marc Cohen, "Aristotle's Metaphysics," in *The Stanford Encyclopedia of Philosophy*, ed. Edward N. Zalta (Stanford, CA: Stanford University, Winter 2016 Edition).

23 *Carey v. Population Services International*, 431 U.S. 678, 685 (1977); *Pierce v. Society of Sisters*, 268 U.S. 510 (1925); and *Meyer v. Nebraska*, 262 U.S. 390 (1923), were described as dealing with childrearing and education; *Prince v. Massachusetts*, 321 U.S. 158 (1944), with family relationships; *Skinner v. Oklahoma ex rel. Williamson*, 316 U.S. 535 (1942), with procreation; *Loving v. Virginia*, 388 U.S. 1 (1967), with marriage; *Griswold v. Connecticut*, supra, and *Eisenstadt v. Baird*, supra, with contraception
24 Bowers, 190.
25 Ibid., 192.
26 Ibid., 198.
27 Ibid., 217–18.
28 Ibid., 196.
29 Colo. Const., Art. II, § 30b., Romer, 624.
30 Romer, 625.
31 Ibid., 638.
32 Ibid., 639.
33 478 U.S. 186 (1986).
34 Ibid., 626.
35 Ibid., 629.
36 Ibid., 628.
37 Ibid., 635.
38 Ibid., 636.
39 Ibid.
40 Ibid.
41 Ibid., 639.
42 Ibid., 640–41.
43 Ibid., 644.
44 Ibid.
45 Ibid., 645.
46 Ibid.
47 Ibid.
48 Ibid., 648.
49 Ibid.
50 114 U.S. 15.
51 *Murphy v. Ramsey*, 114 U.S. 15 (1885).
52 539 U.S. 558 (2003).
53 N. J. Stat. Ann. §§10:5–4 and 10:5–5 (West Supp. 2000)
54 N. J. Stat. Ann. §10:5–4 (West Supp. 2000).
55 BSA, 645–46.
56 Ibid., 663.
57 Ibid., 649.
58 Ibid.
59 Ibid., 651.
60 Ibid., 652.
61 Ibid., 653.
62 Ibid., 654, Reply Brief for Petitioners, 5.
63 Ibid., 668.
64 Ibid., 655–56.
65 Ibid., 661.

66 Ibid., 673.
67 Ibid., 684.
68 Ibid., 696.
69 It is rare for the court to reverse its own precedent, no case more illustrative than *Dred Scott v. Sandford*, 60 U.S. 393 (1857).
70 Lawrence, 567.
71 Tex. Penal Code Ann. § 21.01(1) (2003).
72 *Griswold v. Connecticut*, 381 U.S. 479 (1965).
73 Ibid., 562.
74 Ibid., 586.
75 Ibid.
76 Ibid., 568.
77 Ibid., 571.
78 Ibid., 602.
79 Ibid., 571.
80 Ibid.
81 Ibid., 593. *Washington v. Glucksberg*, 521 U.S., 721. See *Reno v. Flores*, 507 U.S. 292, 303 (1993) (fundamental liberty interests must be "so rooted in the traditions and conscience of our people as to be ranked as fundamental" (internal quotation marks and citations omitted)); *United States v. Salerno*, 481 U.S. 739, 751 (1987) (same). See also *Michael H. v. Gerald D.*, 491 U.S. 110, 122 (1989) ("We have insisted not merely that the interest denominated as a 'liberty' be 'fundamental' ... but also that it be an interest traditionally protected by our society"); *Moore v. East Cleveland*, 431 U.S. 494, 503 (1977) (plurality opinion); *Meyer v. Nebraska*, 262 U.S. 390, 399 (1923).
82 Lawrence, 593; Bowers, 192.
83 Lawrence, 589.
84 Ibid., 590.
85 Ibid., 595.
86 Ibid., 587.
87 Ibid., 571–72.
88 Ibid., 572.
89 Ibid., 573.
90 Ibid., 576.
91 Ibid.
92 Ibid., 574.
93 Ibid.
94 Ibid., 583.
95 Ibid., 588.
96 Ibid., 597.
97 Ibid., 598.
98 Ibid., 599.
99 576 U.S. ___ (2015), slip op. at 6.
100 Roberts, slip op., 2–3.
101 Slip op., 24.
102 Slip op., 7.
103 Slip op., 9.
104 Roberts, slip op., 4.
105 1 U. S. C. §7; slip op., 9.

106 Slip op., 4.
107 Ibid.
108 Slip op., 6.
109 Slip op., 28.
110 Scalia, slip op., 4, 7.
111 Roberts, 29.
112 Slip op., 8.
113 Slip op., 10–11.
114 Slip op., 12.
115 Scalia, slip op., 9.
116 Scalia, slip op., 7.
117 Roberts, slip op., 5.
118 See *Windsor*, 570 U.S., at ___–___ (slip op., at 22–23).
119 Slip op., 13.
120 Slip op., 15–16.
121 Roberts, slip op., 4–5.
122 Roberts, slip op., 8.
123 Roberts, slip op., 9.
124 Slip op., 14.
125 Roberts, slip op., 5.
126 Ibid.
127 St. Thomas, slip op., 2.
128 J. Locke, *Second Treatise of Civil Government*, §4, p. 4 (J. Gough ed. 1947) (Locke). St. Thomas, slip op., 7.

Chapter 5

NATURAL LAW AND THE SUPREME COURT: SUICIDE, EUTHANASIA AND MERCY KILLING

As in all other aspects of contemporary moral culture, the question of suicide, once settled and without dispute, has come under intense scrutiny and questioning. What was once a given in nearly every developed society has bowed to pressure from a host of constituencies, from patient rights groups to individual demands for the freedom to decide if, when and how to die; from libertarians seeking to avoid governmental oversight and intrusion to medical practitioners who see these practices as "merciful" in end-of-life situations. The historic and universal prohibition of suicide, whether by one's own hand or by the use of another person or mechanical device, has come under intense criticism and challenge. Critics of the restriction hold that these resistant views are not only antiquated but also contrary to human dignity and that it is crucial we begin to think about this option in a completely new light. Ben Rich, of the University of California, makes an impassioned plea for more tolerance:

> While there are most certainly sources, aspects, or dimensions of suffering that may at times partake more of the physiological than the emotional or spiritual, the human person is a single embodied self. What affects one aspect of the personal also affects the other, and that is particularly true in the process of dying. Not only do these organizations fail to offer an alternative conceptual analysis of suffering upon which to ground their dichotomization of suffering, but they also fail to articulate the ethical rationale upon which they would deny to any group of dying patients in severe terminal distress a form of relief that would clearly be effective in that it would eliminate the capacity of the patient to experience suffering of any variety.[1]

Rich sees the world moving in his direction by indicating "seismic shifts" in popular opinion regarding physician-assisted suicide or one's own early-life termination.[2]

For the most part, the challenges border on questions of the amorphous liberty theory—as was keenly evident in the abortion debate—a view not shared by all jurists and justices, as well as the argument that the Fourteenth Amendment's equal protection clause is violated because of the prohibition, although it is difficult to connect these particular dots.[3]

In a narrow way, where a patient pulls the plug from the mechanical propping up of a physical life can be and usually is permissible. However, ending life early by an active intervention is distinctly different than "allowing nature to take its course."[4]

Given the turbulent history of *Roe v. Wade*, readers of the two major decisions of the Supreme Court on this subject matter will quickly discern a formidable hesitancy to venture down the path that Roe traversed. Both sides of the aisle can never deny the unsettledness that Roe continues to stoke in our culture. Nor is it possible to claim that Roe has resolved the issue. Instead, it is very fair to observe that Roe and its progeny have done little to provide peace in this complex and very ethically laden matter. Add to this the recent spate of states, like Oregon, Vermont, California, Montana and Washington,[5] all appearing to go their own way in the matter—even to the point of relying on state constitutional principles for the justification[6]—the court confirms its overall hesitancy to rule nationally. To muddy the waters even more, the debate over suicide and the physician-assisted version of it employ euphemisms and doublespeak as the standard for describing the act. For example, a statute that calls for "aid in dying" or "mercy killing" gives the interpreter a sense of nothing more than empathy. Some have called these "monstrous" euphemisms for these words sanitize an intentional decision to accelerate a person's death—something all too foreign to natural law jurisprudence.[7] To the contrary, the Montana Supreme Court found a connection between "individual privacy and human dignity" and the right to end one's life prematurely.[8]

While the fires of disagreement and collective angst still rage on the abortion question, this court in Vacco and Glucksberg, both decided unanimously by a 9–0 tally—the preeminent cases on the matter of suicide—manifests a complete unwillingness to go down this new path to constitutional protections. Curiously and almost inconsistently, various members of the court cannot find or discover any rationale for legitimating the practice. The unanimous *Washington v. Glucksburg* decision, a tally quite unique for a court not naturally inclined to read moral consensus on any matter, rejected the constitutionalization of suicide. In response to the question of whether the Fourteenth Amendment's due process claim applies or the denial of the right violative of equal protection principles, the court declares, "We hold that it does not."[9]

The clarity of the pronouncement is just as rare as the court's general simplicity in not extending liberty and equal protection principles. When the court rejected the constitutional law challenge to New York laws forbidding the practice of physician-assisted suicide, the court lucidly dispenses with the plea for permissibility:

> New York statutes outlawing assisting suicide affect and address matters of profound significance to all New Yorkers alike. They neither infringe on fundamental rights nor involve suspect classifications.[10]

From its perspective, the court may have concluded subconsciously or consciously that extending the Roe and Stenberg constitutional dynamics to end-of-life determinations is simply a bridge too far. Or one might infer that the legal wreckage of *Roe v. Wade* is so obvious in the beginning of human life that the court aims to not compound these problems by providing another means and mechanism to inflict an even greater level of human injustice.

Vacco v. Quill, 521 U.S. 793 (1997)

The court's encounter with a plea to constitutionally protect the right to end one's life prematurely was its 1997 ruling in *Vacco v. Quill*.[11] In Vacco, New York's view was universally shared by all other states as well, and while there are subtle differences and distinctions between prematurely ending one's life and refusing extraordinary measures to sustain a life by mechanical or pharmacological means, the state plainly codifies the criminality of affirmatively aiding and assisting in the death of another. The statute under consideration stated in part:

> "A person is guilty of manslaughter in the second degree when [...] (3) He intentionally causes or aids another person to commit suicide. Manslaughter in the second degree is a class C felony." Section 120.30, Promoting a suicide attempt, states: "A person is guilty of promoting a suicide attempt when he intentionally causes or aids another person to attempt suicide. Promoting a suicide attempt is a class E felony."[12]

Aside from Vacco's general resistance to extend the liberty and fundamental rights principles to assisted suicide, the court's language and rationale for upholding the ban contains various precepts of natural law thinking. First and foremost, the court acknowledges how nature and the biological order systematically and predictably play out in this latter phase of human existence. The tenor and tone of the decision is quite striking when you compare it to the sterile verbiage of *Roe v. Wade*. Second, the court's emphasis on the self-preservation and dignity of human life at even its latest station.

Nature, self-preservation and respect for life

From the outset of Vacco, the court is well aware of the complexity of end-of-life decisions—a reality made all the more morally and ethically complicated by the use of machines and mechanical intervention to keep parts of the body still functioning. The court fully recognizes the "legitimate interests in protecting life and protecting vulnerable persons."[13]

New York and every other state have a natural and compelling interest in the preservation of its citizenry rather than its ultimate destruction. Death is a condition that should be avoided since it is contrary to self-preservation—one of the primordial tenets of natural law thinking. Chief Justice Rehnquist, author of the full majority opinion, stresses at various points how life and its preservation should be the court's primary aim since that is part of our "legal traditions."[14] A party who chooses to "hasten" death by the rejection of extraordinary medical interventions cannot be equated with a physician or other party who orchestrates that earlier passing.[15] The majority opinion also construes that any decision to terminate exceptional or extraordinary treatment may not necessarily be grounded or motivated by a decision to die or end one's life but instead be driven by quality-of-life issues such as pain and functionality of the human person. That party so choosing is not necessarily intent on ending human life and may "fervently wish to live, […] free of unwanted medical technology, surgery or drugs."[16] In this sense, the court confirms the difference between living naturally and "killing."[17]

One other life-affirming aspect of Vacco references the role of the medical professionals—the doctors and nurses whose central purpose targets the maintenance and preservation of life, not its destruction. The court offers clear advice on this role when it remarks,

> New York's reasons for recognizing and acting on this distinction—including prohibiting intentional killing and preserving life; preventing suicide; maintaining physicians' role as their patients' healers; protecting vulnerable people from indifference, prejudice, and psychological and financial pressure to end their lives; and avoiding a possible slide towards euthanasia—are discussed in greater detail in our opinion in Glucksberg, ante. These valid and important public interests easily satisfy the constitutional requirement that a legislative classification bear a rational relation to some legitimate end.[18]

Avoiding the "slide" toward euthanasia has been accomplished in Vacco since its foundational rationale for rejecting suicide is that inherent inclination of every human being, indeed every creature, to preserve and maintain existence—something every natural law thinker fully comprehends.

Washington v. Glucksberg, 521 U.S. 702 (1997)

While a companion case to Vacco, it is clear from the outset of the opinion that the court will delve deeply and comprehensively into this ethical quandary. Glucksberg receives a full and unbridled examination of all the legal issues involved in physician-assisted suicide, and here as in Vacco, the court decides unanimously, although there are distinct rationales posed by selected justices. From its earliest paragraphs, the court differentiates the idea of withdrawal from extraordinary treatment or medical regimens that are so mechanical as to make the continuation of life an impossibility without said intervention. The court is adamant when it references the Washington State's Natural Death Act[19] that allows the right to withhold or withdraw from "life-sustaining treatment" as not being the statutory construction under constitutional challenge.[20] Rather, the court evaluates a criminal codification, designated a felony when any party is "promoting a suicide attempt when he knowingly causes or aids another person to attempt suicide."[21]

Petitioners in this case employ and utilize the identical "liberty" arguments rooted in previous court rulings such as in Lawrence and Obergefell, asserting that the right to end one's life should be a protected fundamental right as well as the substantive due process argument arising from a denial of this particular choice. The majority opinion clearly lays out its overall hesitancy: But we "ha[ve] always been reluctant to expand the concept of substantive due process because guideposts for responsible decision making in this unchartered area are scarce and open-ended."[22]

By extending constitutional protection to an asserted right or liberty interest, we, to a great extent, place the matter outside the arena of public debate and legislative action. We must therefore "exercise the utmost care whenever we are asked to break new ground in this field,"[23] lest the liberty protected by the Due Process Clause be subtly transformed into the policy preferences of the members of this court.[24]

In both arguments, the court emphatically displays a resistance to extending these "liberties" or any willingness to foster and further due process advocacy it has never really been comfortable with. Nor does the court manifest much sympathy for the social change theory espoused in the 9th Circuit Court of Appeals holding favorably for a constitutional protection for this form of suicide. The Supreme Court fully rejected the lower court's judgment upholding a "right to die":

> The court also discussed what it described as "historical" and "current societal attitudes" toward suicide and assisted suicide,[25] and concluded that "the Constitution encompasses a due process liberty interest in controlling the time and manner of one's death—that there is, in short, a constitutionally-recognized 'right to die.'"[26]

The natural law implications for Glucksberg are just as compelling as Vacco. However, Glucksberg displays a far more aggressive willingness to tackle this legal dilemma from a moral and philosophical perspective.

Natural law, legal tradition and history

Natural law jurisprudence readily depends on tradition, historical continuity and custom in human operations. Natural law reasoning never resides with relative or instantaneous decision making but is fully discoverable and discernible over time. How human beings live out their lives and how the typical family, community and nation-state conduct their business over the long continuum of time instruct on what can be properly called natural or unnatural. Natural law reasoning depends on the predictable, the customary and expected choices in human operations, not the moral outlier who tests what humanity typically does. So, in Glucksberg, the emphasis on legal tradition and historical patterns of human choice is witnessed at many locations within the opinion. At the first section of the case, the majority proclaims, "We begin, as we do in all due process cases, by examining our Nation's history, legal traditions, and practices."[27]

Not unexpectedly, the court correctly observes that assisted suicide has been and is a crime in every American jurisdiction, which evidence a "longstanding expressions of the States' commitment to the protection and preservation of all human life."[28] The criminalization of suicide, in all its forms, is not a matter of recent innovation or whim but a condemnation of a long part of Western jurisprudence. The court could not be more eloquent:

> Indeed, opposition to and condemnation of suicide-and, therefore, of assisting suicide-are consistent and enduring themes of our philosophical, legal, and cultural heritages.
>
> More specifically, for over 700 years, the Anglo-American common-law tradition has punished or otherwise disapproved of both suicide and assisting suicide.[29]

The court liberally references Bracton and Blackstone as further support for a historic prohibition and proof of a long and very settled legal tradition on this question. Labeling suicide one of the "highest crimes" and nothing but an act of "real cowardice," the greats of Western jurisprudence have never treated suicide with anything short of condemnation.[30] Citing *Hales v. Petit*, an early English decision on suicide, the court displays zero tolerance for the practice declaring that suicide is an "offence against Nature, against God and against the King. To destroy oneself is contrary to Nature, and Thing most horrible."[31]

The pattern of full prohibition continued into the American Colonial experience.[32] That legal tradition and custom never evolves in any other direction even as American states grapple with the practice. In the final analysis, every American jurisdiction, by the nineteenth century, will prohibit suicide in any context.[33] That legal tradition continues to the present day and is fully encapsulated in the provisions of the Model Penal Code that proscribes the conduct.[34] The MPC provision states in part: "A person who purposely aids or solicits another to commit suicide is guilty of a felony in the second degree if his conduct causes such suicide or an attempted suicide, and otherwise of a misdemeanor."[35]

In sum, the court is quite satisfied that the legal tradition and history regarding the practice of suicide, in all its forms, remains "deeply rooted" and as a result, unwise to alter or challenge. To hold favorably for those seeking its protection as a constitutional right would require the court to "reverse centuries of legal doctrine and practice."[36] And while there may be higher levels of tolerance or individual comfort with the termination of life, especially under the guise of "mercy killing" or euthanasia, the court is convinced that those attitudes cannot shift the validity of this legal tradition, nor should the court give fleeting allegiance to this entrenched and very viable history—a history that provides "guideposts for responsible decision making."[37] The Court states,

> Attitudes toward suicide itself have changed since Bracton, but our laws have consistently condemned, and continue to prohibit, assisting suicide. Despite changes in medical technology and notwithstanding an increased emphasis on the importance of end-of-life decision making, we have not retreated from this prohibition. Against this backdrop of history, tradition, and practice, we now turn to respondents' constitutional claim.[38]

Both legal history and tradition "provide ample support for refusing to recognize an open-ended constitutional right to commit suicide."[39]

Natural law, self-preservation, family life and the value of every human being

Those seeking the legalization of physician-assisted suicide play quaint with legal semantics by employing the principle of self-sovereignty—that notion of self-determination and individual freedom and autonomy which entails personal liberty.[40] However, the court rejects this argument in the context of ending one's life for sovereignty assumes maintenance of a human life not its destruction. Since self-destruction lacks any historical continuity or support—that it be so deeply rooted in our history and traditions—it is a claim that cannot be effectively or accurately made. In place of this alleged self-sovereignty, the court properly concludes a complete lack of support for this proposed autonomy—which includes self-death since "this country has been and continues to be one of the rejection of nearly all efforts to permit it."[41]

The Glucksberg majority displays a complete unwillingness to bend to the pressure of self-autonomy given the severity of the practice and its inherent terminality. Citing the case's lower court reasoning, it appears far more comfortable aligning with a series of state interests that justify the ban on assisted suicide:

> In reaching this conclusion, the opinion discussed in some detail this Court's substantive-due-process tradition of interpreting the Due Process Clause to protect certain fundamental rights and "personal decisions relating to marriage, procreation, contraception, family relationships, child rearing, and education,"[42] and noted that many of those rights and liberties "involv[e] the most intimate and personal choices a person may make in a lifetime."[43]

Against this backdrop, and almost perplexingly given the court's historic tolerance for all things relating to abortion, the court shifts to sanctity of life arguments and then references various cases that promote the sanctity of life. For example, citing *Martin v. Commonwealth*, the court essentially affirms the transcendent nature of human life and the critical demand to preserve it. Martin states in part, "The right to life and to personal security is not only sacred in the estimation of the common law, but it is inalienable."[44]

If one is looking for consistency between Roe and its progeny and the Glucksberg undeniable rejection of assisted suicide, that find will be elusive. Citing the Model Penal Code, the majority references commentary that seems lifted from a theological or ethical text: "The interests in the sanctity of life that are represented by the criminal homicide laws are threatened by one who expresses a willingness to participate in taking the life of another."[45]

Terms like "sanctity of life" rarely weave into the text of a Supreme Court decision and this almost inordinate affinity for self-preservation based on this sanctity is not a common line of reasoning in court decisions. Astoundingly the court observes the value of life and its preservation at these latter stages of human existence, although this same zeal is fully lacking in most abortion decisions. The court even references on the continuum of life:

> Washington, however, has rejected this sliding-scale approach and, through its assisted-suicide ban, insists that all persons' lives, from beginning to end, regardless of physical or mental condition, are under the full protection of the law.[46]

So out of the mainstream are suicidal acts that these results are inconsistent with how reason ordinarily deliberates and even in cases of intense physical pain and the torment natural to many diseases, the medical and pharmacological treatments can alleviate pain at these severe levels. Suicide cannot be promoted, the court indicates, because those "who attempt suicide—terminally ill or not—often suffer from depression of other mental disorders."[47]

The court is keenly aware of the many vulnerable population groups that would be negatively impacted by an open-ended physician-assisted suicide policy. Too many patients laboring under pain, that could be managed more effectively, would make premature and unnecessary decisions to terminate life and these judgments are absolutely contrary to the "state's interests in protecting those who might seek to end life mistakenly or under pressure."[48]

Justice Stevens, hardly a natural law adherent in his judicial philosophy, centers his attention on the value of every human life and its "right for preservation."[49] His concurring opinion stresses the unique and valuable contributions of every human being, as he explains,

> The State has an interest in preserving and fostering the benefits that every human being may provide to the community—a community that thrives on the exchange of ideas, expressions of affection, shared memories, and humorous incidents, as well as on the material contributions that its members create and support. The value to others of a person's life is far too precious to allow the individual to claim a constitutional entitlement to complete autonomy in making a decision to end that life.[50]

Even the terminally ill patient has as much "value" as the "lives of those who are healthy."[51] How this language can be reconciled with *Roe v. Wade* remains a complete mystery. The only distinct difference is the timing of death—not the end result. In the Roe environment, fetal life is subordinated to the "choice" artifice and unequivocally not placed on the same plane of value of the women who adjudges to abort or not. Yet that same mentality is inescapably missing in Glucksberg replaced with a wholly different valuation of life. That valuation is highlighted in the case's discussion of the mentally ill, the mentally incompetent, the mentally challenged individual whose potential for victimization by physician-assisted suicide is far more likely than any party in possession of their full faculties. Justice Stevens lays out the wisdom on why physician-assisted suicide is ripe for abuse against selected clientele.

> Similarly, the State's legitimate interests in preventing suicide, protecting the vulnerable from coercion and abuse, and preventing euthanasia are less significant in this context. I agree that the State has a compelling interest in preventing persons from committing suicide because of depression or coercion by third parties.[52]

Vulnerable populations, the sick and the infirm, the mentally unbalanced and emotionally depressed all are subject to manipulation and suggestion in terms of early termination of human life. "The State has an interest in protecting vulnerable populations—including the poor, the elderly, and disabled persons—from abuse, neglect and mistakes."[53]

The court is attuned to the rippling impact of suicide as well—not as some caricatured "victimless" event but rather a circumstance that inflicts lifelong emotional influences on family and friends. Suicide, in whatever capacity carried out, has its battle casualties, and none are more harmed and injured than close family members. Suicide decisions are rarely carried out in a vacuum and while the motivations among family members will vary widely and interpretations of self-preservation be just as varied, it is simply another danger in the mix of things emerging from physician-assisted suicide. Family members may act as surrogates—a dangerous position to speak on behalf of another in the matter of life and death. The net effect, Glucksberg's majority holds, is to cast a wider net than originally envisioned and, as a result, cause even greater harm. The court correctly observed:

> The court noted, for example, that the "decision of a duly appointed surrogate decision maker is for all legal purposes the decision of the patient himself,"[54] that "in some instances, the patient may be unable to self-administer the drugs and ... administration by the physician ... may be the only way the patient may be able to receive them,"[55] and that not only physicians, but also family members and loved ones, will inevitably participate in assisting suicide.[56] Thus, it turns out that what is couched as a limited right to "physician-assisted suicide" is likely, in effect, a much

broader license, which could prove extremely difficult to police and contain.[57] Washington's ban on assisting suicide prevents such erosion.[58]

The emotional impact can be even more pressing and deleterious to immediate family members. Whether by one's own hand or with the assistance of another, to terminate life in advance of a natural end, to thwart the base and seminal instinct of self-preservation, wreaks havoc on the natural order of things. Family life is turned on its head for its very aim is preservation, procreation and care and love of offspring. Suicide undercuts these fundamental natural law instincts. Glucksberg cites the very powerful legal opinion of an eighteenth-century jurist from Connecticut—Zephaniah Swift who described suicide and its impact on the family in very graphic and disturbing terms.

> There can be no act more contemptible, than to attempt to punish an offender for a crime, by exercising a mean act of revenge upon lifeless clay, that is insensible of the punishment. There can be no greater cruelty, than the inflicting [of] a punishment, as the forfeiture of goods, which must fall solely on the innocent offspring of the offender ... [Suicide] is so abhorrent to the feelings of mankind, and that strong love of life which is implanted in the human heart, that it cannot be so frequently committed, as to become dangerous to society. There can of course be no necessity of any punishment.[59]

In this piercing insight, Justice Swift portrays the natural deficit caused to the suicide actor's family—an act that will "punish the suicide's family for his wrongdoing."[60]

Throughout the Glucksberg decision, one witnesses a court on edge regarding the power of physicians to assume the role of arbiter in matters of life and death and second, what Justice Souter labels a "slippery slope" arising from the "lawfulness" of assisted suicide. For example, Justice Souter prophesizes the possibility:

> Physicians, and their hospitals, have their own financial incentives, too, in this new age of managed care. Whether acting from compassion or under some other influence, a physician who would provide a drug for a patient to administer might well go the further step of administering the drug himself; so, the barrier between assisted suicide and euthanasia could become porous, and the line between voluntary and involuntary euthanasia as well. The case for the slippery slope is fairly made out here, not because recognizing one due process right would leave a court with no principled basis to avoid recognizing another, but because there is a

plausible case that the right claimed would not be readily containable by reference to facts about the mind that are matters of difficult judgment, or by gatekeepers who are subject to temptation, noble or not.[61]

In this sense, the preservation of life cannot be assured and in fact the legalization of physician-assisted suicide may be more likely its ruin or end. Granting power to make those life and death decision connotes a dangerous moral praecipe that even well-intentioned physicians can fall from. On top of this, how consistent is this sought-after practice with the general nature of a healer-physician? Justice Stevens questions whether or not legalizing the practice of physician-assisted suicide might undermine "the traditional integrity of the medical profession."[62] His response manifests an ambivalence since he argues that conditions leading up to the request for assisted suicide might be manageable or correctable enough to avoid the decision. It is an interesting argument. Justice Breyer reaches a similar conclusion pointing out that "medical technology ... Makes the administration of pain-relieving drugs sufficient."[63]

From these various vantage points, the court's decision stresses the maintenance of life, its preservation and continuance, rather than its premature ending—all of which mirror the natural law tenet of self-preservation.

Conclusion

Both Vacco and Glucksberg display scant inclination to legitimate or authorize the practice of physician-assisted suicide. While never explicitly stated, the court heavily relies upon some specific natural law tenets including legal tradition, custom and history, self-preservation and family order. To end one's life prematurely and unnaturally confronts these principles and is strangely different that the court's jurisprudence in other moral and ethical cases. Despite the parallel arguments that arise and emerge from homosexuality, same-sex marriage, the decriminalization of sodomy and abortion rights, the court almost bizarrely wants to avoid this expansion in the matter of fundamental rights and the recognition of another substantive due process right. In both cases, the justices unanimously rule—an event quite rare for this contentious court. Inferences are many, but it appears certain that the court does not wish to travel down that road—particularly the road intersecting at life's later and more vulnerable stages. The Glucksberg majority is particularly attentive to the plight of those likely targeted by the machinery of physician-assisted suicide:

> The State's interest here goes beyond protecting the vulnerable from coercion; it extends to protecting disabled and terminally ill people from

prejudice, negative and inaccurate stereotypes, and "societal indifference."[64] The State's assisted-suicide ban reflects and reinforces its policy that the lives of terminally ill, disabled, and elderly people must be no less valued than the lives of the young and healthy, and that a seriously disabled person's suicidal impulses should be interpreted and treated the same way as anyone else's.[65]

Or it may be because the court has already too often experienced and observed the negative impacts of expanded rights in many areas of behavior. If 9-month-old fetuses can be delivered in a breech position for brain evacuation, an obvious violation of Roe in both term and spirit—what stands in the way of bureaucratic euthanasia governed by cost-benefit principles? Or when will older or elderly life simply lack value for its preservation? Or it may be that early death—the disallowance of allowing nature to take its proper and very inevitable course—may never find a home in a country rooted in its legal tradition and its history. For every asserted right, somehow and in some way, must prove that it is derived from the "traditions from which the Nation developed."[66]

Notes

1 Ben A. Rich, "A Death of One's Own: The Perils and Pitfalls of Continuous Sedation as the Ethical Alternative to Lethal Prescription," *American Journal of Bioethics*, 11, no. 6 (2011): 52, 53.
2 Ibid.
3 See Melvin I. Urofsky, "Do Go Gentle into That Good Night: Thoughts on Death, Suicide, Morality and the Law," *Arkansas Law Review*, 59 (2007): 819, 838; Compare "Oregon Death with Dignity Act," *Oregon Rev. Stat.* §§ 127.800–.897 (2011), with "Washington Death with Dignity Act," *Wash. Rev. Code Ann.* §§ 70.245.010–.904 (West 2011).
4 *Vacco v. Quill*, 521 U.S. 793, 798 (1997).
5 Oregon Death with Dignity Act, *Or. Rev. Stat.* §§ 127.800–.897 (2011); Patient Choice and Control at End of Life Act, *Vt. Stat. Ann.* tit. 18 § 5281–5292 (Supp. 2013); Washington Death with Dignity Act, *Wash. Rev. Code Ann.* §§ 70.245.010–.904 (West 2011).
6 See Arthur G. Svenson, "Montana's Courting of Physician Aid in Dying: Could Des Moines Follow Suit?" *Politics and the Life Sciences*, 29, no. 2 (2010): 2.
7 Ibid., 7.
8 *Baxter v. State*, No. ADV-2007-787, 2008 Mont. Dist. LEXIS 482, at *36 (1st Jud. Dist. Ct. Mont. Dec. 5, 2008), *aff'd in part, rev'd in part*, 2009 MT 449, 224, P.3d 1211; Christina White, "Comment: Physician Aid-in-Dying," *Houston Law Review*, 53, no. 2 (2015): 595.
9 *Washington v. Glucksberg*, 521 U.S. 702, 706 (1997).
10 *Vacco v. Quill*, 521 US 793, 739 (1997).
11 Ibid.

12 New York Penal Law § 125.15 (McKinney 1987).
13 Vacco, 798.
14 Ibid., 800.
15 Ibid.
16 Ibid., 802; *Superintendent of Belchertown State School v. Saikewicz*, 373 Mass. 728, 743, n. 11, 370 N. E. 2d 417, 426, n. 11 (1977).
17 Vacco, 806.
18 Ibid., 808–9.
19 Wash. Rev. Code § 70.122.070(1).2.
20 *Washington v. Glucksberg*, 521 U.S. 702, 707 (1997); Wash. Rev. Code § 70.122.070(1).2.
21 Glucksberg, 707.
22 *Collins v. Harker Heights*, 503 U.S. 115, 125 (1992).
23 Ibid.
24 Glucksberg, 720; *Moore v. City of East Cleveland*, 431 U.S. 494, 502 (1977) (plurality opinion).
25 *Compassion in Dying v. Washington*, 79 F.3d 790, 806–812 (1996).
26 Glucksberg, 709; Compassion, 816.
27 Glucksberg, 710.
28 Ibid.
29 Ibid., 711.
30 Ibid., 712.
31 Ibid., 712; *Hales v. Petit*, 1 Plowd. Com. 253, 261, 75 Eng. Rep. 387, 400 (1561–1562).
32 A. Scott, *Criminal Law in Colonial Virginia* (Chicago, IL: University of Chicago Press), 108, n. 93, 198, n. 15 (1930).
33 Glucksberg, 715.
34 Model Penal Code § 210.5(2) (Official Draft and Revised Comments, 1980).
35 Ibid.
36 Glucksberg, 723.
37 Ibid., 721.
38 Ibid., 719.
39 Ibid., 740.
40 Ibid., 724.
41 Ibid., 728.
42 *Planned Parenthood of Southeastern Pa. v. Casey*, 505 U.S. 833, 846 (1992).
43 Ibid., 851.
44 *Martin v. Commonwealth*, 184 Va. 1009, 10181019, 37 S. E. 2d 43, 47 (1946)
45 Model Penal Code § 210.5, Comment 5, at 100. *People v. Kevorkian*, 447 Mich. 478–479, and nn. 53–56, 527 N. W. 2d, at 731–732, and nn. 53–56.
46 Glucksberg, 729.
47 Ibid., 730.
48 Ibid., 737.
49 Ibid., 738.
50 Ibid., 741.
51 Ibid., 746.
52 Ibid., 747.
53 Ibid., 731.
54 79 F. 3d, at 832, n. 120
55 Ibid., at 831.

56 Ibid., at 838, n. 140.
57 Justice Souter concludes that "the case for the slippery slope is fairly made out here, not because recognizing one due process right would leave a court with no principled basis to avoid recognizing another, but because there is a plausible case that the right claimed would not be readily containable by reference to facts about the mind that are matters of difficult judgment, or by gatekeepers who are subject to temptation, noble or not." Post, at 785 (opinion concurring in judgment). We agree that the case for a slippery slope has been made out but—bearing in mind Justice Cardozo's observation of "the tendency of a principle to expand itself to the limit of its logic," The Nature of the Judicial Process 51 (1932)—we also recognize the reasonableness of the widely expressed skepticism about the lack of a principled basis for confining the right. See Brief for United States as Amicus Curiae 26 ("Once a legislature abandons a categorical prohibition against physician assisted suicide, there is no obvious stopping point"); Brief for Not Dead Yet et al. as Amici Curiae 21–29; Brief for Bioethics Professors as Amici Curiae 23–26; Report of the Council on Ethical and Judicial Affairs, App. 133, 140 ("If assisted suicide is permitted, then there is a strong argument for allowing euthanasia"); New York Task Force 132; Kamisar, The "Right to Die"; On Drawing (and Erasing) Lines, 35 Duquesne L. Rev. 481 (1996); Kamisar, Against Assisted Suicide—Even in a Very Limited Form, 72 U. Det. Mercy L. Rev. 735 (1995).
58 Glucksberg, 733.
59 2 Z. Swift, *A System of the Laws of the State of Connecticut* 304 (1796).
60 Glucksberg, 713.
61 Ibid., 784–85.
62 Ibid., 747.
63 Ibid., 791.
64 49 F. 3d, at 592.
65 Glucksberg, 732.
66 Ibid., 767; Poe, 367 U.S., at 542 (Harlan, J., dissenting).

Chapter 6

NATURAL LAW, RELIGIOUS EXPRESSION AND THE FREEDOM TO BELIEVE

While the natural law is commonly associated with some major tenets, such as self-preservation and procreation, as well as those activities discoverable in the natural order, the jurisprudence also contains a spiritual element or quality. Within the fundamental and primary principles espoused concerning the natural law, a person's spiritual integrity, their natural ordination to believe in a Deity, a higher power and transcendent authority, is central to the content of the natural law. St. Thomas lists and references this natural quality in every human person—to believe in the Creator who fashioned the believer—a type of indelible imprint of the author of human life and existence.[1] Human experience corroborates this view since literally every culture and country displays and manifests a religious or spiritual dimension. It is not any particular or specific spirituality but the undeniable recognition that every person and every nation-state weighs the divine in some manner. Even thinking of God, as Anselm would make in his ontological proof of God's existence, demonstrates the naturalness of believing.[2]

For natural law jurisprudence, the higher, the more transcendent dimension provides the justification for any fixed or meaningful rights—not merely because the positivist enacts it or because the mob screams loudly enough to force the passage. In natural law, the rights descend downward from an eternal God to a very temporal human person—and that Creator who shapes and makes all things impresses upon us these principles known as the natural law. Being created in the imagery of God means just that—and our natural law imprint includes the natural belief in the Creator—a divine reflection that mirrors an omnipotent God.

Hence, the natural law tenet of believing in a Deity sits at center in the world of natural law jurisprudence; it depends upon the belief for the principles to be fixed and immutable and finds God not only necessitous in this line of thought but said belief to make sense of the rest of the principles of the natural law.

Frequently, the US Supreme Court encounters cases touching belief and religious expression. It is an oft-litigated and challenged practice in communities, the workplace and public activity. Since the early 1960s, religious expression and the free exercise thereof have been the too often, unfortunate subject matter for our courts. While there is natural resistance to the idea of government "establishing" a religion—an ambition expressly forbidden under our Constitution—the court's overall difficulties deal with the right to express or exercise particular aspects of a specific faith. The overall tenor of religious challenge on constitutional grounds is grounded in the explicit language in our foundational documents.

> Congress shall make no law respecting an establishment of religion, or prohibiting the free exercise thereof; or abridging the freedom of speech, or of the press; or the right of the people peaceably to assemble, and to petition the government for a redress of grievances.[3]

In assessing any religious case when tangled up with governmental questions, the courts have a two-prong inquiry: first, whether the action of government leads to some manner of "establishment"; and second, whether governmental action impedes, intrudes upon or restricts the "free exercise" of religion. For natural law purposes, the second part of the inquiry is always more relevant since the spiritual dimensions of a human person are under governmental siege or restriction or that government finds a way to punish or negatively harm someone who believes and practices a particular faith. Thus, most of this chapter's attention resides in the free exercise problem for it is exercise of that faith that is grounded in or upon a belief in some Deity—a natural state in the human actor.

The Supreme Court's lineage of cases on religion since *Roe v. Wade* is formidable in size and scope. Most of the case law has been guided by the *Lemon v. Kurtzman's* three-pronged test, announced in the court's 1971 decision regarding the use of state funds for textbooks in religiously affiliated schools.[4] That test consists of three standards:

> First, the statute must have a secular legislative purpose; second, its principal or primary effect must be one that neither advances nor inhibits religion; finally, the statute must not foster an excessive government entanglement with religion.[5]

In this context, the court is forever concerned about whether or not the practice of the state fosters, creates, nurtures or establishes a religion and whether or not the practice may advance and, in the alternative, inhibit one's faith.

To inhibit is to meddle with belief or to undercut one's capacity to freely exercise faith and belief. While Kurtzman unanimously upheld state funds for textbooks, since the practice satisfied all three tests, other cases are far more complicated and nuanced. In *Wisconsin v. Yoder*,[6] the court unanimously agreed that Amish children, due to specific, religiously based beliefs, could not be forced or subject to compulsory education past the eighth grade. The exemption carved out for the Amish manifests the balance between governmental intrusion and right to free exercise. Clearly, that balance has become even more pronounced today as will be evident in the cases to be reviewed. Cases involving prayer, invocations, placement of religious symbols and erecting crèches during holidays will all be on the Supreme Court's docket over recent history.[7] The bulk of those decisions shall deal with the "establishment side" of the question rather than its free exercise. Hence, there are a host of decisions that deal with governmental support for religious entities and institutions, such as school bus service for parochial school and other religiously affiliated schools,[8] the funding of playgrounds,[9] textbooks,[10] medical and special education needs[11] as well as cases concerning educational funding formulas for special programs.[12] At this end of the spectrum, the court has tended to be more tolerant than most would imagine since it sees those types of programs as serving the students rather than establishing a particular religion. As noted above, this chapter will stress those cases that have a natural feel in light of free exercise and the natural law precept—belief in a Deity.

Marsh v. Chambers, 463 U.S. 783 (1983)

A frequent issue before the U.S. Supreme and other federal courts deals with the matter of prayer and the use of Chaplains in legislative houses. For nearly all of this nation's history, both Congress and legislative houses in the states begin or commence their session with a daily prayer or invocation. Prayer and invocation, on its face, says something about how government entangles itself with religion and it is perfectly understandable when parties object to this type of intertwining—a government that provides a forum and space for prayer. In this way, the matter has "establishment" concerns. However, side by side with entanglement is the inevitable concept of "belief." For establishment would not emanate from a completely secular society but instead generally arises because of some belief system that prompts the prayer and invocation. Thus, it is impossible to sever the interplay between "establishment" and "belief" or "free expression" completely. The Marsh decision, concerning the longstanding Nebraska Statehouse prayer protocol, edifies this natural dependency between these two legal issues. Chief Justice Burger, the author of the majority opinion, appreciates the symbiotic relationship and provides the key reason why Marsh is not only about a religious practice but even more keenly about belief.

> The opening of sessions of legislative and other deliberative public bodies with prayer is deeply embedded in the history and tradition of this country. From colonial times through the founding of the Republic and ever since, the practice of legislative prayer has coexisted with the principles of disestablishment and religious freedom.[13]

In this way, the opening prayer in legislative chambers, courthouses and governmental agencies has long been part of our national fabric.

Natural law, legal tradition and religious belief

Part of Marsh's insight is the rightful stress on history and tradition in upholding the right to this form of religious free expression. The idea of prayer in the public square is neither novel nor radical for the bulk of the American citizenry. The court's majority view traces the long and emphatic history of prayer since earlier British history to the colonial period and the founding days of the American republic.[14] None of the Founding Fathers perceived the exercise of some religious practice or belief system as being contradictory or unlawful to the Constitution. The court makes specific reference to these early deliberations in the republic:

> Standing alone, historical patterns cannot justify contemporary violations of constitutional guarantees, but there is far more here than simply historical patterns. In this context, historical evidence sheds light not only on what the draftsmen intended the Establishment Clause to mean, but also on how they thought that Clause applied to the practice authorized by the First Congress—their actions reveal their intent.[15]

The role of this early tolerance and acceptability of prayer illustrates the root nature in natural law analysis—giving credit or credence to practices that are part law but even more compellingly "customary." Most of what the natural law propounds finds a willing and compatible history to confirm and corroborate the sensibility of the practice. The majority here, citing hundreds of years of tradition and practice, rejects the effort to "cast aside" a common prayer in opening the governmental session.[16] The dissenters like Justice Brennan and Marshall conclude that history and tradition tends to be "ambiguous and not relevant to a society far more heterogeneous than that of the Framers"[17]—a finding so at odds with the permanency of natural law principles for the natural law is the same in Rome as in Athens—it does not vary by place or locale.

In this way, the majority holds, the prayer cannot be typed as an establishment of any particular state-run religion but in its place, the court argues, prayer becomes a simple reflection of the beliefs of the citizenry, part of our fabric. Justice Burger eloquently writes,

> In light of the unambiguous and unbroken history of more than 200 years, there can be no doubt that the practice of opening legislative sessions with prayer has become part of the fabric of our society. To invoke Divine guidance on a public body entrusted with making the laws is not, in these circumstances, an "establishment" of religion or a step toward establishment; it is simply a tolerable acknowledgment of beliefs widely held among the people of this country. As Justice Douglas observed, "[w]e are a religious people whose institutions presuppose a Supreme Being."[18]

Nor can it be said that this prayer seeks to advance a particular religious sect or belief system, nor does it hope to convert others, nor do these prayers desire to isolate religious differences or theological postures. Instead, the prayer Marsh refers to is about the most generic recognition that our republic believes in a transcendent power that guarantees the inalienable rights that no state can really grant. It is common knowledge that the framers were a diverse lot with hardly any uniformity when it came to a specific theological bent— and in fact their Deist tendencies speak loudly about their general religious aloofness. However, the Founding documents and all the aligned correspondence leading up to the creation of the new nation never intimate or expressly sever ties with a higher power. Prayer surely reflects this overall belief more than it does a clamor for any state religion. The majority opinion summarizes this observation:

> The content of the prayer is not of concern to judges where, as here, there is no indication that the prayer opportunity has been exploited to proselytize or advance any one, or to disparage any other, faith or belief. That being so, it is not for us to embark on a sensitive evaluation or to parse the content of a particular prayer. [...] The unbroken practice for two centuries in the National Congress and for more than a century in Nebraska and in many other states gives abundant assurance that there is no real threat "while this Court sits."[19]

History, according to the dissent, cannot save any posed rationale in the majority. As noted by Justice Brennan, prayer is not necessarily a matter of belief as much as it is a religious activity the state should always avoid. Prayer is religious activity under the approval and sanction of the state and, as a result, excessively entangles the state and religion. Believing, either singularly or collectively, does not negate this entanglement nor the aim and thrust of the religious activity. Justice Brennan argues,

> That the "purpose" of legislative prayer is preeminently religious, rather than secular, seems to me to be self-evident.[20] "To invoke Divine guidance on a public body entrusted with making the laws,"[21] is nothing but a religious act. Moreover, whatever secular functions legislative prayer might play—formally opening the legislative session, getting the members of the body to quiet down, and imbuing them with a sense of seriousness and high purpose—could so plainly be performed in a purely nonreligious fashion that to claim a secular purpose for the prayer is an insult to the perfectly honorable individuals who instituted and continue the practice.[22]

Brennan sees the state "linking" religious activity with the power of the state. For the majority, the idea that what one believes cannot be firewalled from state influence belies the freedom of belief—a true natural law precept that does not depend on state sanction in any context. Ironically, the Brennan dissent seems to acknowledge the incapacity of the temporal governmental authority to really change the beliefs of any human agent. In fact, Brennan caustically remarks that the closer government gets to any religion, that faith will suffer "trivialization and degradation by too close an attachment to the organs of government."[23] And the good justice even admits it an impossibility to compose a nonsectarian prayer for all prayer has the potential to rankle another whose theological perceptions may differ just enough for insult or harm to the nonbeliever.[24] Those who argue that a lack of opportunity "robs the Nation of its spiritual identity"[25] fail to understand prayer's implications as if prayer was demonstrably a ruinous undercurrent to our free society.

For all of this sanctimony, Brennan misses the real issue that prayer is a matter of internal reflection and interior contemplation—a condition that each human being possesses because of his or her natural law imprint. The dissent incorrectly applies prayer as an individual act—approaching one's higher power in one's own way for there is no prayer template promulgated by governmental authority and no requirement that the participant or nonparticipant "commit [...] on fundamental theological issues."[26]

Believing in a higher power, a transcendent being encompasses the most fundamental precept of the natural law—a precept that our founders were well aware of. Prayer is a reflection of that belief and not an endorsement of an established or soon to be founded state religion.

Employment Division v. Smith, 494 U.S. 872 (1990)

The idea that religious expression knows no bounds or restrictions is the hallmark legacy of Employment Division. In reading both sides of the dispute, it is clear that decision is not only mindful of the gravity and seriousness of religious expression but also how faith and belief are to be presumptively protected except in exceptional circumstances. In Employment Division, an applicant for unemployment benefits appealed his denial based on the division's rationale for rejection, namely drug usage, specifically peyote, during religious exercises of the Native American Church whose liturgy sought communion with the "Great Spirit" and peyote was an agent in that process. The court describes the interplay between peyote and the rubrics employed:

> To the members, peyote is consecrated with powers to heal body, mind and spirit. It is a teacher; it teaches the way to spiritual life through living in harmony and balance with the forces of the Creation. The rituals are an integral part of the life process. They embody a form of worship in which the sacrament Peyote is the means for communicating with the Great Spirit.[27]

In the State of Oregon, and at the federal level, usage of peyote was considered a felony and a criminal act under the Controlled Substances Act.[28]

When workers for a drug rehab facility were fired for their usage of peyote, their application for unemployment was denied due to work-related "misconduct."[29] On appeal, the workers allege their free expression rights, their beliefs and practice of faith, guaranteed on the First Amendment, were being undermined by the division's decision. Since the Native American Church depended upon the use of peyote in its rituals and liturgical practices, it cannot punish any party from adhering to these drug-based requirements. In the majority opinion, authored by Justice Scalia, one witnesses a conundrum—whether faith and belief as well as its practice is an unbridled right and whether an illegal act as part of ritual shapes, controls or limits the free exercise. In the matter of belief, Justice Scalia argues that under no circumstances may government "compel affirmation of religious belief."[30] As to free exercise, a limitation may arise depending on the conduct or action called for in the religious service. In this case, the usage of peyote, a controlled substance outlawed by both state and federal statutes, makes the free exercise claim a bit more muddled. In the end, Justice Scalia concludes that these criminal proscriptions cause the usually protected religious expression to be on the defense. He states,

> Because respondents' ingestion of peyote was prohibited under Oregon law, and because that prohibition is constitutional, Oregon may, consistent with the Free Exercise Clause, deny respondents unemployment compensation when their dismissal results from use of the drug. The decision of the Oregon Supreme Court is accordingly reversed.[31]

Natural law, religious freedom and belief in a Deity

The natural law's very essence depends on its divine underpinnings—the idea that it be a reflection of the divine Creator, that it be an imprint of the eternal law and that its content be impressed in reason for all people and in all places. Natural law cannot subsist on its own but symbiotically is tethered to the highest order, the highest and eternal God. The framers of our Constitution and some of the court's earliest decisions focused on this critical quality—that right to believe and practice. In general, it is only right that the government stay out of religious dogma and doctrine and in its place allow free beings to believe in accordance with their own understanding of God in the world and to practice that faith in an unfettered way. This is utterly and completely natural to the human person.

In Employment Division, we encounter a rare case where government trumps religious expression in favor of a human right—in this case an unemployment benefit program. In both the majority and dissenting opinions, it is clear how fundamental religious liberty is—to discern the respect naturally shown for such a naturally endowed right under our system of government. Justice Scalia observes,

> It would be true, we think (though no case of ours has involved the point), that a state would be "prohibiting the free exercise [of religion]" if it sought to ban such acts or abstentions only when they are engaged in for religious reasons, or only because of the religious belief that they display. It would doubtless be unconstitutional, for example, to ban the casting of "statues that are to be used for worship purposes," or to prohibit bowing down before a golden calf.[32]

However, when belief is put into practice, the protection is not as absolute. This seeming contradiction to the freedom to exercise in a particular way is not all that contradictory. In the court's 1879 resolution of polygamy, as espoused by the Mormon Church, the court did not protect the criminal act of polygamous marriage from the general obligation to allow full and free exercise.[33] In *United States v. Lee*, the court rejected the Amish request not to withhold social security from its employee checks since it did not participate in the Social Security program[34]—two cases that illustrate that violations of the law will not afford a safe harbor under the guise of religious expression and exercise. The use of peyote is a practice directly violating a criminal act and hence not exercisable under a compulsory natural law principle. In other words, the natural law cannot be utilized to advance a wrong, to provide justification and rationale for criminality or illegality and since the tenets of the natural law reflect the imprint of the divine and eternal, it is difficult to find justification of drug usage under a natural law jurisprudence. In this fashion, the prohibition of the drug usage provides the government with the "compelling state interest" to restrict that practice.[35] Otherwise, society would be using religion to court "anarchy."[36] Justice O'Connor's concurring opinion displays this necessity in curbing an alleged religious practice to avoid the pains and negative effects of the criminality.

> Indeed, the Court holds that, where the law is a generally applicable criminal prohibition, our usual free exercise jurisprudence does not even apply.[37] To reach this sweeping result, however, the Court must not only give a strained reading of the First Amendment but must also disregard our consistent application of free exercise doctrine to cases involving generally applicable regulations that burden religious conduct.[38]

Given how natural religious beliefs and expressions are, the court cannot restrict those beliefs unless its restriction is caused by a greater harm or societal injury.[39] In the use of peyote, the court gives proper context to the sanctity and importance of religious expression but cautions that the right may see restriction, not as to belief but as to actual practice and free exercise. Justice O'Connor declares,

> To say that a person's right to free exercise has been burdened, of course, does not mean that he has an absolute right to engage in the conduct. Under our established First Amendment jurisprudence, we have recognized that the freedom to act, unlike the freedom to believe, cannot be absolute.[40] Instead, we have respected both the First Amendment's express textual mandate and the governmental interest in regulation of conduct by requiring the Government to justify any substantial burden on religiously motivated conduct by a compelling state interest and by means narrowly tailored to achieve that interest.[41]

In both the majority and dissenting views, the justices are hesitant, even reticent, to alter the naturalness of free exercise. So fundamental is the right that every restriction on its exercise must be weighed and evaluated in the narrowest and strictest scrutiny possible. Belief and religious expression deserve a special place, "beyond the reach of the majorities and officials."[42] Justice O'Connor eloquently describes our willingness to accommodate the inherent nature of belief and its practice.

> "One's right to life, liberty, and property, to free speech, a free press, freedom of worship and assembly, and other fundamental rights may not be submitted to vote; they depend on the outcome of no elections."[43] "The Fathers of the Constitution were not unaware of the varied and extreme views of religious sects, of the violence of disagreement among them, and of, the lack of any one religions creed on which all men would agree. They fashioned a charter of government which envisaged the widest possible toleration of conflicting views." The compelling interest test reflects the First Amendment's mandate of preserving religious liberty to the fullest extent possible in a pluralistic society.[44]

Even despite this extraordinary deference, the court can properly declare that a religious practice that violates existing laws, in this case being prohibited and controlled substances, and after an assessment of the demonstrable health risks associated with peyote's usage, is not protected under free exercise jurisprudence, nor would it be consistent with natural law reasoning. To worship with a dangerous drug, such as peyote, flies counter to the natural law's self-preservation principles since the usage is destructive to the human person. The court labels the practice "inherently harmful and dangerous."[45] Put another way, the natural law will never advance a behavior that would be inconsistent with our natural disposition or advance vice over virtue or human flourishing over inevitable harm or ruin. As a result, proclaiming peyote usage at religious ceremony as consistent with the natural law is not a defensible argument.

Justices Blackmun, Brennan and Marshall are not all that convinced about the ill effects of peyote usage or how significant the impact would be if an exemption be made for its usage in religious ceremonies. For them the war on drugs and illicit drug usage may be a compelling interest on the part of the state, but First Amendment evaluation also insists that if a least restrictive alternative could be possible than complete ban or prohibition, the latter case of least restrictive alternative could be the better route. And this mentality is fostered by the crucial position belief and free exercise have in constitutional history. Intolerance in every form must be impermissible. The dissent argues,

I do not believe the Founders thought their dearly bought freedom from religious persecution a "luxury," but an essential element of liberty—and they could not have thought religious intolerance "unavoidable," for they drafted the Religion Clauses precisely in order to avoid that intolerance.[46]

Nor is the dissent all that convinced of the health consequences as extremely characterized by the majority since it "offers, however, no evidence that the religious use of peyote has ever harmed anyone."[47] Nor can the majority's view that drug prevention and control outweigh the centrality of religious belief and expression since belief matters more than temporal affairs. For in matters of faith, however "unorthodox they may be," the individual freedom, inherently part of the nature of the human person, always takes precedence over a legislative enactment.[48]

Locke v. Davey, 540 U.S. 712 (2003)

Whether or not a university student could participate in a Washington State Promise Scholarship Program who was majoring in "theology" consumed the court's attention in *Locke v. Davey*. Holding that the Washington State Promise Scholarship Program's exclusion did not violate the free exercise clause of the Constitution, the court rejected the student's appeal. The Promise Program eligibility requirements stated in part the following:

> Intent—Finding.
>
> The legislature intends to strengthen the link between postsecondary education and K-12 education by creating the Washington promise scholarship program for academically successful high school graduates from low and middle-income families. The legislature finds that, increasingly, an individual's economic viability is contingent on postsecondary educational opportunities, yet the state's full financial obligation is eliminated after the twelfth grade. Students who work hard in kindergarten through twelfth grade and successfully complete high school with high academic marks may not have the financial ability to attend college because they cannot obtain financial aid or the financial aid is insufficient.[49]

The program's overall purpose is neutral and inclusive—allowing both religiously affiliated college attendees and public and private students to apply without exception.

When the student wishing to enroll in an undergraduate program in theology applies, the program administrators denied the application based on the State of Washington's own Constitution, the relevant provision stating, "No public money or property shall be appropriated for or applied to any religious worship, exercise or instruction, or the support of any religious establishment."[50] A review of the state constitutional limitation bears little probative support for this view. The majority in Locke cite, although incorrectly, the Washington State Administrative Code that guides the Promise Scholarship Program, implying that specific programs may be excluded when the Code merely declares what constitutes an eligible student.

(12) "Eligible student" means a person who:
   (a) Graduates from a public or private high school located in the state of Washington; and
   (b) Is in the top fifteen percent of his or her 2000 graduating class; or
   (c) Attained a cumulative score of 1200 or better on the Scholastic Assessment Test I (SATI) on the first attempt; or
   (d) Attained a cumulative score of 27 or better on the American College Test (ACT) on the first attempt; and
   (e) Has a family income less than one hundred thirty-five percent of the state's median; and
   (f) Enrolls at least half time in an eligible postsecondary institution in the state of Washington; and
   (g) Is not pursuing a degree in theology[51]

Hence, the court's assertion that the award would be constitutionally impermissible may have less persuasive power than to make said award violative of the Administrative Code.

Other issues emerge as to free exercise and belief in light of the natural law theory.

Natural law, free exercise and belief

At the heart of natural law reasoning rests an unbridled recognition that human law cannot subsist on its own or in some vacuum where its justness and validity depend solely on the promulgative process. It is self-evident that the entire superstructure of natural law jurisprudence depends upon a transcendent and higher power in the nature of God. From this vantage point, theology—the science of God—and in earlier times, considered the highest intellectual pursuit because of its subject matter, namely the highest good, the perfect and omnipotent and all-powerful God, makes the Promise Program exclusion shortsighted and at complete odds with what the natural law dictates.

Even the pagans of Rome and Greece grasped tightly to a metaphysical order in their view of nature and law.[52]

The concept of order in the universe presumed a guiding power—almost an intelligent design. While more modern thinkers in the mode of Lloyd Weinreb and Lon Fuller use the language of natural law in an almost exclusively secular way, the bottom line is that human personhood and how it operates suffices to guarantee natural rights. Weinreb states that his inquiry is "not religious but intellectual."[53] More curiously, Weinreb thinks Aquinas would have reached similar conclusions without the benefit of his faith if he was not exposed to its tenets for the "natural law did not lead Thomas to that faith."[54] One can surely sympathize with that view, yet the fullness of natural law reasoning would never have reached its glorious result in the Middle Ages without that faith. Belief in a Deity, the highest and ultimate good, vivifies all the other precepts in the natural law—for without the foundational understanding that human law depends upon the eternal law, and eternal law that descends and is imprinted in every human creature in the form of the natural law, the entire jurisprudence falters.

At the lower court level, a divided Ninth Circuit took two positions: first, some arguing that to disburse funds had the net effect of establishing a religious setting supported by state taxpayer dollars, while the contrary view was by this exclusion, the "state had singled out religion for unfavorable treatment" without a "compelling state interest."[55] And in a way, it is difficult to accept this narrow exclusion without feeling the vibrations of constitutional infraction. The majority opinion's understanding of "theology" displays a myopic and almost ignorant view of what the academic discipline encompasses. If the court realized that undergraduate studies in theology would include but not be limited to Dogmatics and Ecclesiology, Sacred Scripture and Church History, Moral Philosophy and Social Justice as well as close reviews of intellectual giants like Augustine, Aquinas and the Church Fathers, it would not paint this caricature of theology as being "devotional" alone. The court uncannily concludes that there must be a wall between any chance for occupational preparation for "religious and secular professions."[56] The court seems incapable of finding that some students study theology without the slightest ambition for an occupation related to it.

But the majority, authored by Chief Justice Rehnquist, does not see this unfair projection and caricature, then citing the college catalog that holds that the college is "distinctly Christian in the evangelical sense."[57] This statement affirms the belief system—and the natural law right to not only believe but also practice freely and without governmental intrusion. Would the court reach a similar conclusion about an exceptional Catholic university like Notre Dame or a Jewish institution like Yeshiva? Even the majority's listing of courses in the curriculum manifests the complete and thorough lack of understanding of what the academic discipline of theology really is. Courses like "Christian Doctrine" and "Principles of Spiritual Development" are paraded out as proof on why this degree is an enemy of freedom and the American way.[58] An objective reading of the majority leaves the reader with a sense that its authors lack any meaningful conception of what theological studies truly are—and by giving greater deference to the Administrative Code of Washington State than the First Amendment, should raise the red flag for protectors of religious belief and its practice.

Both Justice Scalia and Thomas, in their dissent, insist that any restriction on a belief system must "undergo the most rigorous of scrutiny."[59] Both claim that the Washington program intentionally discriminates against theology precisely because it is a belief system. When the state provides a general benefit for the general citizenry, it cannot target religious expression for exclusion and, in doing so, impose an unconstitutional burden on that free exercise and belief. Scalia and Thomas comment,

> When the State makes a public benefit generally available, that benefit becomes part of the baseline against which burdens on religion are measured; and when the State withholds that benefit from some individuals solely on the basis of religion, it violates the Free Exercise Clause no less than if it had imposed a special tax.
>
> That is precisely what the State of Washington has done here. It has created a generally available public benefit, whose receipt is conditioned only on academic performance, income, and attendance at an accredited school. It has then carved out a solitary course of study for exclusion: theology.[60]

In this fashion, the state targets religion for exclusion while our constitutional history and traditions insist on neutrality in the matter of religion.[61]

And the dissent fully appreciates how intimately this program undercuts one's ability to believe and live within the free exercise domain envisioned by our Founding Fathers. Justice Scalia seems impatient with the majority's conclusion that if approved, it would sanction and erect a mechanism for the training of ministers, thereby violating the establishment clause. In the final analysis, this decision is more about believing than establishing and with a concerted, clear-cut effort to exclude, one can only impute a singling out of a belief system. Justice Scalia observes,

> No, the interest to which the Court defers is not fear of a conceivable Establishment Clause violation, budget constraints, avoidance of

endorsement, or substantive neutrality—none of these. It is a pure philosophical preference: the State's opinion that it would violate taxpayers' freedom of conscience not to discriminate against candidates for the ministry. This sort of protection of "freedom of conscience" has no logical limit and can justify the singling out of religion for exclusion from public programs in virtually any context.[62]

This program exclusion is not even inferential or unintentional but expressly and unequivocally precise on who gets the money and who does not. Believers, in one way or the other, are relegated to select discriminatory status precisely because of what they believe. Justice Scalia describes this as an "indignity."

> Discrimination on the face of a statute is something else. The indignity of being singled out for special burdens on the basis of one's religious calling is so profound that the concrete harm produced can never be dismissed as insubstantial.[63]

Hence, the majority view in Locke runs deeply and contrarily to the natural law tenet of "Belief in a Deity" and any restriction, without a "valid compelling state interest," would undermine the free expression of belief and religion. A scholarship program cannot intentionally exclude students engaged in the study of our highest science or, as defined by Justice Thomas, as "the study of the nature of God and religious truth" and the "study of God and his relation to the world."[64]

Christian Legal Society of the University of California v. Leo P. Martinez, 561 U.S. 661 (2010)

Religious belief and expression are subject to state and governmental action at many levels, from the *Employment Division v. Smith*,[65] which disallowed the use of peyote for religious ritual, to the denial of prayer at public events such as sports and graduations.[66]

It is equally clear that the public longs for a time when religion and the expression of spirituality were part of our communal, national fabric rather than an arena fraught with contentious challenges every time someone freely expresses a theological belief. Our culture has become increasingly litigious regarding the suppression of belief and while there is a perfectly understandable firewall between what the state establishes and what its citizenry must believe, the idea that the free exercise of religious beliefs could be quashed by governmental action is completely at odds with the nation's constitutional heritage.[67] Like so many legal decisions emanating from the mid-twentieth century, and certainly after the *Roe v. Wade*, mentality became a fixture in legal analysis, the animus to belief simply accelerated. In Christian Legal Society (CLS), a group of Christian believers were directly told they could not believe as they believe or else. Put another way, this group of law students, who tended to the evangelical tradition of religious belief, were told by the hand of government that its society had to accept "all-comers" and whether those applicants believed similarly or even believed with vociferous opposition really was not the point. In CLS, the opinion's primary author, Justice Ruth Bader Ginsburg, lays out the governmental suppression of specific beliefs unless those beliefs can be diluted with those who think otherwise. In full reliance on the Hastings College of Law nondiscriminatory policy, Justice Ginsburg insists that religious expression and belief be subject to the negative effects of the very policy seeking to protect all students. The policy states,

> [Hastings] shall not discriminate unlawfully on the basis of race, color, religion, national origin, ancestry, disability, age, sex or sexual orientation. This nondiscrimination policy covers admission, access and treatment in Hastings-sponsored programs and activities.[68]

At its core, the society seeks members who adhere and concur with the basic tenets of religious expression common to the evangelical tradition. Each applicant must sign a Statement of Faith, which includes the following principles of belief:

- One God, eternally existent in three persons, Father, Son and Holy Spirit.
- God the Father Almighty, Maker of heaven and earth.
- The Deity of our Lord, Jesus Christ, God's only Son conceived of the Holy Spirit, born of the virgin Mary; His vicarious death for our sins through which we receive eternal life; His bodily resurrection and personal return.
- The presence and power of the Holy Spirit in the work of regeneration.
- The Bible as the inspired Word of God.[69]

In addition to these faith principles, the society expects its members to live in accordance with traditional moral rules and guidelines long associated with Christian ethical tradition. The court notes this expectation:

> Among those tenets is the belief that sexual activity should not occur outside of marriage between a man and a woman; CLS thus interprets its bylaws to exclude from affiliation anyone who engages in "unrepentant homosexual conduct."[70]

Hence, in order for a student organization to operate, under the aegis of the University of California, every student, believers or otherwise, must be welcomed into the fold. To have any rules of exclusion, that is a criterion that expects ethical compliance with the principles espoused by the CLS, alters diversity and the inclusiveness policy of Hastings. This all-comers policy is challenged by the society as fundamentally undercutting the group's right of religious expression and free exercise.

Since Hastings College of Law, part of the University of California system, is a public entity, the majority appears in a fog over whether this be an establishment or an association case for religious expression. And even foggier phases of the opinion lay out the court's general tendency to review governmental restrictions with the strict scrutiny rule and demand a compelling state interest for its imposition. The court pays lip service to these general constitutional dynamics and then disregards when announcing its agreement with the silencing of the CLS. Throughout the majority opinion, Justice Ginsburg touts diversity as the driving force behind its rationale—that all points of view are better than just one, although ironically, that one point of view cannot be tolerated. In his dissent, Justice Alito, joined by Justices Scalia and Thomas, target this irony:

> Today's decision rests on a very different principle: no freedom of expression that offends prevailing standards of political correctness in our country's institutions of higher learning.[71]

That standard of suppression does not appear to impact the full array of student groups that presently reside on the Hastings campus—because, as Justice Alito rightfully infers, these "other" groups do not have deficit of true understanding and tolerance. Some of the groups that appear not subject to university oversight are:

- Hastings Democratic Caucus
- Hastings Republicans
- Hastings Jewish Law Students Association
- Hastings Association of Muslim Law Students
- pro-choice
- pro-life groups
- Black Law Students Association
- Korean American Law Society
- La Raza Law Students Association
- Middle Eastern Law Students Association
- Clara Foltz Feminist Association
- Students Raising Consciousness at Hastings[72]

The question about whether or not certain religious beliefs are acceptable to governmental authorities seems self-evident because the CLS belief system has been deemed unacceptable in a public setting. At the deposition phase of these proceedings, even the dean at Hastings could not avoid the inevitable trap of selective religious belief enforcement when noting,

> "It is my view that in order to be a registered student organization you have to allow all of our students to be members and full participants if they want to."[73] [...] "Hastings interprets the Nondiscrimination Policy as requiring that student organizations wishing to register with Hastings allow any Hastings student to become a member and/or seek a leadership position in the organization."[74]

Hence, Hastings demands that an evangelical group of students, all willingly enrolled and without any coercion to others, accept those into the organization whose belief system directly contravenes the core mission of the CLS—even allowing its opposition parties to assume leadership roles. This extraordinary policy triggers a host of quandaries for religious expression and belief—all of which will be inconsistent with the natural law's tenet regarding our natural instinct to know and believe in God.

The natural law, religious expression and belief

The natural inclination, predisposition and inherency regarding our knowledge of God is part and parcel our natural law design. Thwarting and suppressing religious expression and belief are governmental acts utterly and totally inconsistent with natural law jurisprudence. Efforts by governmental authorities to restrict the practice of any sort of religion in the public square have been intense and continuous since the school prayer cases of the 1960s. In many cases, the intensity of this anti-religion mentality has morphed into its own sort of religion—a secularism that purges anything remotely metaphysical.[75]

This secular zeal also weaves its way in the CLS case and hides behind the benign and well-intentioned purpose of diversity policy to suppress religious expression.

The dissent appears to have focused its rationale on the unseemly nature of this suppression. Justice Alito compares and contrasts other groups on campus that have no such obligation to accept those antagonistic to the group's cause. He remarks,

> Only religious groups were required to admit students who did not share their views. An environmentalist group was not required to

admit students who rejected global warming. An animal rights group was not obligated to accept students who supported the use of animals to test cosmetics. But CLS was required to admit avowed atheists. This was patent viewpoint discrimination. "By the very terms of the [Nondiscrimination Policy], the University [...] select[ed] for disfavored treatment those student [groups] with religious [...] viewpoints."[76] It is no wonder that the Court makes no attempt to defend the constitutionality of the Nondiscrimination Policy.[77]

Alito further claims that the target is primarily religion—not fraternities or sports clubs—but those associations that bind one another, join with one another, to advance the tenets of their faith in light of the group itself. This "associational" quality deserves heightened protection under our constitutional tradition. As in *Boy Scouts v. Dale*, the associational qualities, based on a particular set of beliefs that may or may not be universally agreed to, cannot afford government the right to suppress these ideas. In matters of religion, the problem becomes even more acute because faith, religion and the belief in a Deity are naturally inherent in every human agent.[78]

Alito also argues that the free expression of a religious idea and any aligned associational entity may include ideas that others reject—and if this be so, the power of the state to alter those viewpoints must rest on more than a diversity policy or a nondiscrimination statement. It is that viewpoint, rooted in religious expression, that presumptively needs protection from suppression. The majority in CLS simply side steps this essential and very bedrock First Amendment concept. Justice Alito lays out the inconsistency when it comes to sexual morality:

> The Hastings Nondiscrimination Policy, as interpreted by the law school, also discriminated on the basis of viewpoint regarding sexual morality. CLS has a particular viewpoint on this subject, namely, that sexual conduct outside marriage between a man and a woman is wrongful. Hastings would not allow CLS to express this viewpoint by limiting membership to persons willing to express a sincere agreement with CLS's views. By contrast, nothing in the Nondiscrimination Policy prohibited a group from expressing a contrary viewpoint by limiting membership to persons willing to endorse that group's beliefs. A Free Love Club could require members to affirm that they reject the traditional view of sexual morality to which CLS adheres. It is hard to see how this can be viewed as anything other than viewpoint discrimination.[79]

At its heart, the majority in CLS gives little credence to a belief system that guides the religious citizen—and guides that citizen in unique ways that emanate from the tenets of that particular faith. No state, no government has the power to minimize or degrade that belief system; no governmental entity can erase or modify those beliefs because the free exercise of those beliefs causes alienation to those who deny those beliefs. An often heard comment in the modern world is how the Christian critique knows no bounds—that hostility to those beliefs fosters a judicial inconsistency that would not be tolerated in other faiths. The dissenters focused on this inconsistency:

> Religious groups like CLS obviously engage in expressive association, and no legitimate state interest could override the powerful effect that an accept-all-comers law would have on the ability of religious groups to express their views. The State of California surely could not demand that all Christian groups admit members who believe that Jesus was merely human. Jewish groups could not be required to admit anti-Semites and Holocaust deniers. Muslim groups could not be forced to admit persons who are viewed as slandering Islam.[80]

In sum, the implications of the decision chill religious expression and its associational implications since the policy seeks to correct beliefs that do not fit squarely in modern moral relativity. Tolerance becomes the higher, state-sanctioned and approved belief that corrects the intolerance of biblical moral precepts. In this way, the policy or suppression directly and antagonistically challenges that natural law principle on belief. To be sure, the CLS held firm to its principle tenets of belief and, as a result, would only accept members who found those principles agreeable and consistent with their theological outlook. Under the First Amendment, such a policy fully comports and to decide otherwise is a "serious setback for freedom of expression in this country."[81]

Burwell v. Hobby Lobby Stores, 134 S.Ct. 2751 (2014)

Efforts by governmental authorities to impose ideological tests against individuals and business entities became a regular event during the presidency of Barack Obama. With the implementation of the Affordable Care Act,[82] popularly known as Obamacare, came a host of governmental demands regarding provisions for health care that were mandated on every party. Especially apparent were the incessant demands that all had to participate and support the practice of abortion and birth control. The moral implications soon became quite obvious and efforts to carve out exemptions and exceptions based on religious beliefs and religious faith were generally met with governmental hostility. The court had to consider whether the mandatory provisions of the Affordable Care Act and the regulatory processes implemented by the federal Health and Human Service Agency violated the religious rights enunciated in the Religious Freedom Restoration Act of 1993 (RFRA),[83] which was enacted to thwart efforts by governmental authorities to restrict religious rights. The Act states in part

> that "Government shall not substantially burden a person's exercise of religion even if the burden results from a rule of general applicability."[84] If the Government substantially burdens a person's exercise of religion, under the Act that person is entitled to an exemption from the rule unless the Government "demonstrates that application of the burden to the person—(1) is in furtherance of a compelling governmental interest; and (2) is the least restrictive means of furthering that compelling governmental interest."[85]

The Act affirms traditional constitutional parlance and measures in questions regarding religious liberty and its free exercise. First, the Act demands that governmental action not substantially burden free exercise and religious belief; second, if the government needs to restrict religious liberty in any form, it will have to demonstrate a "compelling" state interest and proof that the imposition of this restriction be the least restrictive means of doing so.[86]

Compliance under the Affordable Care Act called for provision for contraceptive services and devices and provided no religious exception except for churches and select nonprofits. Those exemptions and exceptions did not extend to commercial, business or proprietary interests whose owners might have the same belief system.[87] Other exemptions related to business size, number of employees, time of plan implementation and the like. In this case, the chain known as Hobby Lobby failed to qualify for any exemption and despite its managerial objections was forced to dispense contraceptive materials and abortifacients like the "day after pill."

Aside from the impositions of fines for failure to comply with forced provisions for artificial birth control, the heavy hand of the government, by its forced and clearly non-discretionary enforcement, manifests less regard for the freedom to religiously object to contraception and, in turn, undercuts and undermines sincere and deeply felt religious beliefs that object to artificial birth-control measures including abortifacients.

Owners of Hobby Lobby and the aligned case of Conestoga Wood Specialties objected to this imposition on strictly free exercise and religious belief grounds. In Conestoga, the owners were guided by the Mennonite doctrine on the matter of human life whereby "the fetus in its earliest stages

[...] shares humanity with those that conceived it."[88] Conestoga even issued a "Statement on the Sanctity of Human Life" because their business must be run as their faith and belief system demands. For these Mennonites, "human life begins at conception" and to disregard this conclusion is to "sin against God to which they are held accountable."[89] In both settings, the business owners felt compelled to the point of "complicity" with a moral evil or a wrong that was directly repugnant to their religious faith and beliefs and a form of "scandalous participation."[90]

Similar facts exist in the case of Hobby Lobby—a national chain of more than 500 stores whose owners are evangelical Christians. Part of being an evangelical Christian is to obey the commands of both the Bible and the moral precepts that guide the overall belief system. The owners' objections are deeply rooted in their faith and the majority opinion lays out how this faith influences business.

> Like the Hahns, the Greens believe that life begins at conception and that it would violate their religion to facilitate access to contraceptive drugs or devices that operate after that point.[91] They specifically object to the same four contraceptive methods as the Hahns and, like the Hahns, they have no objection to the other 16 FDA-approved methods of birth control.[92]

For Hobby Lobby, compliance with a law that challenged their faith and belief system was simply an impossibility. And as the Affordable Care Act mandated, heavy fees and fines were imposed on those that did not comply—in this case being in excess of $475,000,000.

How this type of governmental punishment—exacting fees for nonparticipation—can be said proper under RFRA, strikes at the very heart of religious freedom. Here the majority readily concludes that the burden imposed on the free exercise of religious belief was substantial; the government cannot provide any compelling rationale as to why this tact must be done; and last, the government's failure to implement less restrictive means makes the policy flawed at every level. The court summarily dispenses its judgment by noting, "We have little trouble concluding that it does."[93]

Natural law, religious expression and belief

During the last decade, the tone and tenor of governmental authority have become more and more intolerant of those seeking to exercise good faith and faith-based objections to governmental authority. In natural law jurisprudence, the primacy of the eternal, transcendent, higher power always trumps the power of any human enactment. No case more keenly edifies this contrast in legal authority than Hobby Lobby where individual religious conscience is overwhelmed by the power of governmental authority that seeks to impose a requirement that conflicts with a person's faith or belief. The majority in Hobby Lobby is keenly aware of this conflict and but is even more attuned to how this confrontation so fundamentally alters the usual deference and respect shown to those beliefs. In the natural law, belief in a Deity rests at its jurisprudential center, and if this inherent state of belief can be disregarded, there are no safe rights and surely no inalienable rights to speak about. Justice Kennedy's concurring opinion captures this aspect of natural law reasoning most eloquently:

> In our constitutional tradition, freedom means that all persons have the right to believe or strive to believe in a divine creator and a divine law. For those who choose this course, free exercise is essential in preserving their own dignity and in striving for a self-definition shaped by their religious precepts. Free exercise in this sense implicates more than just freedom of belief.[94]

From its earliest pages, the majority opinion, Justice Alito outlines the dilemma of belief, faith and religious exercise with the power of government to undermine these firmly held principles. He notes,

> This belief implicates a difficult and important question of religion and moral philosophy, namely, the circumstances under which it is wrong for a person to perform an act that is innocent in itself but that has the effect of enabling or facilitating the commission of an immoral act by another.[95] Arrogating the authority to provide a binding national answer to this religious and philosophical question, HHS and the principal dissent in effect tell the plaintiffs that their beliefs are flawed. For good reason, we have repeatedly refused to take such a step.[96]

To fashion a legal remedy that sweeps away these beliefs, without a compelling state interest, really begs whether there is any religious freedom remaining under historic First Amendment principles. Justice Alito cautions governmental authority to not cross "this forbidden line" and to not conclude that these "religious beliefs are mistaken or insubstantial."[97] Imposing $475,000,000 in fees and fines for the exercise of that religious conviction is properly typed a "substantial burden" on the free exercise of religion.[98]

To overcome this basic presumption of belief, the governmental authority shall have to provide a "compelling" reason for the intrusion on that faith.

Justice Kennedy appreciates the role of religious freedom in shaping the overall character of this nation and allowing or tolerating restrictions to this most fundamental right may change that character. "Among the reasons the United States is so open, so tolerant, and so free is that no person may be restricted or demeaned by government in exercising his or her religion."[99]

While the majority targets the right to believe and exercise one's faith, in accordance with natural law jurisprudence, the dissenters, Justices Ginsburg, Breyer, Kagan and Sotomayor, treat the reader to every imaginable positive law theory, utilitarian argument, convenience rationale and feminist critique that essentially dwell in individual circumstances exclusively. Paying lip service to religious freedom and the exercise thereto, the dissent surely tolerates the view that all must agree with the policy but cannot carve out the smallest niche for those who object on religious grounds. Of course, as all overly zealous governmental policies usually opine, a failure to participate is an imposition on "employees who hold other beliefs."[100] Ginsburg strangely deduces that the exercise of religion and faith shorts the "uniform compliance with the law" and will cause "adverse health consequences."[101] Instead of focusing on the matter at hand, namely religious freedom, belief and the right to exercise those tenets of faith, the dissenting opinion favors a social-political manifesto of injustices that are likely to emerge if everyone does not participate in artificial birth control. Rather than giving any deference to the free exercise of religion, Justice Ginsburg, citing HHS internal studies, called for

> the HRSA adopted guidelines recommending coverage of "[a]ll [FDA-] approved contraceptive methods, sterilization procedures, and patient education and counseling for all women with reproductive capacity."[102]

As a result of any denial of reproductive health funding and choices, the dissent asserts that endgame will be disastrous by denying coverage to "legions of women who do not hold their employers' beliefs access to contraceptive coverage that the ACA would otherwise secure."[103] Hence, the compelling rationale rests in the obtuse and indefinable "public health and women's well-being."[104] Within this context of religious expression and contraceptive rights, the dissent seems strangely fearful of the implications and influences Hobby Lobby might inflict as to their reproductive cause. Yet in the grand legal scheme of things, few would argue that contraception assumes preeminent favor over religious expression as a primordial and most fundamental right, although that is precisely what Justice Ginsburg seems to believe.[105]

Aside from this hyperbole, especially when one considers the general availability of contraception, even dispensed without cost from organizations like Planned Parenthood, and the many organizations and entities that provide free reproductive services, the "compelling" claim seems more exaggerated than real. The dissent appears quite certain of the uniform policy to be imposed on the world at large but then uncannily reticent when figuring whether RFRA has been violated—all the more curious when RFRA was enacted to prevent the very governmental tyranny so evident in this case. Given that RFRA exists to evaluate burdensome governmental actions in the matter of religious expression, how sensible is the dissenting view that it may be incapable of "divin{ing} which religious beliefs are worthy of accommodation, and which are not?"[106]

Side by side with the women's rights critique—and those rights evaluated not in light of any constitutional parameters but more social commentary—the dissent cannot brook any company, business or for-profit entity having a claim rooted in religious expression. While both the majority and dissent discuss and dissect the idea of a "corporate person"—an issue not central to natural law analysis—the question of whether of an owner—particularly the proprietor of a for-profit business having the right to free exercise beliefs seems impossible for the dissent.

> The distinction between a community made up of believers in the same religion and one embracing persons of diverse beliefs, clear as it is, constantly escapes the Court's attention. One can only wonder why the Court shuts this key difference from sight.[107]

Justice Ginsburg further finds incredulous the idea that any corporation might be run and operated by individuals, officers and board members who guide their enterprise using religious principles as the compass for day-to-day operations. To argue that every business entity and its principal players must sever their managerial policies from their belief systems would advance a capitalism exclusively rooted in secular purposes. The dissent remarks that religion may exist in other entities such as not-for-profits, although for-profit "corporations do not fit that bill."[108]

Here the effort to detach the human person from their natural law instinct to know God, to believe, is replaced by a sterile vision of human agency—blank, neutral and incapable of integrating faith dimensions into this and many other aspects of life. In the natural law, there is no such severance but a perpetual integration of life's activities and applications with how one believes. That person, if acting consistently with the natural law, cannot avoid the precepts embedded in every person; cannot blot out their content; cannot forget or erase these imprints; and most importantly, cannot eradicate the most natural reflection impressed on the mind of every human agent—the image and likeness of God.

Masterpiece Cakeshop v. Colorado Civil Rights Commission, 138 S.Ct. 1719 (2018)

The mixture of discriminatory protections in the law, based on civil rights remedies, and the natural and highly constitutional protections in religious belief and the freedom to exercise said beliefs encompasses the dilemma posed in Masterpiece Cakeshop. No matter what position regarding same-sex marriage is taken, the Cakeshop case once again highlights the "intersection of same-sex marriage and issues of religious freedom" and how "notions of traditional morality" influence gay and lesbian constitutional rights.[109]

In Colorado, like most American jurisdictions, discrimination based on race, creed, gender, religion and ethnic background is prohibited. Of more recent inclusion has been discriminatory practices based on sexual orientation. In Masterpiece, when a male, gay couple were planning their wedding at a future date, soon to be married under Massachusetts law, asked a local baker to provide the wedding cake, he balked and respectfully advised these consumers that, due to his religious beliefs, same-sex weddings are not valid and directly in contravention to his religious precepts. The baker, being a devout Christian, could not cooperate in this service and respectfully declined the business based on his belief system. Here, the baker held firm to the traditional definition of marriage, only possible between a man and woman and any participation in this type of marital service would "be contrary to his most deeply held beliefs."[110]

As a result of this rejection of requested services, the parties filed a discrimination complaint with the Colorado Civil Rights Commission. The complaint expressly relied on the following statutory language:

> It is a discriminatory practice and unlawful for a person, directly or indirectly, to refuse, withhold from, or deny to an individual or a group, because of disability, race, creed, color, sex, sexual orientation, marital status, national origin, or ancestry, the full and equal enjoyment of the goods, services, facilities, privileges, advantages, or accommodations of a place of public accommodation.[111]

In the commission's review, it was clear that the bakery owners sought the complete integration of personal, Christian faith with their business operation. The commission expended very little energy on the free exercise side of the complaint and most of its deliberative assessment focused on the sexual orientation side of the dilemma. The commission found the bakers discriminated against the same-sex couple "for refusing to sell them wedding cakes [...] they would sell to heterosexual couples."[112] From this determination, the appeal eventually arrived at the highest court, and in a 7–2 decision, the majority, written by Justice Kennedy, struck down the administrative determination of the commission and the lower court affirmations citing the First Amendment's free expression and free exercise rights regarding religion and belief. From early in his analysis, Justice Kennedy seeks to balance these rights—not minimize or categorize either in a subservient position. He comments,

> Our society has come to the recognition that gay persons and gay couples cannot be treated as social outcasts or as inferior in dignity and worth. For that reason the laws and the Constitution can, and in some instances must, protect them in the exercise of their civil rights. The exercise of their freedom on terms equal to others must be given great weight and respect by the courts. At the same time, the religious and philosophical objections to gay marriage are protected views and in some instances protected forms of expression.[113]

The tension between these two positions—that of religious freedom and the right to be free of discrimination based on sexual orientation—constitutes the classic comparison of distinct individual rights. Justice Kennedy, long a sympathetic ear in matters involving sexual orientation, displays a deep and heartfelt empathy for the baker—whose belief system would be undermined by the coercive power of the state to act against one's conscience. His insight is obvious,

> In this context the baker likely found it difficult to find a line where the customers' rights to goods and services became a demand for him to exercise the right of his own personal expression for their message, a message he could not express in a way consistent with his religious beliefs.[114]

In the final analysis, Masterpiece Cakeshop captures both worlds quite remarkably—the one world where inner belief, internal spirituality operates free from the intrusive and heavy-handed governmental authority and the other domain where a conflict of moral beliefs emerges—a party choosing the belief over the state mandate.

Natural Law, belief in a Deity, sexual attraction and procreation

Various threads of the natural law weave through the Masterpiece Cakeshop decision. Aside from the majority's profound respect for religious belief and its corresponding constitutional protections, and in this case, rooted in the traditional, Christian vision of marriage, the court takes offense at governmental authority that appears to denigrate this central right in the American constitutional system. It targets, in particular, the commission's blatant animus to the exercise of this right—by a commission that quite clearly has contempt for these religious ideals of marriage between one man and one woman. As the bakery points out, this is part of God's plan—the attraction to opposite sexes and the procreative purpose of marriage—all of which encapsulate natural law precepts. Instead of respecting these positions, the commission equates these views with the institution of slavery and the Holocaust. The majority cites the decision:

> I would also like to reiterate what we said in the hearing or the last meeting. Freedom of religion and religion has been used to justify all kinds of discrimination throughout history, whether it be slavery, whether it be the holocaust, whether it be—I mean, we—we can list hundreds of situations where freedom of religion has been used to justify discrimination. And to me it is one of the most despicable pieces of rhetoric that people can use to—to use their religion to hurt others.[115]

Justice Kennedy zeroes in on the obvious animus—aghast that any governmental authority would characterize these spiritual beliefs as "despicable pieces of rhetoric."[116] Here the heavy hand of the government—oppressing the free exercise of religion and the belief system that religion depends upon—could not be more obvious. Government has no role, under natural law principles "sitting in judgment" as to religious beliefs.[117]

While the commission clamored for respect and dignity for every same-sex marriage couple, it found no room for even a modicum of respect to the religious believer. Hurling insult and indignities at a party exercising a natural inclination to belief and a higher power, cannot pass muster in a free and open society. This case, Justice Kennedy argues, should have been resolved "with tolerance, without undue disrespect to sincere religious beliefs."[118]

Even the traditionally liberal justices Breyer and Kagan concurred in the judgment for what can only be deemed a governmental intrusion in the interior belief system of a faith-based actor. Government cannot invade this territory and should not "show hostility to religious views."[119] The centrality of the free exercise clause in matters of religious belief and practice cannot be overemphasized enough. Gorsuch describes the commission's action as a "judgmental dismissal of a sincerely held religious belief, [...] antithetical to the First Amendment."[120] Failure to show this right proper deference will likely lead to a governmental mindset that has little regard for any other aligned rights. Justice Gorsuch and Alito, also concurring, appreciate the critical subject matter before the court.

> But we know this with certainty: when the government fails to act neutrally toward the free exercise of religion, it tends to run into trouble. Then the government can prevail only if it satisfies strict scrutiny, showing that its restrictions on religion both serve a compelling interest and are narrowly tailored.[121]

Hence it is clear that government failed to act or resolve these competing interests in a neutral and fair manner but instead favored the rights under sexual orientation principles while simultaneously denigrating religious belief and its free exercise. That, in the end, connotes an antagonistic view of the traditional and natural law view of what marriage means. Under the commission's decision, the right to believe as Western tradition has believed for nearly 5,000 years is no longer on the list of acceptable beliefs—it must be "irrational" to conclude in this manner; it must be driven by hate or outright virulent condemnation of a lifestyle to which Justice Gorsuch retorts,

> Many may agree with the Commission and consider Mr. Phillips's religious beliefs irrational or offensive. Some may believe he misinterprets the teachings of his faith. And, to be sure, this Court has held same-sex marriage a matter of constitutional right and various States have enacted laws that preclude discrimination on the basis of sexual orientation. But it is also true that no bureaucratic judgment condemning a sincerely held religious belief as "irrational" or "offensive" will ever survive strict scrutiny under the First Amendment. In this country, the place of secular officials isn't to sit in judgment of religious beliefs, but only to protect their free exercise.[122]

Having government decide what is acceptable religiously can only be seen as an affront to basic notions of free exercise and religious belief. Even educational accreditors for colleges and universities have used the power of accreditation to force educational institutions to adopt "prevailing social norms" or else—a clear suppression of religious belief at the expense of quasi-governmental authority.[123]

"Civil authorities," Justice Gorsuch writes, "whether 'high or petty,' bear no license to declare what is or should be 'orthodox' when it comes to religious beliefs, or whether an adherent has 'correctly perceived' the commands of his religion."[124] Concurring overall, Justice Thomas is taken aback by the animus and hostility shown these Christian believers—as if what they believe was not worth any meaningful consideration and, as a result, "flouts bed-rock principles" in the matter of religious expression.[125] The notion that government might invade the inner sanctum of faith, of belief and spirituality, and substitute a more favorable measure of sexual orientation as the justification cannot be defended under historic and even contemporary free exercise jurisprudence. Indeed, as Justice Alito so prophetically remarked in Obergefell, the net intention of forcing the belief is to "stamp out every vestige of dissent" and to "vilify Americans who are unwilling to assent to the new orthodoxy."[126]

Interestingly, the dissenting opinion by Justices Ginsburg and Sotomayor acts as if religious belief and its free exercise were not part of the mix, nor are they even willing to entertain the idea that a positive approval of once-held prohibited behavior might cause social disruption or foster an out of sight and out of mind mentality in the implementation of this new definition.[127] Justice Scalia has long critiqued the court's willingness to socially engineer changes without the sense or sensibility of what could, might or may happen. In *Lawrence v. Texas*, he used the term "massive social disruption."[128]

All that matters in this context is the purported or actual rights of same-sex couples—not that religious objection has any relevance to the question at all. The dissent is so silent on the matter of religious expression that it confirms the new world order of political correctness, where belief is replaced with a political and social orthodoxy—something so transient and ephemeral that no "right" has any foundation at all. The bottom line, Justice Ginsburg argues, is that the cake was not sold to these consumers "for no other reason other than their sexual orientation, a cake of the kind he regularly sold to others."[129] In this context, Justices Ginsburg and Sotomayor have little, if any, regard for the religious counterbalance, the measure of how these various rights might respectfully compete. In their sterile, positive world of promulgation and enactment, religion plays little if any role in this dilemma. In its place, the human agent is treated to a world devoid of belief—a condition so at odds that the natural law could not and would not recognize it.

Conclusion

Any fair reading of these legal cases on religious belief and free exercise manifests the court's overall respect for this most fundamental form of personal and spiritual expression. Whether in majority or dissent, the court rightfully grant a presumptive view on the nature of belief and its expression. And while there is no universal agreement on specific outcomes, there is a clearly identifiable deference shown for this natural right, a right inherent in the natural law imprint in every human agent—to belief not only in a Deity but to simultaneously express those beliefs in a particular faith-based rubric or exercise. Efforts to clamp it down under the compelling state interest standard are further mollified by the demand for strict scrutiny or the insistence on the least restrictive means possible test. None of these legal measures assures perfection in the outcome but all the decisions posed in this chapter demonstrate an underlying regard for the right to free exercise under the First Amendment. The Marsh decision solidified the idea of a spiritual nation, a religious people by tradition and the upholding of simple, nondenominational prayer before the commencement of activities in the Nebraska legislative session. With this decision, the court affirms the transcendent, higher-power jurisprudence that shaped and founded this nation. In *Employment Division v. Smith*, the court grappled with the right to use peyote and ruled that its proscription outweighed the religious practice, although both dissent and majority saw the natural conflict with interfering with a belief system.

In *Locke v. Ramsey*, the court struggled with a Washington State College Scholarship program that excluded students in the academic discipline of theology—a decision that is more valuable for its dissent than its majority. The dissenters clearly prioritized faith and belief above the secular world order. In CLS, the court contorted its reasoning to restrict funding to a Christian law student association that would not accept the state All-Comers policy—the net effect watering down the very basic beliefs of the society. After these two less expansive cases regarding religion, the court moved toward a pro-belief and pro-exercise direction, ruling in Hobby Lobby that the owners of a company may not be compelled to dispense abortifacients and birth control under the Affordable Care Act nor should a bakery owner be compelled to bake cakes for same-sex marital consumers in Masterpiece Cakeshop. In these latest cases, the court reaffirms the preeminency of religion, belief and faith in each and every person and fully accepts that these beliefs are part and parcel of every human person, as natural as the natural law itself.

As a short side, the court recently ruled, in a procedural finding, in the Little Sisters of the Poor case, *Zubik v. Burwell*.[130] The Little Sisters of the Poor are a religious order that were heavily fined unless and until their compliance with the Affordable Care Act was demonstrated—a compliance directly at odds with the order's religious viewpoint. While the court did not rule on the full merits, it sent it back to the Ninth Circuit Court of Appeals for a better and more consistent resolution with free exercise and religious expression principles. As of this date, the court has yet to hear the resolution from the Ninth Circuit. But given the court's 9–0 insistence on reconsideration, it is unlikely that the Little Sisters of the Poor will feel the heavy hand of government oppressing their deeply felt faith and the corresponding right to practice what it believes. The end result could not be more consistent with the natural law.

Notes

1 See St. Thomas Aquinas, *Summa Theologica*, trans. English Dominican Friars (New York: Benziger, 1947).
2 St. Anselm, "Cur Deus Homo," in *Opera Omnia*, trans. Franciscus Salesius Schmitt (Rome: Ex Officina San Saini et Soc., 1940).
3 US Constitution, amend. 1.
4 *United States v. Freed*, 401 U.S. 601, 602 (1971).
5 Ibid.
6 406 U.S. 205 (1972).
7 *Reynolds v. United States*, 98 U.S. 145 (1879); *West Virginia State Board of Education v. Barnette*, 319 U.S. 624 (1943); *Cantwell v. Connecticut*, 310 U.S. 296 (1940); *Everson v. Board of Education*, 330 U.S. 1 (1947); *Braunfeld v. Brown*, 366 U.S. 599 (1961); *Torcaso v. Watkins*, 367 U.S. 488 (1961); *Engel v. Vitale*, 370 U.S. 421 (1962); *Sherbert v. Verner*, 374 U.S. 398 (1963); *School District of Abington Township, Pennsylvania v. Schempp*, 374 U.S. 203 (1963); *Murray v. Curlett*, 374 U.S. 203 (1963); *Epperson v. Arkansas*, 393 U.S. 97 (1968); *Lemon v. Kurtzman*, 403 U.S. 602 (1971); *Wisconsin v. Yoder*, 406 U.S. 205 (1972); *McDaniel v. Paty*, 435 U.S. 618 (1978); *Stone v. Graham*, 449 U.S. 39 (1980); *Mueller v. Allen*, 463 U.S. 388 (1982); *Lynch v. Donnelly*, 465 U.S. 668 (1984); *Wallace v. Jaffree*, 472 U.S. 38 (1985); *Estate of Thornton v. Caldor, Inc.*, 472 U.S. 703 (1985); *Goldman v. Weinberger*, 475 U.S. 503 (1986); *Edwards v. Aguillard*, 482 U.S. 578 (1987); *County of Allegheny v. ACLU*, 492 U.S. 573 (1989); *Board of Education of Westside Community Schools v. Mergens*, 496 U.S. 226 (1990); *Employment Division v. Smith*, 494 U.S. 872 (1990); *Lee v. Weisman*, 505 U.S. 577 (1992); *Church of the Lukumi Babalu Aye v. City of Hialeah*, 508 U.S. 520 (1993); *Zobrest v. Catalina Foothills School District*, 509 U.S. 1 (1993); *Kiryas Joel School District v. Grumet*, 512 U.S. 687 (1994); *Capitol Square Review and Advisory Board v. Pinette*, 515 U.S. 753 (1995); *Santa Fe Independent School District v. Doe*, 530 U.S. 290 (2000); *Mitchell v. Helms*, 530 U.S. 793 (2000); *Good News Club v. Milford Central School*, 533 U.S. 98 (2001); *Zelman v. Simmons-Harris*, 536 U.S. 639 (2002); *Elk Grove Unified School District v. Newdow*, 542 U.S. 1 (2004); *Locke v. Davey*, 540 U.S. 712 (2004); *Van Orden v. Perry*, 545 U.S. 677 (2005); *McCreary County v. American Civil Liberties Union of Ky.*, 545 U.S. 844 (2005); *Cutter v. Wilkinson*, 544 U.S. 709 (2005); *Gonzales v. O Centro Espírita Beneficente União do Vegetal*, 546 U.S. 418 (2006); *Hein v. Freedom from Religion Foundation*, 551 U.S. 587 (2007); *Christian Legal Society v. Martinez*, 561 U.S. 661 (2010).
8 See *Everson v. Board of Education*, 330 U.S. 1 (1947), https://supreme.justia.com/cases/federal/us/330/1/.
9 See *Trinity Lutheran Church of Columbia, Inc. v. Comer*, 582 U.S. ____ (2017), Slip opinion No. 15–577, https://www.supremecourt.gov/opinions/16pdf/15-577_khlp.pdf.
10 See *Cochran v. Louisiana State Board of Education*, 281 U.S. 370 (1930), https://caselaw.findlaw.com/us-supreme-court/281/370.html; *Board of Education v. Allen*, 392 U.S. 236 (1968), https://supreme.justia.com/cases/federal/us/392/236/.
11 See *Agostini v. Felton*, 521 U.S. 203 (1997), https://supreme.justia.com/cases/federal/us/521/203/.
12 See *Mitchell v. Helms*, 530 U.S. 793 (2000), https://supreme.justia.com/cases/federal/us/530/793/.
13 *Marsh v. Chambers*, 463 U.S. 783, 786 (1983).
14 Marsh, 787–89.
15 Ibid., 790.
16 Ibid.

17 Ibid., 791.
18 Ibid., 792; *Zorach v. Clauson*, 343 U.S. 306, 343 U.S. 313 (1952).
19 Ibid., 794–95; *Panhandle Oil Co. v. Mississippi ex rel. Knox*, 277 U.S. 218, 277 U.S. 223 (1928) (Holmes, J., dissenting).
20 See *Stone v. Graham*, 449 U.S. 39, 449 U.S. 41 (1980).
21 Marsh, 792.
22 Ibid., 797–98.
23 Ibid., 804.
24 Ibid., 821.
25 Ibid.
26 Ibid., 808.
27 *Employment Division v. Smith*, 494 U.S. 872, 919 (1990).
28 Ore. Rev. Stat. § 475.992(4) (1987), Federal Controlled Substances Act, 21 U.S.C. §§ 811–812 (1982 ed. and Supp. V), as modified by the State Board of Pharmacy. Ore. Rev. Stat. § 475.005(6) (1987).
29 Smith, 874.
30 Ibid., 877.
31 Ibid., 890.
32 Ibid., 877–78.
33 *Reynolds v. United States*, 98 U.S. 145 (1879).
34 *United States v. Lee*, 455 U.S. 252, 455 U.S. 263, n. 3 (1982).
35 Smith, 888.
36 Ibid., 889.
37 Ibid., 884.
38 Ibid., 892.
39 In the dissent, the court takes great pains to delineate the many religious exemptions carved out over the years. See, e.g., *Olsen v. Iowa*, 808 F.2d 652 (CA8 1986) (marijuana use by Ethiopian Zion Coptic Church); *United States v. Rush*, 738 F.2d 497 (CA1 1984), cert. denied, 470 U.S. 1004 (1985) (same); *United States v. Middleton*, 690 F.2d 820 (CA11 1982), cert. denied, 460 U.S. 1051 (1983) (same); *United States v. Hudson*, 431 F.2d 468 (CA5 1970), cert. denied, 400 U.S. 1011 (1971) (marijuana and heroin use by Moslems); *Leary v. United States*, 383 F.2d 851 (CA5 1967), rev'd on other grounds, 395 U.S. 6 (1969) (marijuana use by Hindu); *Commonwealth v. Nissenbaum*, 404 Mass. 575, 536 N.E.2d 592 (1989) (marijuana use by Ethiopian Zion Coptic Church); *State v. Blake*, 5 Haw.App. 411, 695 P.2d 336 (1985) (marijuana use in practice of Hindu Tantrism); *Whyte v. United States*, 471 A.2d 1018 (D.C.App.1984) (marijuana use by Rastafarian); *State v. Rocheleau*, 142 Vt. 61, 451 A.2d 1144 (1982) (marijuana use by Tantric Buddhist); *State v. Brashear*, 92 N.M. 622, 593 P.2d 63 (1979) (marijuana use by nondenominational Christian); *State v. Randall*, 540 S.W.2d 156 (Mo.App.1976) (marijuana, LSD and hashish use by Aquarian Brotherhood Church). See generally Annotation, Free Exercise of Religion as Defense to Prosecution for Narcotic or Psychedelic Drug Offense, 35 *A.L.R.3d* 939 (1971 and Supp. 1989).
40 See, e.g., *Cantwell*, supra, 310 U.S. at 310 U.S. 304; *Reynolds v. United States*, 98 U.S. 145, 98 U.S. 161–67.
41 Smith, 894.
42 Ibid., 901.
43 319 U.S. at 319 U.S. 638. See also *United States v. Ballard*, 322 U.S. 78, 322 U.S. 87 (1944).

44. Ibid., 903.
45. Ibid., 905.
46. Ibid., 909.
47. Ibid., 912.
48. Ibid., 921.
49. RCW 28B.119.005.
50. Washington State Constitution, Article 1 at section 11.
51. Wash. Admin. Code §250–80–020(12) (2003).
52. Charles P. Nemeth, *A Comparative Analysis of Cicero and Aquinas: Nature and the Natural Law* (London: Bloomsbury, 2017).
53. Lloyd L. Weinreb, "A Secular Theory of Natural Law," *Fordham Law Review*, 72, no. 6 (2004): 2287; Charles Covell, ed., "Lon L. Fuller and the Defence of Natural Law." In *The Defence of Natural Law* (London: Palgrave Macmillan, 1992).
54. Weinreb, "Secular," 2287.
55. *Locke v. Davey*, 540 U.S. 712, 718 (2003).
56. Ibid., 721.
57. Ibid., 724.
58. Ibid., 725.
59. Ibid., 726; *Church of Lukumi Babalu Aye, Inc. v. Hialeah*, 508 U.S. 520 (1993).
60. Ibid., 726–27; Wash. Rev. Code §28B.119.010(8) (Supp. 2004); Wash. Admin. Code §250–80–020(12)(g) (2003).
61. Ibid., 728.
62. Ibid., 730.
63. Ibid., 731.
64. Ibid., 734–35.
65. 494 U.S. 872 (1990).
66. See note 34, *infra*, for a comprehensive list.
67. Trinity Lutheran.
68. *Christian Legal Society of the University of California v. Leo P. Martinez*, 561 U.S. ___ (2010), Ginsburg, slip op., 4.
69. App. 226. Ginsburg, slip op., 5, n. 3.
70. Ibid., 5–6.
71. Alito, slip op., 1.
72. Ibid., 3–4; See App. 236–245; Brief for Petitioner, 3–4.
73. App. 343.
74. Ibid., 349; Alito, slip op., 6.
75. See Samuel R. Bagenstos, "The Unrelenting Libertarian," *Stanford Law Review*, 66, no. 6 (2014): 1205, 1230.
76. *Rosenberger v. Rector and Visitors of Univ. of Va.*, 515 U.S. 819, 831 (1995).
77. Alito, slip op., 19–20.
78. Ibid., 22.
79. Ibid., 22–23.
80. Ibid., 27.
81. Ibid.
82. Patient Protection and Affordable Care Act, 42 U.S.C. § 18001 et seq. (2010).
83. 107 Stat. 1488, 42 U. S. C. §2000bb et seq.
84. §2000bb–1(a).
85. §2000bb–1(b). *Burwell v. Hobby Lobby Stores*, 134 S.Ct. 2751 (2014), slip op., 5.

86   Burwell, Alito, slip op., 2.
87   Ibid., 9.
88   Ibid., 11; Mennonite Church USA, "Statement on Abortion," online at http://www.mennoniteusa.org/resource-center/resources/statements-and-resolutions/statement-on-abortion/.
89   Burwell, Alito, slip op., 12.
90   Kaleb Brooks, "Too Heavy a Burden: Testing Complicity-Based Claims under the Religious Freedom Restoration Act," *Indiana Law Journal*, 92, no. 5 (2016): 40, 46.
91   723 F. 3d, 1122.
92   Ibid., 1125. Burwell, Alito, slip op., 14.
93   Ibid., 31.
94   See *Cantwell v. Connecticut*, 310 U.S. 296, 303 (1940); Kennedy, slip op., 1–2.
95   See Oderberg, "The Ethics of Co-Operation in Wrongdoing." In *Modern Moral Philosophy*, edited by A. O'Hear, 203–28 (Cambridge: Cambridge University Press, 2004); T. Higgins, *Man as Man: The Science and Art of Ethics* (Rockford, IL: Tan Books, 1949), 353, 355; 1 H. Davis, *Moral and Pastoral Theology* (New York: Sheed and Ward, 1935), 341.
96   See, e.g., *Smith*, 494 U.S., at 887; *Hernandez v. Commissioner*, 490 U.S. 680, 699 (1989); *Presbyterian Church in U. S. v. Mary Elizabeth Blue Hull Memorial Presbyterian Church*, 393 U.S. 440, 450 (1969); Alito, slip op., 36–37.
97   Burwell, Alito, slip op., 37.
98   Ibid., 38.
99   Burwell, Kennedy, slip op., 4.
100 Burwell, Ginsburg, slip op., 32.
101 Ibid., 1, 5.
102 Ibid., 5.
103 Ibid., 8.
104 Ibid., 24.
105 For an interesting assessment of Hobby Lobby's influence in the State of Texas, see Kimberly Saindon, "Religious Freedom Legislation in Texas Takes Aim at Same-Sex Marriage," *Texas Journal on Civil Liberties & Civil Rights*, 23, no. 2 (2018): 165.
106 Burwell, Ginsburg, slip op., 33.
107 Ibid., 17.
108 Ibid., 18.
109 Tobin A. Sparling, "The Odd Couple: How Justices Kennedy and Scalia, Together, Advanced Gay Rights in Romer v. Evans," *Mercer Law Review*, 67 (2016): 305, 329.
110 *Masterpiece Cakeshop v. Colorado Civil Rights Commission*, 138 S.Ct. 1719 (2018), slip op., 3.
111 Colo. Rev. Stat. §24–34–601(2)(a) (2017).
112 Cakeshop, slip op., 8.
113 Ibid., 9.
114 Ibid., 11.
115 Ibid., 11–12, 13.
116 Ibid.
117 Ibid., 15.
118 Ibid., 18.
119 Cakeshop, Kagan, slip op., 1.
120 Cakeshop, Gorsuch, slip op., 2.

121 *Church of Lukumi Babalu Aye, Inc. v. Hialeah*, 508 U.S. 520, 546 (1993). Burwell, Gorsuch, slip op., 1.
122 Cakeshop, Gorsuch, slip op., 7.
123 Michael Schay, "Gordon College, Religious Liberty and Accreditation," *Journal of Law & Education*, 47, no. 2 (2018): 275, 281.
124 Cakeshop, Gorsuch, slip op., 9.
125 Cakeshop, Thomas, slip op., 2.
126 *Obergefell v. Hodges*, 135 S.Ct. 2071 (2015) (dissenting opinion) (slip op., 14).
127 Ibid.
128 *Lawrence v. Texas*, 539 U.S. 558, 1815 (2003); See also Maura J. Strassberg, "Scrutinizing Polygamy: Utah's *Brown v. Buhman* and British Columbia's Reference RE: Section 293," *Emory Law Journal*, 64, no. 6 (2015): 1815.
129 Cakeshop, Ginsburg, slip op., 5.
130 578 U.S. ___ (2016).

POSTSCRIPT TO *ROE v. WADE*: THE *DOBBS* DECISION

The influence of *Roe v. Wade*[1] cannot be overstated, especially when one considers how it influences constitutional thinking regarding unenumerated rights. It is doubtful if many of the cases considered in this text would have generated the decisions as issued without *Roe* as a reference point. Questions involving same-sex marriage and consensual homosexuality without criminal proscription, to name a few, have ties to a *Roe* mentality.

And in the end, this was part of *Roe*'s difficulty, for the decision ventured into a world of legal creationism—a sort of invented right, at least in a constitutional sense alone, for states were and have been free to deal with issues far longer than a federal, one size fits all. Here too, *Roe* never calmed the waters of dissent and division. *Roe* has never brought peace by any means on these contentious issues nor has *Roe* developed a consensus in the citizenry. The majority clearly and unequivocally noted the lack of any constitutional claim for an abortion right throughout the entire American experience. It was only until 1973 that *Roe* supplanted a pretty dependable understanding, The Court notes:

> Without any grounding in the constitutional text, history, or precedent, *Roe* imposed on the entire country a detailed set of rules for pregnancy divided into trimesters much like those that one might expect to find in a statute or regulation. See 410 U.S., at 163–164. *Roe*'s failure even to note the overwhelming consensus of state laws in effect in 1868 is striking, and what it said about the common law was simply wrong.[2]

Given this, the *Dobbs*[3] decision, issued in 2022, rattled the cages dramatically when it announced that *Roe* was over and of no further significance. In *Dobbs*, the abortion debate was de-federalized and sent back to the individual states. This decision has been both praised and pilloried but there were a host of forces that made it inevitable. Even the Court knew the endless litigation and rehashing of the abortion trauma was unhealthy and unproductive and from a more textualist wing, the *Dobbs* decision simply concluded that the express language of the U.S. Constitution provided no explicit or implicit constitutional right to an abortion. In essence the 50-year ideological war between pro-life and pro-choice forces was to hopefully come to an end, although the verdict is out on the eventuality of that result. In *Dobbs*, the U.S. Supreme Court recognized the tumultuous history when it concluded:

> Americans continue to hold passionate and widely divergent views on abortion, and state legislatures have acted accordingly. Some have recently enacted laws allowing abortion, with few restrictions, at all stages of pregnancy. Others have tightly restricted abortion beginning well before viability. And in this case, 26 States have expressly asked this Court to overrule *Roe* and Casey and allow the States to regulate or prohibit pre-viability abortions. Before us now is one such state law. The State of Mississippi asks us to uphold the constitutionality of a law that generally prohibits an abortion after the 15th week of pregnancy—several weeks before the point at which a fetus is now regarded as "viable" outside the womb.[4]

While no express mention of the natural law ever occurs in *Dobbs*, one characteristic of natural law jurisprudence was always on display, namely tradition, historical placement and legal lineage and definition relating to abortion as a practice. The *Dobbs* decision expends considerable energy laying out the overall condemnation of abortion in the history of English common law and the American experience. Justice Alito remarks:

> Not only was there no support for such a constitutional right until shortly before *Roe*, but abortion had long been a crime in every single State.[5]

From another angle the Court looks at the dilemma through an historical prism and again finds support for the right fully lacking. The majority concludes:

> Next, the Court examines whether the right to obtain an abortion is rooted in the Nation's history and tradition and whether it is an essential component of "ordered liberty." The Court finds that the right to abortion is not deeply rooted in the Nation's history and tradition. The underlying theory on which Casey rested—that the Fourteenth Amendment's Due Process Clause provides substantive, as well as procedural, protection for "liberty"—has long been controversial.[6]

The term "deeply rooted" and part of our tradition, is central when considering the claim of a fundamental constitutional right. For the majority, the evidence is simply lacking, with the Court commenting:

> Until the latter part of the 20th century, there was no support in American law for a constitutional right to obtain an abortion. No state constitutional provision had recognized such a right. Until a few years before *Roe*, no federal or state court had recognized such a right. Nor had any scholarly treatise. Indeed, abortion had long been a crime in every single State. Under common law, abortion was criminal in at least some stages of pregnancy and was regarded as unlawful and could have very serious consequences at all stages. American law followed the common law until a wave of statutory restrictions in the 1800s expanded criminal liability for abortions. By the time the Fourteenth Amendment was adopted, three-quarters of the States had made abortion a crime at any stage of pregnancy. This consensus endured until the day *Roe* was decided. *Roe* either ignored or misstated this history, and Casey declined to reconsider *Roe*'s faulty historical analysis.[7]

Relevant to natural law jurisprudence would be the issue of quickening or viability or personhood based on the concept of quickening. Quickening was the imprecise measure of whether a human being was confirmed by movement. And even in the ancient and medieval world, thinkers like Aristotle or Aquinas would hold a non-quickening fetus had yet to be viable and hence not subject to murder. However, Aquinas would argue that all abortion at even this stage is unnatural and a mortal sin. That Thomistic view appears unimportant in the Court's assessment of abortion practice since the nation's founding. It is fascinating to read the Court's assessment of quickening being pertinent to the legitimacy of abortion. Interestingly, the Court recounts how abortion in either the quickening or non-quickening version made little difference to the states that banned the practice. The Court mentions these distinctions at various places, such as:

> Although a pre-quickening abortion was not itself considered homicide, it does not follow that abortion was *permissible* at common law—much less that abortion was a legal *right*. Cf. *Glucksberg*, 521 U.S., at 713 (removal of "common law's harsh sanctions did not represent an acceptance of suicide"). Quite to the contrary, in the 1732 case mentioned above, the judge said of the charge of abortion (with no mention of quickening) that he had "never met with a case so barbarous and unnatural."[8]

As a result, *Dobbs* turns the abortion world on its head because of what the majority perceives as major deficiencies to any constitutional claim for a designated right. History does not support this view, nor does common law tradition. In fact, for most of Western tradition, the act of abortion was subject to criminal prosecution. Thus, *Dobbs* in a curious sort of way, returns the issue for state-by-state analysis. This is nothing new under the sun, because for most of our legal history, this is precisely how the matter was handled. Justice Alito, author of the majority opinion, highlights the irony of decision and why *Roe* could not or should not last.

> For the first 185 years after the adoption of the Constitution, each State was permitted to address this issue in accordance with the views of its citizens. Then, in 1973, this Court decided *Roe* v. Wade, 410 U.S. 113. Even though the Constitution makes no mention of abortion, the Court held that it confers a broad right to obtain one.[9]

Notes

1. *Roe v. Wade*, 410 U.S. 113 (1973).
2. *Dobbs v. Jackson*, No. 19-1392, slip op. syllabus at 5 (U.S. June 24, 2022).
3. *Id*
4. *Id.*, slip op. Alito at 4.
5. *Id.*, slip op. Alito at 16.
6. *Id.*, slip op. syllabus at 2.
7. *Id.*, at 3.
8. *Id.*, slip op. Alito at 18.
9. *Id.*, at 1.

INDEX

1st Amendment 145
   Establishment Clause 183, 192
   religious expression 187, 194, 195, 203, 206
9th Amendment 63
14th Amendment 76
   Due Process Clause 62, 134, 169
   Equal Protection 141, 166

abortion 40, 58, 65
   on demand 59, 71, 94
   facilities 75
   first trimester 60
   informed consent 79, 90, 93
   life-saving exception 72, 78, 83, 102
   parental/spousal consent 79, 90, 95
   public funding 79, 85
Abortion Control Act 79
Affordable Care Act 200
Alexander of Hales 11
Aristotle 132
   forms 5
   quickening 58

Bowers v. Hardwick 125, 127
Boy Scouts of America v. Dale 141
Burwell v. Hobby Lobby Stores 200

Christian Legal Society of the University of California v. Leo P. Martinez 195
Cicero 1, 61, 65, 132

Defense of Marriage Act 153
divine law 46, 188
Doe v. Bolton 75

Employment Division v. Smith 187
ensoulment 66

eternal law 7, 11, 31, 32, 45, 188, 202,
   See also Lex Aeterna

free exercise of religion 182, 191, 201, 208

Gonzales v. Carhart 109
Gratian 10
Griswold v. Connecticut 63

habituation 61, *See also* Aristotle
hierarchy of laws. *See also* St. Thomas
   Aquinas
Hippocratic Oath 65
homosexuality 41, 125, 131, 136,
   141, 148
   Equal Protection 137
   gay rights 135, 150
   marriage 152, 155, 206
human law 8, 11, 18, 32, 47, 192
   derivative nature 49
   necessity of 48

incest 41
Isidore of Seville 8

jurisprudence
   schools of 2

Lawrence v. Texas 126, 146
lex aeterna 7, 17
lex naturalis 7
Locke v. Davey 191

marriage 42
Marsh v. Chambers 183
Masterpiece Cakeshop v. Colorado Civil Rights Commission 206

mediate animation 66, 71
Murphy v. Ramsey 140

natural law 12, 34
  Aristotle 5
  Cicero 5, 6
  common good. *See also* human law
  content of 36
  intellect 12
  19th Century America 1
  origin 1
  Plato 3
  primary tenets 2, 10,
    31, 94
  promulgation 3
  rule and measure of reason 3, 36
  St. Augustine 6
  St. Thomas Aquinas 8
  secondary precepts 31, 37, 128, 132,
    139, 143, 154
  supreme law 6

Obergefell v. Hodges 151

partial birth abortion 100, 109
personhood 58, 73, 85, 90
Peter Abelard 9
Planned Parenthood v. Casey 69,
  89, 104
Plato 1
  nature in law 4
polygamy 43, 140, 188
positive law 5
positivism 3, 31

quickening theory 66, 71

reason 16, 30, 47
recta ratio 11
religious expression 187
Religious Freedom Restoration Act 201
right reason. *See also* Cicero
right to privacy 59
Roe v. Wade 57, 166, 173
Romer v. Evans 135

salvation 46
secondary precepts 94, 157
  belief in a diety 45, 181, 193, 205
  care of offspring 42, 77, 83, 101, 112
  communal life 44
  procreation 41, 126, 132, 208
  self-preservation 39, 86, 93, 101, 111,
    168, 172
  sexual attraction 125, 144
sexual orientation
  discrimination 135, 206
sodomy 41, 125, 127, 137, 147
  historical laws 129
  natural order 131
  privacy 130, 149
St. Albert the Great 12
St. Anselm 8
St. Augustine 1
St. Bonaventure 11
St. Thomas Aquinas 2, 13, 60, 65,
  132, 181
  divine exemplar 16
  the good 15, 19
  hierarchy of laws 18
  rule and measure of reason 14
  virtue 18
Stenberg v. Carhart 100
suicide 39, 165
  assisted 167, 169
supreme exemplar 33
synderesis 11

teleology 2, 17
the good 61
*Thornburgh v. American College of Obstetricians
  and Gynecologists* 79

unjust law 8, 11, 49
utilitarianism 3

Vacco v. Quill 167
viability 72, 80, 85, 86, 92, 101, 103

Washington v. Glucksberg 166, 169
Webster v. Reproductive Health Systems 85

www.ingramcontent.com/pod-product-compliance
Lightning Source LLC
Chambersburg PA
CBHW021140230426
43667CB00005B/193